New Longman

Othello

William Shakespeare

Series and Volume Editor: John O'Connor

6

Longman

Edinburgh Gate

Pearson Education Limited
Edinburgh Gate
Harlow
Essex
CM20 2JE
England and Associated Companies throughout the World

ISBN 0582–48883–4

First published 2003
Second impression 2003
Text Editor: Monica Kendall
Printed in China
SWTC/02

The Publisher's policy is to use paper manufactured from
sustainable forests.

Acknowledgements

We are grateful to the following for permission to reproduce
photographs:

Jennifer Beaumont page 60; John Bunting pages 104, 142,
152, 246, 249; Donald Cooper courtesy Shakespeare's Globe
page vi (bottom); Greg Evans International page vi (top);
Fotomas Index page 214; Richard Mildenall pages 49, 64,
168, 205, 226; Shakespeare Centre Library pages 16 (Reg
Wilson), 26 (Malcolm Davies), 82 (Malcolm Davies), 116
(Malcolm Davies), 124 (Malcolm Davies), 155 (Reg Wilson);
The Shakespeare Institute, The University of Birmingham
page 255.

Front cover: Ronald Grant Archive (Rank/Castlerock/Turner)

Laurence Fishburne as Othello in the 1995 film directed by
Oliver Parker

A0140 4

Contents

Introduction

This book in the *New Longman Shakespeare* series has been designed to meet the varied and complex needs of students who are making the transition from GCSE to AS Level and then on to A Level itself. Each feature – the *notes, commentaries, activities, critical extracts* and *background information* – will help you to meet the new **Assessment Objectives** at both AS and A2 Levels.

The textual notes

These in-depth notes, freshly written with the new-style examinations in mind, provide understandable explanations which are easily located on the page:
- **notes** are placed opposite the text with clear line references
- **explanations** of more complex words are given in context and help is provided with key imagery and historical references
- a **critical commentary**, which accompanies the textual notes, raises important critical and performance issues.

The activities

At the end of each Act – and also at the end of the book – there are activities which require AS and A2 style responses. These help you to meet the Assessment Objectives by asking for:
- **close study of particular extracts**, *focusing on dramatic technique, language, themes, structure and audience response*
- **responses to the play as a whole**
- **comments on staging and performance.**

Critical context

In your exam you will be required to express your own opinions, taking into account other readers' interpretations. This mini **critical anthology** provides you with extracts from the key critical works on the play in question, from the earliest essays to the most recent studies. There is also a suggested **Further reading** list with brief explanations of what each title is about.

Background

There are detailed sections which help you to understand the relationships between this play and others, as well as the cultural and historical contexts in which it was written. You will find sections on:
- the **date** of the play, its **sources** and where it was first performed
- the **Renaissance** (or early modern period) and key dates
- other **playwrights** from the period
- the **social and historical background** *to this particular play.*

In some other books in this series (for example, *The Winter's Tale*) you will also find expanded sections on:
- Shakespeare's life and career
- playhouses, players and publishing.

Characters and language

Focusing on the play itself there are comprehensive sections on:
- the **characters** – *with all the key references*
- the **language, structure and imagery**.

Performance

This feature of the book describes the **performance history** of the play and also provides details of productions currently available on video.

Studying and writing about the play

To give you further support as you prepare for the examinations, there are sections on:
- **Shakespeare's verse** *with examples from this particular play*
- **Study skills**: *titles and quotations*.

Date and first performances

Othello was performed at court in the autumn of 1604 – but there is no evidence that this was its first performance. It might have been written as early as 1601. However, looking at the style of the writing and considering some of the works that Shakespeare might well have consulted, most critics have come to the conclusion that it was written between the end of 1603 and early 1604.

Othello was performed by the King's Men (Shakespeare's company) at the outdoor Globe Theatre in Maiden Lane, Bankside in Southwark, and later at their indoor theatre, Blackfriars. The Globe opened in 1599, burnt down in 1613, was rebuilt, and was finally pulled down during the Civil War (in the 1640s). Plays were shown in the afternoon. The photographs show the reconstructed Globe which was built in the 1990s, on the south bank of the Thames, near the site of the original Globe.

Characters in the play

RODERIGO, *a Venetian gentleman*
IAGO, *'ancient' or ensign to Othello*
BRABANTIO, *a Venetian senator, Desdemona's father*
OTHELLO, *'the Moor', a general in the service of Venice*
CASSIO, *Othello's lieutenant*
DUKE OF VENICE
First and Second SENATOR, *of Venice*
DESDEMONA, *a Venetian lady, Othello's wife and Brabantio's daughter*
MONTANO, *Governor of Cyprus*
First, Second and Third GENTLEMAN, *with Montano*
EMILIA, *Iago's wife*
a CLOWN, *Othello's servant*
BIANCA, *a woman of Cyprus*
LODOVICO, *a high-ranking Venetian noble*
GRATIANO, *Brabantio's brother*
OFFICER, *in Venice*
SAILOR, *in Venice*
MESSENGER, *in Venice*
HERALD, *in Cyprus*
MUSICIAN, *in Cyprus*

In Venice: servants to Brabantio, attendants, officers, other senators

In Cyprus: attendants, gentlemen, musicians, officers

———————

Act 1 takes place in Venice; the rest of the play on the island of Cyprus.

1.1 *Iago defends himself against Roderigo's complaints that he had not informed him about Othello's marriage to Desdemona*

1   **Tush! Never tell me** Rubbish! Don't give me that! *(Roderigo does not believe what Iago has been telling him)*

3   **As if the strings...** as though you had control of it *(purses were tied by cords)*

     this the fact that Othello has been planning to elope with Desdemona

4   **'Sblood** God's blood!

5   **abhor** hate

7   **great ones** important people

8   **In personal suit** making a personal request

     lieutenant second-in-command

9   **Off-capped** took off their caps *(as a sign of respect)*

11   **as** as though

12   **Evades...circumstance** avoids answering directly, using an exaggerated and long-winded excuse *(bombast was a cotton material used for padding or stuffing; the word came to be used for 'puffed-up' language)*

13   **epithets of war** military language

14   **Nonsuits my mediators** rejects the people pleading on my behalf

     Certes certainly

16   **Forsooth** truly *(used here sarcastically)*

     arithmetician (1) somebody who is good at the theory of war, but has had no experience; (2) an accounts clerk *(Florence was known as a great banking centre; see line 28)*

18   **almost damned...** No one has been able to explain what this means, since Cassio appears not to be married. Perhaps it is a reference to his fondness for women (explicitly Bianca); or perhaps Shakespeare intended to include Cassio's wife in the story and then changed his mind.

20–21   **Nor the division...spinster** he doesn't know any more about fighting in the front line than a home-loving woman does

21–23   **unless...as he** unless we're talking about theory out of books – in which the toga-wearing senators can make suggestions as informed as his

23–24   **Mere prattle...soldiership** as a soldier, he's all talk and no action

24   **had th'election** was chosen *(as lieutenant)*

25   **proof** proof of my ability as a soldier

26   **grounds** battlefields

27   **belee'd and calmed** *images from sailing: Cassio's ship had sailed 'under Iago's lee', cutting off the wind from Iago's sails, and preventing him from advancing any further*

28   **debitor and creditor...counter-caster** *more references to Cassio as an accounts clerk or bookkeeper, only good at adding up figures*

30   **God bless the mark!** God help us!

     his Moorship's *a sarcastic play on the phrase 'his worship'; Iago mockingly refers to Othello's ethnic origins ('Moor' was used by Shakespeare for any black African) and his high status*

     ancient ensign; standard-bearer; personal attendant *(an inferior rank to Cassio's)*

Dramatic structure

As an audience we are initially puzzled by this conversation: all we know is that one is plainly angry with the other for having kept something from him. But Shakespeare very quickly establishes the relationship between the speakers and some key background facts, not least that Iago has had access to Roderigo's purse, and has been passed over for promotion.

2

Act 1

(handwritten top margin) bleur / also absurd: Othello (bad / Othello ended 2 scene*

(circled) **1.1**

Scene 1

Venice. A street.

Enter RODERIGO and IAGO.

RODERIGO Tush! Never tell me. I take it much unkindly
That thou, Iago, who hast had my purse
As if the strings were thine, shouldst know of this.

IAGO 'Sblood, but you'll not hear me! If ever I did dream
Of such a matter, abhor me.

RODERIGO   Thou told'st me   5
Thou didst hold him in thy hate.

IAGO   Despise me
If I do not. Three great ones of the city, *(handwritten: catastrophe)*
In personal suit to make me his lieutenant, *(handwritten left: I implicat)*
Off-capped to him; and by the faith of man,
I know my price; I am worth no worse a place.   10
But he, as loving his own pride and purposes, *(handwritten: ironic 2)*
Evades them with a bombast circumstance,
Horribly stuffed with epithets of war,
Nonsuits my mediators. For, 'Certes,' says he,
'I have already chose my officer.' And what
     was he?   15
Forsooth, a great arithmetician,
One Michael Cassio, a Florentine, *(handwritten: plosive)*
(A fellow almost damned in a fair wife) *(handwritten left: imple / negative / Naval)*
That never set a squadron in the field,
Nor the division of a battle knows *(handwritten: sarcasm)*   20
More than a spinster, unless the bookish theoric,
Wherein the togèd consuls can propose *(handwritten: contrasting pair)*
As masterly as he. Mere prattle without practice
Is all his soldiership. But he, sir, had th'election;
And I, of whom his eyes had seen the proof   25
At Rhodes, at Cyprus, and on other grounds
(handwritten left: contrast) Christian and heathen, must be belee'd and calmed
By debitor and creditor. This counter-caster, *(handwritten: Alliteration)*
He, in good time, must his lieutenant be,
And I – God bless the mark! – his Moorship's *(handwritten: persuasive)*
     ancient. *(handwritten: exclamatory)*   30
(handwritten left: 3 Power + Position)

RODERIGO By heaven, I rather would have been his hangman.

3

(handwritten right margin: self obsessed / Putting self up / others down)

Bitter that he has not been promoted as Othello's lieutenant, Iago declares his intention to stay with Othello for his own advantage

33 **Preferment...affection** you only get promotion because of who you know and favouritism

34 **gradation** step-by-step promotion; seniority

36 **in any just term** on any reasonable grounds

   affined bound

38 **content you** rest assured

39 **serve my turn upon him** get what I want out of him

40–41 **nor...Cannot** and neither can

42 **knee-crooking knave** someone who masks his dishonesty by bowing and fawning

43 **doting...bondage** loving his own servile captivity

45 **naught but provender** nothing but his feed

   cashiered sacked; dismissed

47 **trimmed...duty** well practised in looking dutiful

48 **Keep yet...themselves** make sure that, inwardly, they are looking after themselves

49 **throwing but shows of service** appearing to be dutiful

50 **Do well thrive** get on very well

   lined their coats lined their pockets; benefited themselves

51 **Do themselves homage** pay some respect to themselves; or serve their own interests

   soul spirit

56–57 **not I for...end** I am not following him out of affection or duty; I am merely pretending to do so, to get what I want

59 **native act...heart** my true actions and real nature

60 **complement extern** outward appearance; external show

60–61 **'tis not...But** it won't be long before

61 **I will wear...sleeve** I will show my real feelings openly

62 **For daws...at** for any fool to take advantage of (**daws** = [1] jackdaws; [2] fools)

   I am not what I am I am not what I appear to be *(see note on line 54 below)*

63–64 **What a full...thus!** How lucky the 'thick-lips' is if he can get away with this! *(thick-lips is an offensive reference to the fact that Othello is a black African)* **owe** = own

65 **him** Othello

Iago

50 Roderigo is too stupid to realise that Iago's description of followers who deceive their masters is an account of what Iago is doing to him.

54 'It may be that Shakespeare seems to have deliberately given Iago a trick of speech by which he makes remarks which appear at first hearing well turned and significant, and on examination turn out to mean very little' (M R Ridley). Iago's comment possibly means either: 'If I were Othello, I wouldn't employ me!' or 'If I were a general, I wouldn't want to be a subordinate.'

62 Iago announces himself with this admission that he is not what he appears to be: *I am not what I am*. It might also mean that, if he were to show his feelings openly, he would not be his true self.

Act 1 Scene 1

IAGO   Why, there's no remedy. 'Tis the curse of service:
Preferment goes by letter and affection,
And not by old gradation, where each second
Stood heir to th'first. Now, sir, be judge yourself,   35
Whether I in any just term am affined
To love the Moor.

RODERIGO   I would not follow him then.

IAGO   O sir, content you.
I follow him to serve my turn upon him.
We cannot all be masters, nor all masters   40
Cannot be truly followed. You shall mark
Many a duteous and knee-crooking knave
That, doting on his own obsequious bondage,
Wears out his time, much like his master's ass,
For naught but provender; and when he's old,   45
   cashiered.
Whip me such honest knaves! Others there are
Who, trimmed in forms and visages of duty,
Keep yet their hearts attending on themselves,
And, throwing but shows of service on their lords,
Do well thrive by them, and when they have lined
   their coats   50
Do themselves homage. These fellows have some
   soul,
And such a one do I profess myself. For, sir,
It is as sure as you are Roderigo,
Were I the Moor, I would not be Iago.
In following him, I follow but myself.   55
Heaven is my judge, not I for love and duty,
But seeming so, for my peculiar end;
For when my outward action doth demonstrate
The native act and figure of my heart
In complement extern, 'tis not long after   60
But I will wear my heart upon my sleeve
For daws to peck at; I am not what I am.

RODERIGO   What a full fortune does the thick-lips owe
If he can carry't thus!

IAGO   Call up her father,
Rouse him, make after him, poison his delight,   65

5

1.1 *Iago persuades Roderigo to wake Desdemona's father, Brabantio, and tell him what has happened*

67–68 though he...flies he has a nice life now, but we'll plague him!

69 chances of vexation opportunities for causing him misfortune

70 lose some colour be spoilt; lose its lustre

72–74 with like...spied with the same terrifying sound that people make at night when they spot a fire caused by carelessness

79 terrible frightening

80 What is the matter...? What's your business?

83 Zounds God's wounds! *(a strong oath)*

86 tupping copulating with

87 snorting snoring

88 the devil...grandsire the devil will make you a grandfather *(like **old black ram**, line 85, another offensive reference to Othello's colour: the devil was supposed to be black)*

Iago's language

64–70 The quicker, staccato verse in Iago's speech reflects the way in which he injects an urgency here.

68 Iago's use of animal imagery perhaps reflects his view of human relations and passions as merely bestial and based on physical desire. Some actors have uttered words like *tupping* with relish, as though Iago is simultaneously condemning sex and enjoying the thought of it.

Proclaim him in the streets. Incense her kinsmen,
And though he in a fertile climate dwell,
Plague him with flies; though that his joy be joy,
Yet throw such chances of vexation on't
As it may lose some colour.　　　　　　　　70

RODERIGO　　Here is her father's house. I'll call aloud.

IAGO　　Do, with like timorous accent and dire yell
As when, by night and negligence, the fire
Is spied in populous cities.

RODERIGO　　What, ho, Brabantio! Signior Brabantio, ho!　75

IAGO　　Awake! What ho, Brabantio! Thieves, thieves!
Look to your house, your daughter, and your bags!
Thieves, thieves!

BRABANTIO above, at a window.

BRABANTIO　　What is the reason of this terrible summons?
What is the matter there?　　　　　　　　80

RODERIGO　　Signior, is all your family within?

IAGO　　Are your doors locked?

BRABANTIO　　　　　　　　　Why, wherefore ask you this?

IAGO　　Zounds, sir, y'are robbed! For shame, put on your
　　　gown!
Your heart is burst, you have lost half your soul.
Even now, now, very now, an old black ram　85
Is tupping your white ewe. Arise, arise!
Awake the snorting citizens with the bell,
Or else the devil will make a grandsire of you.
Arise I say!

BRABANTIO　　　　　　　What, have you lost your wits?

RODERIGO　　Most reverend signior, do you know my voice?　90

BRABANTIO　　Not I; what are you?

RODERIGO　　My name is Roderigo.

93   **charged** ordered

95   **is not for thee** will not marry you

96   **distemp'ring draughts** drinks that have stirred you up

97   **Upon malicious knavery** with the intention of causing trouble

98   **start my quiet** disturb my rest

100–101   **My spirits...to thee** my feelings – and the influence I wield – have power enough to punish you for this

102–103   **This is Venice...** I live in a busy city – not an isolated farmhouse (**grange**)

106   **if** even if

107   **do you service** help you

108   **covered with** mated by

109   **Barbary** from the Barbary coast of North Africa, famous for horse-breeding *(another reference to Othello's background – see lines 63 and 85 and the map on page 253)*

nephews any descendants

110   **coursers** fast horses

111   **gennets for germans** small Spanish horses for blood relations

112   **profane** obscene; foul-mouthed

114   **making the beast...** *a slang term for having sexual intercourse*

115   **You are** – *Iago might possibly be pausing, as though about to insult Brabantio.*

Iago's language

109 Having described Othello as *a Barbary horse*, Iago develops the theme with references to Brabantio's future descendants and relations as horses.

114 A further example (see 68) of Iago's view of human beings as animals.

Iago in performance

Frank Finlay's performance (filmed in 1964) showed how totally convincing Iago can be in this scene. Bob Hoskins, on the other hand (BBC TV, 1981), revealed early indications of the psychopath which was later to emerge.

BRABANTIO	The worser welcome!
	I have charged thee not to haunt about my doors.
	In honest plainness thou hast heard me say
	My daughter is not for thee; and now, in madness,
	Being full of supper and distemp'ring draughts,
	Upon malicious knavery dost thou come
	To start my quiet.
RODERIGO	Sir, sir, sir –
BRABANTIO	But thou must needs be sure
	My spirits and my place have in their power
	To make this bitter to thee.
RODERIGO	Patience, good sir.
BRABANTIO	What tell'st thou me of robbing? This is Venice;
	My house is not a grange.
RODERIGO	Most grave Brabantio,
	In simple and pure soul I come to you.
IAGO	Zounds, sir, you are one of those that will not
	serve God if the devil bid you. Because we come to
	do you service and you think we are ruffians,
	you'll have your daughter covered with a
	Barbary horse, you'll have your nephews neigh
	to you, you'll have coursers for cousins, and
	gennets for germans.
BRABANTIO	What profane wretch art thou?
IAGO	I am one, sir, that comes to tell you your daughter
	and the Moor are making the beast with two backs.
BRABANTIO	Thou art a villain.
IAGO	You are – a senator.
BRABANTIO	This thou shalt answer. I know thee, Roderigo.
RODERIGO	Sir, I will answer anything. But I beseech you,
	If't be your pleasure and most wise consent,
	As partly I find it is, that your fair daughter,

95

100

105

110

115

Having convinced Brabantio that his daughter has indeed been secretly married, Iago gives Roderigo further instructions and leaves

120 **At this odd-even...night** at this time between night and morning when most people are asleep

121–122 **Transported...hire** that your daughter should be transported and entrusted to the safety of a servant that anybody can hire

123 **gross clasps of a lascivious** foul embraces of a lustful

124 **and your allowance** and done with your consent

125 **saucy** insolent *(much stronger than today's meaning)*

127 **We have...rebuke** you have rebuked us unjustly

127–129 **Do not believe...reverence** Do not believe that, lacking a sense of decent behaviour, I would trifle with you, your honour.

132–133 **Tying...stranger** placing everything she possesses in the hands of a wandering, roving alien

134 **Straight** straightaway

137 **Strike on the tinder** *to produce fire for a light*

138 **taper** candle

142 **not meet...place** inappropriate and not in keeping with my position *(as Othello's ensign)*

143 **produced** *i.e. as a witness*

144–146 **I do know...cast him** I know that, however much this might cause Othello some annoyance and delay, the state cannot afford to dismiss him

147 **With such loud reason** *In the opinion of all reasonable people, Othello is the obvious choice to lead the Venetian forces against the Turks in Cyprus. (The Venetian republic had been at war with the Ottoman Empire for some time. See pages 253–254.)*

148 **Which even...act** which has already begun

149 **Another of his fathom...** they have no other man of his abilities

154 **but sign** nothing more than an appearance

That so that

155 **Sagittary** *possibly an inn, bearing the sign of a centaur (like the zodiac sign Sagittarius)*

Venice

136 Roderigo invokes *the justice of the state*. Throughout the play, the great city-state of Venice is presented as a place of sophisticated civilisation (see also 102–103), and the manners of its people are often contrasted with those of outsiders (as the Moor Othello is in Roderigo's eyes).

Performance

141–144 Most productions take line 112 to mean that Brabantio cannot see Iago. In films he can be obscured by darkness; on stage he sometimes stands underneath the balcony on which Brabantio appears (see photographs on pages vi and 214). From Iago's point of view, it is important not to be recognised if he is later to maintain his pose of loyalty to Othello; it would not do to be called as a witness.

At this odd-even and dull watch o'th'night,   120
Transported with no worse nor better guard
But with a knave of common hire, a gondolier,
To the gross clasps of a lascivious Moor –
If this be known to you, and your allowance,
We then have done you bold and saucy wrongs;   125
But if you know not this, my manners tell me
We have your wrong rebuke. Do not believe
That from the sense of all civility
I thus would play and trifle with your reverence.
Your daughter, if you have not given her leave,   130
I say again, hath made a gross revolt,
Tying her duty, beauty, wit, and fortunes
In an extravagant and wheeling stranger
Of here and everywhere. Straight satisfy yourself.
If she be in her chamber, or your house,   135
Let loose on me the justice of the state
For thus deluding you.

BRABANTIO   Strike on the tinder, ho!
Give me a taper! Call up all my people!
This accident is not unlike my dream.
Belief of it oppresses me already.   140
Light, I say, light!

Exit above.

IAGO   Farewell, for I must leave you.
It seems not meet, nor wholesome to my place,
To be produced – as, if I stay, I shall –
Against the Moor. For I do know the state,
However this may gall him with some check,   145
Cannot with safety cast him; for he's embarked
With such loud reason to the Cyprus wars,
Which even now stands in act, that for their souls
Another of his fathom they have none
To lead their business; in which regard,   150
Though I do hate him as I do hell-pains,
Yet, for necessity of present life,
I must show out a flag and sign of love,
Which is indeed but sign. That you shall surely
  find him,
Lead to the Sagittary the raisèd search,   155

158   **my despisèd time** the time ahead when I shall be mocked for having a disobedient daughter

166   **treason of the blood** (1) treason against her family; (2) rebellion of her emotions

168   **charms** magic charms; love potions

169   **property** true nature; normal self

172   **O would...** I wish you had married her! *(a change of heart for Brabantio – see lines 93–95)*

173   **Some one way...** *Brabantio sends his men off in different directions.*

175   **discover** find

178   **command at most** call upon help at most houses

180   **deserve your pains** reward you for your trouble

Themes

168 This is the first reference to magic, a theme present throughout the play.

Roderigo

By Iago's exit, Roderigo has been established as the classic 'gull', the rich simpleton whose destiny is to be duped by the clever and unscrupulous Iago. The best-known gull in Shakespeare is Sir Andrew Aguecheek (in *Twelfth Night*).

1.1

And there will I be with him. So farewell.

Exit.

Enter BRABANTIO in his nightgown, with SERVANTS and torches.

BRABANTIO	It is too true an evil. Gone she is,
	And what's to come of my despisèd time
	Is naught but bitterness. Now Roderigo,
	Where didst thou see her? – O unhappy girl! – 160
	With the Moor, say'st thou – Who would be a father? –
	How didst thou know 'twas she? – O, she deceives me
	Past thought! – What said she to you? Get more tapers!
	Raise all my kindred! – Are they married, think you?
RODERIGO	Truly I think they are. 165
BRABANTIO	O heaven! How got she out? O treason of the blood!
	Fathers, from hence trust not your daughters' minds
	By what you see them act. Is there not charms – magic
	By which the property of youth and maidhood
	May be abused? Have you not read, Roderigo, 170
	Of some such thing?
RODERIGO	Yes, sir, I have indeed.
BRABANTIO	Call up my brother. – O, would you had had her! –
	Some one way, some another. – Do you know
	Where we may apprehend her and the Moor?
RODERIGO	I think I can discover him, if you please 175
	To get good guard and go along with me.
BRABANTIO	Pray you lead on. At every house I'll call;
	I may command at most. – Get weapons, ho!
	And raise some special officers of night. –
	On, good Roderigo; I will deserve your pains. 180

Exeunt.

1.2 *Iago feigns concern that Othello might be punished for the marriage, but Othello is confident that his status in Venice will protect him*

1 **Though...** *Again the scene opens in medias res ('in the middle of things'): Iago has been giving Othello his version of events.*

2 **very stuff** the essence

3 **contrived** premeditated; planned beforehand

3–4 **I lack...service** sometimes I am too scrupulous for my own good

5 **yerked** stabbed

6 **prated** said stupid things

7 **scurvy** disgraceful

9 **I did...him** I had real difficulty letting him carry on

10 **fast** properly; definitely

11 **magnifico** *an important person in Venice, i.e. Brabantio*

12–13 **hath...Duke's** potentially he is as powerful as the Duke – with twice the power of other nobles

14–16 **Or put...cable** or impose whatever restraint or hardship the law...will give him scope to do

17 **Signiory** the Venetian government

18 **out-tongue** put up a superior argument than

19–20 **Which...promulgate** and when I know that it is honourable to boast, I will publish it

20–21 **I fetch...siege** I am descended from a royal family, both in name and character

21–23 **and my demerits...reached** my good qualities are equal to the high rank I have achieved *(if you address someone unbonneted – without removing your hat – it is because you are of the same rank and status)*

24–27 **But that...worth** if I did not love Desdemona, I would not put restrictions and limitations on my unconfined freedom for all the treasure in the sea

27 **yond** from over there

Iago's language

16 Although he is a soldier, Iago often uses imagery to do with the sea (a *cable* is a powerful ship's rope).

Othello in performance

Many actors like to portray Othello's power and dignity on their first entrance. Ben Kingsley's Othello (RSC, 1985) was 'an Eastern Moor. In flowing white robes and elegantly turbanned, he seemed to glide downstage, his eyes fixed on some distant fixed point, conveying powerfully the sense of a meditative man untouchable by humdrum reality, almost godlike in his grace and bearing' (Keith Parsons and Pamela Mason). (See photograph on page 16.)

[Handwritten top margin:]
Othello: Love for Desdemona
Romantic - idealism
self - deception
Innocence (simplicity)
Recklness (exoticism)

[Handwritten right top:]
Dignity (self-control)
Passion (imagination)
Reputation

Scene 2

Another street outside the Sagittary. *[handwritten:]* Pub

Enter OTHELLO, IAGO, ATTENDANTS with torches.

IAGO	Though in the trade of war I have slain men,
	Yet do I hold it very stuff o'th' conscience
	To do no contrived murder. I lack iniquity
	Sometime to do me service. Nine or ten times
	I had thought t'have yerked him here, under the
	ribs. 5
OTHELLO	'Tis better as it is.
IAGO	Nay, but he prated,
	And spoke such scurvy and provoking terms
	Against your honour, that with the little godliness I
	have
	I did full hard forbear him. But I pray you sir,
	Are you fast married? Be assured of this, 10
	That the magnifico is much beloved,
	And hath in his effect a voice potential
	As double as the Duke's. He will divorce you,
	Or put upon you what restraint or grievance
	The law, with all his might to enforce it on, 15
	Will give him cable.
OTHELLO	Let him do his spite.
	My services which I have done the Signiory
	Shall out-tongue his complaints. 'Tis yet to know –
	Which when I know that boasting is an honour
	I shall promulgate – I fetch my life and being 20
	From men of royal siege; and my demerits
	May speak unbonneted to as proud a fortune
	As this that I have reached. For know, Iago, *[handwritten: I arg.]*
	But that I love the gentle Desdemona,
	I would not my unhousèd free condition 25
	Put into circumscription and confine
	For the seas' worth. But look, what lights come
	yond?

Enter CASSIO, with OFFICERS and torches.

15

30–31 **My parts...rightly** my qualities, my title and confidence will plead for me

32 **By Janus** *Interestingly, Iago swears by the two-faced Roman god.*

36 **haste-posthaste** as fast as possible

38 **divine** assume; guess

39 **heat** urgency

40 **sequent** following one after another

43 **hotly** urgently

45 **several** separate

48 **what makes he here?** what's he doing here?

49 **boarded...carack** taken a treasure ship on dry land *(with a bawdy play on* **boarded** = *had sex with)*

Ben Kingsley as Othello in the 1985 Royal Shakespeare Company production

Iago's language

49 Another example of Iago's use of (a) imagery from ships and the sea; (b) sexual language to describe human relations.

IAGO   Those are the raiséd father and his friends.
            You were best go in.

OTHELLO   Not I. I must be found.
            My parts, my title, and my perfect soul   30
            Shall manifest me rightly. Is it they?

IAGO   By Janus, I think no.

OTHELLO   The servants of the Duke? And my lieutenant?
            The goodness of the night upon you, friends.
            What is the news?

CASSIO   The Duke does greet you, general,   35
            And he requires your haste-posthaste appearance
            Even on the instant.

OTHELLO   What is the matter, think you?

CASSIO   Something from Cyprus, as I may divine.
            It is a business of some heat. The galleys
            Have sent a dozen sequent messengers   40
            This very night at one another's heels,
            And many of the consuls, raised and met,
            Are at the Duke's already. You have been hotly called
                for.
            When, being not at your lodging to be found,
            The Senate hath sent about three several quests   45
            To search you out.

OTHELLO   'Tis well I am found by you.
            I will but spend a word here in the house,
            And go with you.

                                                              Exit.

CASSIO   Ancient, what makes he here?

IAGO   Faith, he tonight hath boarded a land carack.
            If it prove lawful prize, he's made forever.   50

CASSIO   I do not understand.

IAGO   He's married.

52 **Marry** by Mary *(with a play on* **marry** *in the previous line)*

Have with you OK

57 **I am for you** *Iago picks out Roderigo for a pretend fight – for various reasons (see 1.3.377–380), he doesn't want him to be injured.*

59 **years** the respect due to you because of your age

62 **Damned** *because of his black skin, Othello is associated with the devil (a figure* **to fear** *– see line 70)*

enchanted bewitched *(with spells or potions)*

63 **I'll refer...sense** I call upon common sense to be the judge

66 **opposite to** opposed to the idea of

67 **curlèd** with fashionable curled hair *(Roderigo is one example of the 'curlèd darlings' that Desdemona rejected)*

68 **t'incur...mock** to bring public ridicule upon herself

69 **her guardage** my guardianship over her

sooty black *(a further reference to Othello's skin colour – see the note below)*

71 **Judge me...sense** I call upon the world to judge whether it isn't perfectly obvious

72 **practised...charms** put her under disgusting spells

73 **minerals** poisons

74 **disputed on** debated

Cassio

51 It seems odd that Cassio, who has been close to Othello throughout his wooing of Desdemona (see 3.3.94–100), should be unaware of the marriage. Many actors assume that Cassio is pretending ignorance, not wishing to discuss the subject with Iago who is lower than him in rank.

Othello

58 Othello is impressive in his calm authority here. Laurence Olivier (National Theatre, 1964) 'came on smelling a rose, laughing softly with a private delight; barefooted, ankleted, black...He sauntered downstage, with a loose, bare-heeled roll of the buttocks, came to rest feet splayed apart, hip lounging outward' (Ronald Bryden). 'He projected an air of racial confidence and rejected the concerns for his safety expressed by Iago or Cassio' (Keith Parsons and Pamela Mason).

Language

62–98 Brabantio's speeches show his obsession with (a) Othello's blackness (62, 69–70 and 97–98); and (b) the idea that Desdemona must have been subject to witchcraft, magic spells or love potions.

CASSIO	To who?

Enter OTHELLO.

IAGO	Marry, to – Come, captain, will you go?
OTHELLO	Have with you.
CASSIO	Here comes another troop to seek for you.

Enter BRABANTIO, RODERIGO, with OFFICERS and torches.

IAGO   It is Brabantio. General, be advised.
He comes to bad intent.

OTHELLO   Holla! Stand there!   55

RODERIGO   Signior, it is the Moor.

BRABANTIO   Down with him, thief!

They draw swords.

IAGO   You, Roderigo? Come, sir, I am for you.

OTHELLO   Keep up your bright swords, for the dew will rust
them:
Good signior, you shall more command with years
Than with your weapons.   60

BRABANTIO   O thou foul thief, where hast thou stowed my
daughter?
Damned as thou art, thou hast enchanted her!
For I'll refer me to all things of sense,
If she in chains of magic were not bound,
Whether a maid so tender, fair, and happy,   65
So opposite to marriage that she shunned
The wealthy, curlèd darlings of our nation,
Would ever have, t'incur a general mock,
Run from her guardage to the sooty bosom
Of such a thing as thou – to fear, not to delight?   70
Judge me the world if 'tis not gross in sense
That thou hast practised on her with foul charms,
Abused her delicate youth with drugs or minerals
That weaken motion. I'll have't disputed on;

75 **'Tis...palpable to thinking** it makes sense; it's likely

76 **apprehend...attach** arrest

77 **abuser** corrupter

78 **inhibited...warrant** prohibited and illegal *(e.g. black magic)*

80 **at his peril** at his own risk

81 **of my inclining** on my side

85 **course...session** normal process of law

89 **present** immediate; urgent

94 **idle** unimportant

97 **if such...free** if people can be allowed to get away with things like this

98 **pagans** non-Christians *(another insulting reference to Othello's origins)*

Language

82–83 Shakespeare often uses the language of the theatre. Here Othello compares himself to an actor who knows his cue without needing to be prompted.

Venice

98 Slavery was an accepted part of the Venetian constitution: Shylock refers to it in *The Merchant of Venice*: 'You have among you many a purchased slave...' (4.1.90–98). Brabantio expresses the fear, commonly heard by modern racists, of being 'taken over' by 'aliens' considered to be inferior.

'Tis probable, and palpable to thinking.   75
I therefore apprehend and do attach thee
For an abuser of the world, a practiser
Of arts inhibited and out of warrant.

[To the OFFICERS]

Lay hold upon him. If he do resist,
Subdue him at his peril.

OTHELLO   Hold your hands,   80
Both you of my inclining and the rest.
Were it my cue to fight, I should have known it
Without a prompter. Whither will you that I go
To answer this your charge?

BRABANTIO   To prison, till fit time
Of law and course of direct session   85
Call thee to answer.

OTHELLO   What if I do obey?
How may the Duke be therewith satisfied,
Whose messengers are here about my side
Upon some present business of the state
To bring me to him?

OFFICER   'Tis true, most worthy signior.   90
The Duke's in council, and your noble self
I am sure is sent for.

BRABANTIO   How? The Duke in council?
In this time of the night? – Bring him away.
Mine's not an idle cause. The Duke himself,
Or any of my brothers of the state,   95
Cannot but feel this wrong as 'twere their own;
For if such actions may have passage free,
Bondslaves and pagans shall our statesmen be.

Exeunt.

In the palace, the Duke and senators discuss conflicting reports concerning a Turkish invasion fleet

1 **composition** consistency

2 **gives them credit** makes them *(the pieces of news)* believable

   disproportioned inconsistent

5 **jump not...accompt** do not agree on an exact figure

6 **where the aim reports** where the reported figure is an estimate

10 **I do...error** I am not going to let the inconsistent figures cause me to reject the main report *(that there is a Turkish fleet at sea)*

11–12 **But...fearful sense** but I do believe the central, frightening, point

17 **How say...change?** What is your opinion of this change in the news *(that the Turks are heading for Rhodes rather than Cyprus)?*

18 **assay of reason** common sense test

   pageant show; deception

19 **keep...gaze** distract us; keep us looking in the wrong direction

19–30 **When we consider...** *The gist of this speech is that it would be foolish for the Turks to attack Rhodes rather than Cyprus, because (1) Rhodes is more heavily fortified, and (2) Cyprus would be a better prize for the Turks strategically (as it commands the eastern Mediterranean; see the map on page 253). 'We should not underestimate the Turks by believing that they would commit such an error.'*

22 **more concerns** is more important (strategically) to

Venice

The 1995 film (see page 282) brilliantly evokes the power and glory of the Venetian state in this scene, the sumptuously dressed senators thronging a magnificent council chamber in the Doge's (Duke's) palace. Though small geographically, Venice is represented by Shakespeare as a trading republic well capable of opposing the might of the Ottoman Empire in defending its Mediterranean interests. It is, moreover, a place of order and justice.

Scene 3

A council chamber.

The DUKE, SENATORS, and OFFICERS sitting round a table, with lights and ATTENDANTS.

DUKE	There's no composition in these news That gives them credit.
FIRST SENATOR	Indeed, they are disproportioned. My letters say a hundred and seven galleys.
DUKE	And mine a hundred forty.

SECOND SENATOR   And mine two hundred.
But though they jump not on a just accompt –   5
As in these cases where the aim reports
'Tis oft with difference – yet do they all confirm
A Turkish fleet, and bearing up to Cyprus.

DUKE   Nay, it is possible enough to judgment.
I do not so secure me in the error,   10
But the main article I do approve
In fearful sense.

SAILOR   [*Within*]   What, ho! What, ho! What ho!

Enter SAILOR.

OFFICER   A messenger from the galleys.

DUKE   Now? What's the business?

SAILOR   The Turkish preparation makes for Rhodes.
So was I bid report here to the State   15
By Signior Angelo.

DUKE   How say you by this change?

FIRST SENATOR   This cannot be
By no assay of reason. 'Tis a pageant
To keep us in false gaze. When we consider
Th' importancy of Cyprus to the Turk,   20
And let ourselves again but understand
That, as it more concerns the Turk than Rhodes,

23 **more...bear it** capture it with an easier fight

24 **brace** state of defence *(it is less prepared to resist attack)*

26 **dressed in** equipped with

28 **latest** last

29–30 **Neglecting...profitless** giving up an easy and profitable venture in order to risk a dangerous and fruitless one

31 **in all confidence** we can be sure

33 **Ottomites** Turks *(see pages 253–254)*

35 **injointed...fleet** joined up with another, following, fleet

37–38 **restem...course** retrace their earlier course

38 **frank** open *(they are no longer disguising their intentions)*

41 **With his...thus** respectfully offers this information

44 **Marcus Luccicos** *Like Signior Angelo (line 16), we never meet this character or find out anything more about him.*

48 **straight** immediately

49 **general enemy** enemy of the state

Othello

47–48 Note the language used by the Duke and senators when referring to Othello – he plainly commands their respect – and how it contrasts with Brabantio's insults.

Performance

48–50 There is a marked contrast between the Duke's welcome to Othello and to Brabantio. Many productions have emphasised the fact that the Duke considers Othello to be much more important at this point and barely notices Brabantio's arrival.

Venice

49 The reference to *the general enemy Ottoman* underlines the representation of Venice as the champion of Christianity against 'the infidel' (people who did not share the Christian faith).

So may he with more facile question bear it,
For that it stands not in such warlike brace,
But altogether lacks th'abilities　　　　　　　　　　　　25
That Rhodes is dressed in. If we make thought of
　　this,
We must not think the Turk is so unskilful
To leave that latest which concerns him first,
Neglecting an attempt of ease and gain
To wake and wage a danger profitless.　　　　　　　　30

DUKE　　　　　Nay, in all confidence he's not for Rhodes.

OFFICER　　　Here is more news.

　　　　　　Enter a MESSENGER.

MESSENGER　The Ottomites, reverend and gracious,
Steering with due course toward the isle of Rhodes,
Have there injointed them with an after fleet.　　　　35

FIRST　　　　Ay, so I thought. How many, as you guess?
SENATOR

MESSENGER　Of thirty sail; and now they do restem
Their backward course, bearing with frank appearance
Their purposes toward Cyprus. Signior Montano,
Your trusty and most valiant servitor,　　　　　　　　40
With his free duty recommends you thus,
And prays you to believe him.

DUKE　　　　'Tis certain then for Cyprus.
Marcus Luccicos, is not he in town?

FIRST　　　　He's now in Florence.　　　　　　　　　　　　　45
SENATOR

DUKE　　　　Write from us to him; post-posthaste dispatch.

FIRST　　　　Here comes Brabantio and the valiant Moor.
SENATOR

　　　Enter BRABANTIO, OTHELLO, CASSIO, IAGO, RODERIGO, and OFFICERS.

DUKE　　　　Valiant Othello, we must straight employ you
Against the general enemy Ottoman.

25

53   **Neither...business** it wasn't my official position or anything to do with state affairs

56   **of so floodgate...nature** so overwhelming, pushing everything else aside

57   **engluts** swallows up

61   **of mountebanks** from fake doctors (charlatans; quacks)

62–64   **For nature...could not** nature – not being deficient, blind or stupid – could not have made such a ridiculous mistake unless influenced by witchcraft

64   **Sans** without

66   **beguiled** cheated

69   **After...sense** interpreting it *(the law)* as you see fit

69–70   **yea, though...action** yes, even though my own son were facing your accusation

71–73   **whom now...brought** who, it appears, has now been brought here by your special powers concerning affairs of state

Ray Fearon as Othello (RSC, 1999)

[To BRABANTIO*]* I did not see you. Welcome, gentle
    signior.   50
We lacked your counsel and your help tonight.

BRABANTIO	So did I yours. Good your grace, pardon me.

So did I yours. Good your grace, pardon me.
Neither my place, nor aught I heard of business,
Hath raised me from my bed; nor doth the general
    care
Take hold on me; for my particular grief   55
Is of so floodgate and o'erbearing nature
That it engluts and swallows other sorrows,
And it is still itself.

DUKE   Why, what's the matter?

BRABANTIO   My daughter! O, my daughter!

SENATORS   Dead?

BRABANTIO   Ay, to me.
She is abused, stol'n from me, and corrupted   60
By spells and medicines bought of mountebanks;
For nature so prepost'rously to err,
Being not deficient, blind, or lame of sense,
Sans witchcraft could not.

DUKE   Whoe'er he be that in this foul proceeding   65
Hath thus beguiled your daughter of herself,
And you of her, the bloody book of law
You shall yourself read in the bitter letter
After your own sense; yea, though our proper
    son
Stood in your action.

BRABANTIO   Humbly I thank your Grace.   70
Here is the man – this Moor, whom now, it seems,
Your special mandate for the state affairs
Hath hither brought.

ALL   We are very sorry for't.

DUKE   *[To* OTHELLO*]* What in your own part can you say to
    this?

BRABANTIO   Nothing, but this is so.   75

80–81 **The very head...more** That is the fullest extent of my crime.

81 **Rude** rough

83–84 **For since...wasted** for, from the age of seven until roughly nine months ago

83 **pith** strength

85 **dearest action...field** most important action in the field of battle

87 **pertains** relates

90 **round** plain; to the point

92 **conjuration** incantation (uttering spells)

93 **withal** with

95–96 **Of spirit...herself** so quiet and shy in her character that she blushed at her own emotions

97 **credit** personal reputation

98 **what she feared...** *see 1.2.62 and 70*

99–103 **It is...should be** You would have to be warped in your judgement to believe that such a perfect individual could go so far astray, against all the rules of nature; we have to look to hellish witchcraft in order to explain how this could have happened.

103 **vouch** state; assert

104 **blood** passions

105 **dram, conjured** dose, made powerful by a magic spell

106 **wrought** cast a spell

106–109 **To vouch...against him** Accusation is not proof, without fuller and more obvious (**overt**) proof than these shaky theories (**thin habits**) and weak probabilities to do with commonplace happenings (**modern seeming**) offered as evidence against him.

111 **indirect...forcèd courses** cunning manoeuvres

Othello's language

76–94 Addressing the Duke, and completely confident, Othello flavours the opening of his speech with stately and formal terms from Latin and the Romance languages (*potent, grave...reverend signiors...approved...*). He then goes on to use military terms relating to battle-lines (*head...front*). Then, when he refers to the Venetians as *My...masters* (77), it is 'proudly edged: he had been a slave, their inquisition recalled his slavery; he reminded them in turn of his service and generalship' (Ronald Bryden). This powerful language makes it hard for us to accept his statement *Rude am I in my speech...*(81): is he being modest; or does he genuinely believe that he lacks eloquence?

83–85 Throughout the play Othello shows great pride in his profession; his reputation as a soldier is extremely important to him.

Desdemona

94–96 Brabantio's view of his daughter's excessive modesty seems to be at odds with her behaviour during the courtship and the elopement.

OTHELLO	Most potent, grave, and reverend signiors,
	My very noble and approved good masters,
	That I have ta'en away this old man's daughter,
	It is most true; true I have married her.
	The very head and front of my offending	80
	Hath this extent, no more. Rude am I in my speech,
	And little blessed with the soft phrase of peace,
	For since these arms of mine had seven years' pith
	Till now some nine moons wasted, they have
	used
	Their dearest action in the tented field;	85
	And little of this great world can I speak
	More than pertains to feats of broil and battle;
	And therefore little shall I grace my cause
	In speaking for myself. Yet, by your gracious
	patience,
	I will a round unvarnished tale deliver	90
	Of my whole course of love – what drugs, what charms,
	What conjuration, and what mighty magic
	(For such proceeding I am charged withal)
	I won his daughter.

BRABANTIO	A maiden never bold,
	Of spirit so still and quiet that her motion	95
	Blushed at herself; and she, in spite of nature,
	Of years, of country, credit, everything,
	To fall in love with what she feared to look on!
	It is a judgment maimed and most imperfect
	That will confess perfection so could err	100
	Against all rules of nature, and must be driven
	To find out practices of cunning hell
	Why this should be. I therefore vouch again
	That with some mixtures powerful o'er the blood,
	Or with some dram, conjured to this effect,	105
	He wrought upon her.

DUKE	To vouch this is no proof,
	Without more wider and more overt test
	Than these thin habits and poor likelihoods
	Of modern seeming do prefer against him.

| FIRST | But Othello, speak. | 110 |
| SENATOR | Did you, by indirect and forcèd courses |

1.3 *While Desdemona is sent for, Othello describes how he and Desdemona came to fall in love*

113–114 **fair question...affordeth** the pleasant talk that one person has with another

117 **If you...report** if she gives a bad report of my behaviour

128 **Still** constantly

133 **chances** accidents

134 **moving...field** exciting experiences at sea and on land

135 **hairbreadth scapes...breach** escaping by the skin of my teeth from a hole made in a fortress, where death would have been instantaneous

137 **redemption** freedom *(probably after a ransom had been paid)*

138 **portance** behaviour

139 **antres vast...idle** vast caves and barren deserts

141 **hint** occasion

process story

Othello

122–123 We learn from this that Othello is a practising Christian. Olivier emphasised Othello's Christian faith throughout his performance (see page 281) with a prominent cross worn around his neck.

127–144 Othello's heroic past plainly intrigues the Venetians; it has a mythic quality which might remind us of Homer's Odysseus.

> Subdue and poison this young maid's affections?
> Or came it by request, and such fair question
> As soul to soul affordeth?

OTHELLO   I do beseech you,
Send for the lady to the Sagittary   115
And let her speak of me before her father.
If you do find me foul in her report,
The trust, the office I do hold of you
Not only take away, but let your sentence
Even fall upon my life.

DUKE   Fetch Desdemona hither.   120

OTHELLO Ancient, conduct them; you best know the place.

Exit IAGO, with ATTENDANTS.

And till she come, as truly as to heaven
I do confess the vices of my blood,
So justly to your grave ears I'll present
How I did thrive in this fair lady's love,   125
And she in mine.

DUKE   Say it, Othello.

OTHELLO Her father loved me, oft invited me;
Still questioned me the story of my life
From year to year, the battle, sieges, fortune
That I have passed.   130
I ran it through, even from my boyish days
To th'very moment that he bade me tell it.
Wherein I spoke of most disastrous chances,
Of moving accidents by flood and field,
Of hairbreadth scapes i'th'imminent deadly
      breach,   135
Of being taken by the insolent foe
And sold to slavery, of my redemption thence
And portance in my travel's history,
Wherein of antres vast and deserts idle,
Rough quarries, rocks, and hills whose heads touch
      heaven   140
It was my hint to speak. Such was my process.
And of the Cannibals that each other eat,

1.3 *The Duke is satisfied by Othello's account, but Brabantio demands to hear what his daughter has to say*

143 **Anthropophagi** 'people-eaters'

145 **seriously incline** be greatly interested

146 **still** always

148 **again** back

149 **discourse** conversation; story

150 **pliant** favourable

152 **all my pilgrimage dilate** relate all my travels in full

153 **by parcels** in bits and pieces; piecemeal

154 **intentively** paying attention uninterruptedly

155 **did beguile...tears** managed to make her cry

159 **passing** extremely

162 **made her such a man** made her into a man like that

165 **Upon this hint** given this opportunity

171 **take up...best** make the best of a bad job

175–176 **Destruction...the man** may I suffer if I have accused this man wrongly (**Light on** = fall upon)

Desdemona

174 Othello's explanation of their wooing (especially 157–165) has already revealed that Desdemona was, in Brabantio's phrase, *half the wooer.*

The Anthropophagi, and men whose heads
Do grow beneath their shoulders. These things to
    hear
Would Desdemona seriously incline;   145
But still the house affairs would draw her thence;
Which ever as she could with haste dispatch,
She'd come again, and with a greedy ear
Devour up my discourse. Which I observing,
Took once a pliant hour, and found good means   150
To draw from her a prayer of earnest heart
That I would all my pilgrimage dilate,
Whereof by parcels she had something heard,
But not intentively. I did consent
And often did beguile her of her tears   155
When I did speak of some distressful stroke
That my youth suffered. My story being done,
She gave me for my pains a world of sighs.
She swore in faith 'twas strange, 'twas passing
    strange;
'Twas pitiful, 'twas wondrous pitiful.   160
She wished she had not heard it, yet she wished
That heaven had made her such a man. She thanked
    me,
And bade me, if I had a friend that loved her,
I should but teach him how to tell my story,
And that would woo her. Upon this hint I spake.   165
She loved me for the dangers I had passed,
And I loved her that she did pity them.
This only is the witchcraft I have used.
Here comes the lady. Let her witness it.

Enter DESDEMONA, IAGO, ATTENDANTS.

DUKE   I think this tale would win my daughter too.   170
Good Brabantio, take up this mangled matter at the
    best.
Men do their broken weapons rather use
Than their bare hands.

BRABANTIO   I pray you hear her speak.
If she confess that she was half the wooer,
Destruction on my head if my bad blame   175
Light on the man. Come hither, gentle mistress.

1.3 *Desdemona declares that her duty is now to Othello, her husband, and the Duke attempts unsuccesfully to pacify Brabantio*

180   **education** upbringing

181   **learn** teach

182   **lord of duty** the person to whom I owe obedience

186   **challenge** claim

188   **Please it...on to** if your Grace pleases, let us move on to

189   **I had...get it** I wish I had adopted a child, rather than have fathered one.

192   **but thou...already** if you did not already have it

196   **clogs** wooden blocks to restrict movement

197   **lay a sentence** (1) utter a proverbial saying; (2) give my verdict

198   **grise** step

199–200   **When remedies...depended** When things are past remedy, it is better to face the worst, rather than constantly live in hope that they might improve.

201–202   **To mourn...on** Carrying on complaining about something that has happened is the best way to make other bad things happen.

203–204   **What cannot...makes** When you cannot hold on to something, accepting the loss helps to remove the pain.

205–206   **The robbed...grief** You take some of the satisfaction away from the thief, if you show that the robbery has not affected you; but you just harm yourself by indulging in pointless unhappiness.

207   **So let...beguile** so let's allow the Turk to cheat us out of Cyprus

209–212   **He bears...borrow** It's easy to suffer when all you have to put up with is people's advice; but it's hard to suffer a loss and the sorrow that goes with it, when you have to cope with your grief by using up your small stock of patience.

Desdemona

179–187 Desdemona's carefully chosen words about a daughter's conflicting duties towards her father and the man she loves find echo in other plays of Shakespeare, notably in *King Lear* and *Romeo and Juliet.*

Do you perceive in all this noble company
Where most you owe obedience?

DESDEMONA   My noble father,
I do perceive here a divided duty.
To you I am bound for life and education;   180
My life and education both do learn me
How to respect you. You are the lord of duty,
I am hitherto your daughter. But here's my husband,
And so much duty as my mother showed
To you, preferring you before her father,   185
So much I challenge that I may profess
Due to the Moor my lord.

BRABANTIO   God be with you. I have done.
Please it your Grace, on to the state affairs.
I had rather to adopt a child than get it.
Come hither, Moor.   190
I here do give thee that with all my heart
Which, but thou hast already, with all my heart
I would keep from thee. For your sake, jewel,
I am glad at soul I have no other child,
For thy escape would teach me tyranny   195
To hang clogs on them. I have done, my lord.

DUKE   Let me speak like yourself and lay a sentence
Which, as a grise or step, may help these lovers.
When remedies are past, the griefs are ended
By seeing the worst, which late on hopes
    depended.   200
To mourn a mischief that is past and gone
Is the next way to draw new mischief on.
What cannot be preserved when fortune takes,
Patience her injury a mock'ry makes.
The robbed that smiles, steals something from the
    thief;   205
He robs himself that spends a bootless grief.

BRABANTIO So let the Turk of Cyprus us beguile: — *rhyming couplets*
We lose it not so long as we can smile.
He bears the sentence well that nothing bears
But the free comfort which from thence he hears;   210
But he bears both the sentence and the sorrow

213–214 These sentences...equivocal These proverbs can be interpreted sweetly or bitterly: they carry equal weight either way (**gall** = bitterness).

215–216 I never...ear It's news to me that pain can be alleviated by words.

219 fortitude strength; military defences

221 substitute...sufficiency a deputy whose competence is widely acknowledged *(this is Montano, who appears in Act 2)*

222–223 opinion...on you public opinion, which is very powerful, would feel safer with you in charge

224–225 slubber...fortunes spoil your recent good fortune

225–226 stubborn...expedition rough and violent speed

227 tyrant custom habit, which forces us to do things

228 flinty hard

229 thrice-driven...down softest bed of eiderdown

229–231 I do agnize...hardness I acknowledge that I take to harsh conditions very readily

233 bending bowing

234 I crave fit disposition I beg that suitable arrangements might be made

235–237 Due reference...breeding treatment, financial provision, accommodation and servants, appropriate to her rank

241 To my unfolding...ear please listen favourably to what I have to say

242 charter permission

243 simpleness innocence

Language

199–216 'The rhymed verse suggests that both the Duke and Brabantio are indulging in proverbial wisdom, and the speeches have a choric effect' (Edwin Muir).

218 The change from verse to prose can help the actor to inject a business-like tone.

That to pay grief must of poor patience borrow.
These sentences, to sugar, or to gall,
Being strong on both sides, are equivocal.
But words are words. I never yet did hear   215
That the bruisèd heart was piercèd through the ear.
I humbly beseech you, proceed to th'affairs of state.

rhyming couplets

Prose

DUKE   The Turk with a most mighty preparation makes
for Cyprus. Othello, the fortitude of the place is
best known to you; and though we have there a   220
substitute of most allowed sufficiency, yet
opinion, a more sovereign mistress of effects,
throws a more safer voice on you. You must
therefore be content to slubber the gloss of your
new fortunes with this more stubborn and   225
boisterous expedition.

OTHELLO   The tyrant custom, most grave senators,
Hath made the flinty and steel couch of war
My thrice-driven bed of down. I do agnize
A natural and prompt alacrity   230
I find in hardness, and do undertake
This present wars against the Ottomites.
Most humbly therefore, bending to your state,
I crave fit disposition for my wife,
Due reference of place, and exhibition,   235
With such accommodation and besort
As levels with her breeding.

DUKE   Why, at her father's.

BRABANTIO   I will not have it so.

OTHELLO   Nor I.

DESDEMONA   Nor would I there reside,
To put my father in impatient thoughts
By being in his eye. Most gracious Duke,   240
To my unfolding lend your prosperous ear,
And let me find a charter in your voice,
T'assist my simpleness.

DUKE   What would you, Desdemona?

245 **downright...fortunes** my drastic actions and the whirlwind of things that have happened to me

246–247 **My heart's...lord** I love Othello's virtues and character

248–250 **I saw...consecrate** I recognised Othello's character in his face *(perhaps with the sense that she fell in love with the inner person)* and dedicated my soul and my future life to his honourable and courageous attributes

252 **moth** lazy creature

253 **rites for...me** *possibly:* I would be deprived of the privileges (sexual and otherwise) a wife ought to have

254 **interim** interval *(time will pass slowly)*

255 **dear** (1) which affects me particularly; (2) of someone dear to me

256 **voice** agreement

257 **Vouch with me** bear me witness

257–260 **I therefore...satisfaction** I am not asking for her to accompany me for my own pleasure, nor to satisfy sexual desire – I am too old for that –

nor because a married man has a right to his wife's company

261 **free** generous

262 **heaven...souls** heaven forbid

263 **scant** neglect

264–267 **when light-winged...business** when the attractions of love-making make my eyes blind, so that my pleasures ruin my professional work (**Cupid** = *the winged god of love;* **seel** = *close up the eyes of a hawk – see 3.3.210;* **wanton dullness** = *lack of concentration brought about by sex;* **speculative and officed instrument** = *the eyes*)

268 **skillet** saucepan

269–270 **all indign...estimation!** may all unworthy and shameful misfortunes attack my reputation!

271 **Be it...determine** I will leave the decision to you

272 **cries** demands; calls for

277 **commission** orders

278–279 **such things...you** and other things of importance and relevance which concern you

Language of soldiership

It has often been observed that Othello's tragedy is closely bound up with the fact that he, Cassio and Iago are all soldiers. This section of the scene is full of soldiers' language, relating to warfare and hardship. It starts with the Duke's speech (218–226: *mighty preparation...fortitude...stubborn and boisterous expedition*), and is picked up by Othello (*flinty and steel couch of war...hardness...a skillet of my helm...Make head against*). Desdemona seems to accept the importance of these soldierly qualities but objects to being left behind *A moth of peace*.

Desdemona

246–247 Although she has disobeyed her father, she feels an emotional subjugation to Othello.

253 She is not afraid to assert her rights as a married woman. While Othello plays down the sexual aspect of their relationship and is keen to establish that marriage will not distract him from his professional duties (257–260), Desdemona herself specifically raises the question of her 'marital rites'.

DESDEMONA	That I did love the Moor to live with him,	
	My downright violence, and storm of fortunes,	245
	May trumpet to the world. My heart's subdued	
	Even to the very quality of my lord;	
	I saw Othello's visage in his mind,	
	And to his honours and his valiant parts	
	Did I my soul and fortunes consecrate.	250
	So that, dear lords, if I be left behind,	
	A moth of peace, and he go to the war,	
	The rites for why I love him are bereft me,	
	And I a heavy interim shall support	
	By his dear absence. Let me go with him.	255
OTHELLO	Let her have your voice.	
	Vouch with me, heaven, I therefore beg it not	
	To please the palate of my appetite,	
	Nor to comply with heat the young affects	
	In my defunct and proper satisfaction;	260
	But to be free and bounteous to her mind;	
	And heaven defend your good souls that you think	
	I will your serious and great business scant	
	When she is with me. No, when light-winged toys	
	Of feathered Cupid seel with wanton dullness	265
	My speculative and officed instrument,	
	That my disports corrupt and taint my business,	
	Let housewives make a skillet of my helm,	
	And all indign and base adversities	
	Make head against my estimation! –	270
DUKE	Be it as you shall privately determine,	
	Either for her stay or going. Th'affair cries haste,	
	And speed must answer it.	
FIRST SENATOR	You must away tonight.	
OTHELLO	With all my heart.	
DUKE	At nine i'th' morning here we'll meet again.	275
	Othello, leave some officer behind,	
	And he shall our commission bring to you,	
	And such things else of quality and respect	
	As doth import you.	

281 **conveyance...** *Iago is to look after Desdemona.*

285 **If virtue...lack** if goodness is not without delightful beauty

290 **faith** faithfulness

292 **I prithee** please (I pray thee)

293 **in the best advantage** when the best opportunity arises

295 **direction** instructions

301 **incontinently** immediately

305 **prescription** (1) a right; (2) a doctor's prescription

---

Language

280 *honesty:* 'the first of the many times in the play that this quality is attributed to Iago' (M R Ridley)

286 'This contrast between black and white recurs frequently in the play' (Edwin Muir).

298 Significantly, having addressed Roderigo as 'you' in 1.1, Iago has now adopted the more familiar 'thou'.

Emilia

292 Does Desdemona know Emilia? In the 1989 RSC production the impression was given that she did not, and this added to Desdemona's isolation as she left her homeland and family.

1.3

OTHELLO	So please your grace, my ancient;
	A man he is of honesty and trust. 280
	To his conveyance I assign my wife,
	With what else needful your good grace shall think
	To be sent after me.
DUKE	Let it be so.
	Good night to every one. [*To* BRABANTIO] And, noble signior,
	If virtue no delighted beauty lack, 285
	Your son-in-law is far more fair than black.
FIRST SENATOR	Adieu, brave Moor. Use Desdemona well.
BRABANTIO	Look to her, Moor, if thou hast eyes to see:
	She has deceived her father, and may thee.

Exeunt DUKE, SENATORS, OFFICERS, etc.

OTHELLO	My life upon her faith. Honest Iago, 290
	My Desdemona must I leave to thee;
	I prithee let thy wife attend on her,
	And bring them after in the best advantage.
	Come, Desdemona, I have but an hour
	Of love, of worldly matter, and direction 295
	To spend with thee. We must obey the time.

Exit OTHELLO with DESDEMONA.

RODERIGO	Iago?
IAGO	What say'st thou, noble heart?
RODERIGO	What will I do, think'st thou?
IAGO	Why, go to bed and sleep. 300
RODERIGO	I will incontinently drown myself.
IAGO	If thou dost, I shall never love thee after. Why, thou silly gentleman?
RODERIGO	It is silliness to live when to live is torment; and then have we a prescription to die when death is 305 our physician.

Dissuading Roderigo from thoughts of suicide, Iago persuades him that his best plan is follow Othello and Desdemona to Cyprus

312   **guinea hen** *dismissive term for a woman*

315   **fond** stupidly infatuated

        virtue power

319   **set** plant

        hyssop...thyme *herbs*

320   **gender** species

        distract spoil

322   **manured** cultivated

323   **corrigible authority** the power to correct things

325   **poise** balance out

328   **carnal stings** physical desires

329   **unbitted** unbridled

330   **sect or scion** cutting or shoot

336   **perdurable** long-lasting

337   **stead** help; be of use to

338–339   **defeat...beard** disguise your appearance with a false beard (**usurped** *also because the weak Roderigo has no right to look like a 'real man'*)

344   **answerable sequestration** a corresponding (*i.e. equally violent*) ending

        put but just put

Iago

307–308   Iago tells us that he is twenty-eight, but he is nearly always played on stage as older, possibly to get across the impression of an embittered man. When Kenneth Branagh played the part in his mid-thirties (in the 1995 film), he was one of the youngest Iagos of modern times. Some actors quite deliberately ignore this statement, in order to play Iago older: Richard McCabe, for example, played him for the RSC in 1999 as 'the wrong side of forty'.

IAGO	O villainous! I have looked upon the world for four times seven years, and since I could distinguish betwixt a benefit and an injury, I never found man that knew how to love himself. Ere I would say I would drown myself for the love of a guinea hen, I would change my humanity with a baboon.

310

RODERIGO	What should I do? I confess it is my shame to be so fond, but it is not in my virtue to amend it.

315

IAGO	Virtue? A fig! 'Tis in ourselves that we are thus, or thus. Our bodies are our gardens, to the which our wills are gardeners; so that if we will plant nettles or sow lettuce, set hyssop and weed up thyme, supply it with one gender of herbs or distract it with many – either to have it sterile with idleness or manured with industry – why, the power and corrigible authority of this lies in our wills. If the balance of our lives had not one scale of reason to poise another of sensuality, the blood and baseness of our natures would conduct us to most preposterous conclusions. But we have reason to cool our raging motions, our carnal stings or unbitted lusts, whereof I take this that you call love to be a sect or scion.

320

325

330

RODERIGO	It cannot be.

IAGO	It is merely a lust of the blood and a permission of the will. Come, be a man! Drown thyself? Drown cats and blind puppies! I have professed me thy friend, and I confess me knit to thy deserving with cables of perdurable toughness. I could never better stead thee than now. Put money in thy purse. Follow thou the wars; defeat thy favour with an usurped beard. I say, put money in thy purse. It cannot be long that Desdemona should continue her love to the Moor – put money in thy purse – nor he his to her. It was a violent commencement in her and thou shalt see an answerable sequestration – put but money in thy purse. These Moors are changeable in their wills –

335

340

345

347	**locusts** *a sweet fruit of the carob tree*
348	**coloquintida** *a bitter apple*
349	**is sated with** has had enough of
351	**damn thyself** *i.e. by committing suicide, a sin against God*
353	**sanctimony** holy ritual *(i.e. the marriage service)*
354	**erring** (1) wandering; vagrant *(see 1.1.132–134)*; (2) sinful; misguided
	supersubtle extremely refined
357–358	**clean out of the way** a ridiculous idea
359	**compassing** obtaining
365	**hearted** heart-felt; vigorous
366	**be conjunctive** work together
367	**cuckold him** turn him into a cuckold *(a husband whose wife has been unfaithful)*
370	**Traverse** About turn!
374	**betimes** early
377	**make my fool my purse** turn the butt of my laughter into a source of money
378	**I mine...profane** I would insult the knowledge I have gained through experience
379	**snipe** fool *(a kind of bird)*

Iago in performance

365 Ian McKellen's delivery (1989) of *My cause is hearted* revealed all Iago's bitter jealousy; he was motivated by deeply felt emotions.

fill thy purse with money. The food that to him
now is as luscious as locusts shall be to him
shortly as bitter as coloquintida. She must change
for youth; when she is sated with his body, she will
find the errors of her choice. Therefore, put money   350
in thy purse. If thou wilt needs damn thyself, do
it a more delicate way than drowning. Make all the
money thou canst. If sanctimony and a frail vow
betwixt an erring barbarian and a supersubtle
Venetian be not too hard for my wits, and all the   355
tribe of hell, thou shalt enjoy her. Therefore, make
money. A pox of drowning thyself, it is clean out
of the way. Seek thou rather to be hanged in
compassing thy joy than to be drowned and go
without her.   360

RODERIGO   Wilt thou be fast to my hopes, if I depend on the
issue?

IAGO   Thou art sure of me. Go, make money. I have told
thee often, and I retell thee again and again, I hate
the Moor. My cause is hearted; thine hath no less   365
reason. Let us be conjunctive in our revenge
against him. If thou canst cuckold him, thou dost
thyself a pleasure, me a sport. There are many
events in the womb of time, which will be
delivered. Traverse, go, provide thy money! We   370
will have more of this tomorrow. Adieu.

RODERIGO   Where shall we meet i'th' morning?

IAGO   At my lodging.

RODERIGO   I'll be with thee betimes.

IAGO   Go to, farewell. Do you hear, Roderigo?   375

RODERIGO   I'll sell all my land.

Exit.

IAGO   Thus do I ever make my fool my purse;
For I mine own gained knowledge should profane
If I would time expend with such a snipe
But for my sport and profit. I hate the Moor,   380

taught   45   ✕ tel
                        raeist .

1.3 *Having expressed his contempt for Roderigo, Iago declares his hatred of Othello and begins to form a plan in which he will make Othello believe that Cassio and Desdemona are having an affair*

381–382 **'twixt my sheets...office** he's done my job as a husband in my bed (i.e. had sex with my wife)

384 **as if for surety** as though it were certain

holds me well regards me highly

386 **proper** good-looking

387 **his place** *the position of lieutenant that Cassio has been given*

plume up my will do exactly what I want

388 **double knavery** *i.e. harming both Cassio and Othello*

389–390 **to abuse...wife** to deceive Othello into believing that Cassio is too familiar with Desdemona

391–392 **a person...suspected** the appearance and smooth manner that might look suspicious

392 **framed** built

Iago

377–398 'In Iago's soliloquy we see him for the first time without a mask' (Edwin Muir). In the scenes that follow, look out for three things: (a) the gradual stages by which Iago's plot takes shape; (b) how far he intends it to go (and how that intention changes); and (c) what motives he claims to have for his actions.

And it is thought abroad that 'twixt my sheets
H'as done my office. I know not if't be true,
But I, for mere suspicion in that kind,
Will do, as if for surety. He holds me well;
The better shall my purpose work on him.   385
Cassio's a proper man. Let me see now:
To get his place, and to plume up my will
In double knavery. How? How? Let's see.
After some time, to abuse Othello's ears
That he is too familiar with his wife.   390
He hath a person and a smooth dispose
To be suspected – framed to make woman false.
The Moor is of a free and open nature
That thinks men honest that but seem to be so;
And will as tenderly be led by th'nose   395
As asses are.
I have't! It is engendered! Hell and night
Must bring this monstrous birth to the world's light.

Exit.

Exam practice

Extracts

1. Reread 1.1.1–39 ('...my turn upon him'). In what ways is a sense of mystery
   and intrigue created in this opening to the play? In your answer you should:
   - show in detail how the language conveys the relationship between the two
     men and the situation they find themselves in
   - describe the ways in which the audience learn only gradually who the two
     men are; what their connection is to the character after whom the play is
     named; and what the 'matter' is that Iago claims he never 'did dream of'
   - show some awareness of the importance of the setting (the time and the
     place).

2. Reread 1.2.58–98 ('Keep up your...statesmen be'). How do the ideas and
   language of these speeches help to reveal the different attitudes we observe
   in the play to Othello's blackness? In your answer you should:
   - make detailed references to the ways in which Brabantio links Othello's
     colour to damnation, magic and witchcraft
   - describe the image that Othello creates through the language of his
     responses
   - express your own reaction to Brabantio's ideas and language, as well as
     suggesting how other readers or audiences might respond to them.

3. Reread 1.3.333–398 ('Come, be a man!...world's light'). In what ways do this
   dialogue and soliloquy develop your understanding of Iago and his role in the
   play? In your answer you should:
   - make detailed references to language, tone and characterisation of both
     Iago and Roderigo
   - describe the ways in which Iago tries to maintain Roderigo's confidence
     and trust
   - show some awareness of the dramatic effects that can be gained through
     the use of soliloquy, drawing comparisons with soliloquies in other plays by
     Shakespeare and the various contexts in which they appear (*Hamlet* or
     Macbeth would be good starting points).

Extended writing

4. How important is Act 1 in establishing the main themes and underlying issues
   of the play? In your answer you should:
   - discuss the ways in which themes (such as witchcraft and deception) are
     introduced and developed

- comment upon the importance of Venice and what it comes to represent
- show understanding of attitudes in Shakespeare's time to issues arising from Othello's colour and origin.

Performance

5. In pairs, reread 1.1.38–70 and the notes on pages 4 and 6. Then rehearse the dialogue in order to bring out:
   - the possible meaning behind Iago's 'significant' utterances
   - the way in which a sense of urgency is injected through the staccato verse of lines 64–70.

6. Look back at the scene in which Roderigo and Iago call out to Brabantio (1.1.75–141). Draw a sketch to show different ways in which the characters might be placed on Shakespeare's stage to ensure that Iago is hidden from Brabantio. (See the photographs on pages vi and 214, and the notes on pages 206 and 208.)

Ian McKellen as Iago (RSC, 1989)

49

2.1 *As Montano, current governor of Cyprus, looks anxiously out to sea, news comes that the Turkish fleet has been destroyed in the storm*

1 **discern** make out

2 **high-wrought flood** turbulent sea

3 **'twixt** between *(from 'betwixt')*

5 **Methinks** it seems to me

7 **ruffianed** raged; behaved violently

8–9 **What ribs...mortise** Which oaken ship's ribs can remain joined together when mountainous seas like these crash down on them?

10 **segregation** dispersal; scattering

12 **The chidden...pelt** the whipped-up waves seem to beat

13 **main** main body of the sea *(with a play on a lion's mane)*

14 **burning Bear** brightly shining Little Bear constellation *(Ursa Minor)*

15 **guards** *the two stars in Ursa Minor next in brightness to the Pole star and used for navigation*

16–17 **I never...flood** I have never seen such turmoil in the angry sea.

18 **embayed** anchored in a bay

21 **desperate** frightening

banged beaten

22 **designment halts** plan is crippled (**halts** = limps along)

23 **sufferance** damage

26 **Veronesa** ship from Verona

Act 2

[handwritten marginalia: Desdemona (devotion) / above (strength) / Courage (strength) / Generosity (goodness) / innocence (delicacy) / Gentlemen (graciousness) / Beauty]

Scene 1

Cyprus.

Enter MONTANO, Governor of Cyprus, and two GENTLEMEN,
[on the balcony].

MONTANO	What from the cape can you discern at sea?
FIRST GENTLEMAN	Nothing at all, it is a high-wrought flood. I cannot 'twixt the heaven and the main Descry a sail.
MONTANO	Methinks the wind hath spoke aloud at land; 5 A fuller blast ne'er shook our battlements. If it hath ruffianed so upon the sea, What ribs of oak, when mountains melt on them, Can hold the mortise? What shall we hear of this?
SECOND GENTLEMAN	A segregation of the Turkish fleet: 10 For do but stand upon the foaming shore, The chidden billow seems to pelt the clouds; The wind-shaked surge, with high and monstrous main, Seems to cast water on the burning Bear And quench the guards of th'ever-fixèd pole. 15 I never did like molestation view On the enchafèd flood.
MONTANO	If that the Turkish fleet Be not ensheltered and embayed, they are drowned; It is impossible to bear it out.

Enter a THIRD GENTLEMAN.

THIRD GENTLEMAN	News, lads! Our wars are done. 20 The desperate tempest hath so banged the Turks That their designment halts. A noble ship of Venice Hath seen a grievous wrack and sufferance On most part of their fleet.
MONTANO	How? Is this true?
THIRD GENTLEMAN	The ship is here put in, 25 A Veronesa; Michael Cassio,

51

29	**is in full commission** has full powers to govern
32	**looks sadly** has a grave expression
38	**throw out our eyes** keep our eyes peeled
39–40	**Even till...regard** until our strained eyes cannot distinguish between the sea and the sky
41–42	**every...arrivance** we are expecting the arrival of more ships every minute
45	**elements** powers of wind and water
47	**well shipped** in a good ship

48	**bark** ship
49	**Of very expert...allowance** experienced and with a good reputation
50–51	**not surfeited...cure** which have not overeaten, but are healthy *(his hopes are not wildly optimistic, but reasonable)*
s.d.	***Within*** offstage *(i.e. within the tiring-house behind the back wall of the stage)*
53	**brow** cliff overlooking the shore
55	**My hopes...for** I hope it is

Lieutenant to the warlike Moor Othello,
Is come on shore; the Moor himself at sea,
And is in full commission here for Cyprus.

MONTANO   I am glad on't. 'Tis a worthy governor.   30

THIRD   But this same Cassio, though he speak of comfort
GENTLEMAN   Touching the Turkish loss, yet he looks sadly
            And prays the Moor be safe, for they were parted
            With foul and violent tempest.

MONTANO   Pray heavens he be;
            For I have served him, and the man commands   35
            Like a full soldier. Let's to the seaside, ho!
            As well to see the vessel that's come in
            As to throw out our eyes for brave Othello,
            Even till we make the main and th'aerial blue
            An indistinct regard.

THIRD   Come, let's do so;   40
GENTLEMAN   For every minute is expectancy
            Of more arrivance.

Enter CASSIO.

CASSIO   Thanks, you the valiant of the warlike isle,
            That so approve the Moor, O, let the heavens
            Give him defence against the elements,   45
            For I have lost him on a dangerous sea.

MONTANO   Is he well shipped?

CASSIO   His bark is stoutly timbered, and his pilot
            Of very expert and approved allowance;
            Therefore my hopes, not surfeited to death,   50
            Stand in bold cure. [*Within* A sail, a sail, a sail!]

CASSIO   What noise?

FIRST   The town is empty; on the brow o'th'sea
GENTLEMAN   Stand ranks of people, and they cry, 'A sail!'

CASSIO   My hopes do shape him for the governor.   55

A shot.

56 **shot of courtesy** welcoming salute from the cannons

61 **achieved** gained

62 **paragons...fame** surpasses descriptions and wild rumours

63 **excels...pens** is even better than the extravagant descriptions of the writers who praise her

64–65 **And in...ingener** and, in her natural outward beauty, she wears out people who try to describe it (**ingener** = inventor)

69–72 **The guttered...natures** the jagged rocks (reefs) and sandbanks, treacherously submerged to hinder innocent ships, forget their deadly natures, as though they are aware of Desdemona's beauty

76–77 **Whose footing...speed** whose landing here is a week earlier than we expected

81 **extincted** dead; extinguished

2.1

SECOND GENTLEMAN	They do discharge their shot of courtesy: Our friends at least.

CASSIO   I pray you, sir, go forth
And give us truth who 'tis that is arrived.

SECOND GENTLEMAN   I shall.

Exit.

MONTANO   But, good lieutenant, is your general wived?   **60**

CASSIO   Most fortunately. He hath achieved a maid
That paragons description and wild fame;
One that excels the quirks of blazoning pens,
And in th'essential vesture of creation
Does tire the ingener.

Enter SECOND GENTLEMAN.

                    How now? Who has put in?   **65**

SECOND GENTLEMAN   'Tis one Iago, ancient to the general.

CASSIO   H'as had most favourable and happy speed: *arrived*
Tempests themselves, high seas, and howling winds,
The guttered rocks and congregated sands,
Traitors ensteeped to enclog the guiltless keel,   **70**
As having sense of beauty, do omit
Their mortal natures, letting go safely by
The divine Desdemona.   *Goddess*

MONTANO   What is she?

                                                    Cassio
                                                    – close
CASSIO   She that I spake of, our great captain's captain,   *to Oth.*
Left in the conduct of the bold Iago,   *and /say* **75**
Whose footing here anticipates our thoughts
A se'nnight's speed. Great Jove, Othello guard,
And swell his sail with thine own pow'rful breath,
That he may bless this bay with his tall ship,
Make love's quick pants in Desdemona's arms,   **80**
Give renewed fire to our extinct spirits,
And bring all Cyprus comfort.

87   **Enwheel thee round** surround you

89–90   **nor know...well** the only information I have is that he is safe

95   **This likewise is** this *(ship)* is also

97   **gall your patience** irritate you

98   **extend my manners** greet your wife in this way *(possibly with a sense of overdoing the courteous behaviour)*

breeding upbringing

100–101   **would she...me** if she gave you as much of her lips as she gives me of her tongue *(by nagging him)*

102   **she has no speech** she is a quiet person *or* she isn't able to reply to that

---

Cassio

98–99 Cassio explains that his upbringing has influenced the way he greets women; is he being snobbish, or simply referring to the fact that he is from Florence, where social customs are different? Whichever it is, his *manners* give Iago just the opportunity he later needs to represent Cassio to Othello as a 'ladies' man' (see 4.1).

Handwritten annotation: Cassio
– Physical appearance
intemperance (either drunken?)
character (repulsive)
sold ship

Enter DESDEMONA, IAGO, RODERIGO, and EMILIA.

> O, behold!
> The riches of the ship is come on shore!
> You men of Cyprus, let her have your knees.

Kneeling.

> Hail to thee, lady! and the grace of heaven,   85
> Before, behind thee, and on every hand,
> Enwheel thee round.

DESDEMONA   I thank you, valiant Cassio.
> What tidings can you tell me of my lord?

CASSIO   He is not yet arrived, nor know I aught
> But that he's well and will be shortly here.   90

DESDEMONA O but I fear. How lost you company?

CASSIO   The great contention of sea and skies
> Parted our fellowship. [*Within* A sail, a sail!]
> [*A shot*]   But hark. A sail!

SECOND   They give this greeting to the citadel;
GENTLEMAN This likewise is a friend.

CASSIO   See for the news.   95

Exit GENTLEMAN.

> Good ancient, you are welcome. [*To* EMILIA] Welcome,
>   mistress.
> Let it not gall your patience, good Iago,
> That I extend my manners. 'Tis my breeding
> That gives me this bold show of courtesy.

Kisses EMILIA.

IAGO   Sir, would she give you so much of her lips   100
> As of her tongue she oft bestows on me,
> You would have enough.

DESDEMONA   Alas, she has no speech.

IAGO   In faith, too much.

57

2.1 *Othello has not yet arrived: to distract herself, Desdemona invites Iago to engage in some wordplay*

104 **still** always

107 **chides with thinking** nags only in her thoughts

108 **pictures** silent

109 **Bells** noisy

110 **Saints in your injuries** you look innocent when you are about to attack somebody

111 **Players in your housewifery** you only play at being skilful housekeepers

housewives in your beds skilful in bed

112 **fie upon thee** shame on you

119 **assay** give it a try

120–121 **beguile The thing I am** (1) disguise my feelings; (2) distract myself

124 **pate** head

birdlime *a sticky substance used to catch birds; very difficult to remove from a coarse cloth like* **frieze**

125–126 **my muse...delivered** my creativity is struggling but this is what it has given birth to

129 **black** brunette *(blondes were fashionable in Shakespeare's time)*

witty intelligent and sharp

Desdemona in performance

116–176 This sequence is helpful in establishing more about Iago (his cheap attitude to women, his tendency to stereotype...), but actors playing Desdemona have often found it difficult to perform. Why should she engage in this silly banter with Iago when she is desperate to know whether Othello has survived the storm? She does give an explanation of her behaviour in 120–121, but it often fails to sound convincing and this remains a curious episode.

Iago's language

125–126 Interestingly, this is the same image *(muse...delivered)* as the one with which he concluded Act 1 (397–398); but there the birth was monstrous and hellish.

I find it still when I have leave to sleep.
Marry, before your ladyship, I grant,   105
She puts her tongue a little in her heart
And chides with thinking.

EMILIA   You have little cause to say so.

IAGO   Come on, come on! You are pictures out of door,
Bells in your parlours, wildcats in your kitchens,
Saints in your injuries, devils being offended,   110
Players in your housewifery, and housewives in
    your beds.

DESDEMONA   O, fie upon thee, slanderer!

IAGO   Nay, it is true, or else I am a Turk:
You rise to play, and go to bed to work.

EMILIA   You shall not write my praise.

IAGO   No, let me not.   115

DESDEMONA   What wouldst write of me, if thou shouldst praise
    me?

IAGO   O gentle lady, do not put me to't,
For I am nothing if not critical.

DESDEMONA   Come on, assay, There's one gone to the harbour?

IAGO   Ay, madam.

DESDEMONA   [Aside]   I am not merry; but I do beguile   120
The thing I am by seeming otherwise. – [To IAGO]
Come, how wouldst thou praise me?

IAGO   I am about it; but indeed my invention
Comes from my pate as birdlime does from frieze;
It plucks out brains and all. But my muse labours,   125
And thus she is delivered:
If she be fair and wise: fairness and wit,
The one's for use, the other useth it.

DESDEMONA   Well praised. How if she be black and witty?

131	**white** *a pun on the word wight (= man)*
135	**folly** sexual irresponsibility
136	**fond paradoxes** foolish riddling contradictions
138	**foul** (1) immoral; (2) ugly
139	**thereunto** as well
140	**pranks** sexual acts
143–145	**one that in the authority...itself** a woman whose virtue was so widely acknowledged that even malicious people would have to admit it
147	**Had tongue at will** spoke when she wanted to; was never lost for words
148	**gay** expensively dressed
149	**Fled from her wish** refrained from indulging her wishes

151	**Bade her wrong...fly** accepted the wrong done her and refused to be angry about it
153	**To change...tail** *possibly:* to swap a foolish husband for a handsome lover (**tail** *often means 'penis' in Shakespeare*)
156	**wight** person *(see line 131)*
158	**chronicle small beer** keep track of trivial things *(an insulting reference to a housewife's account-keeping)*
159	**impotent** weak; anticlimactic
161–162	**profane and liberal** irreverent, disrespectful and licentious (too free and easy)
163	**home** bluntly
163–164	**relish him more in** appreciate him more in the character of

Niamh Cusack as Desdemona (RSC, 1985)

60

| IAGO | If she be black, and thereto have a wit, | 130 |
| | She'll find a white that shall her blackness fit. | |

DESDEMONA   Worse and worse!

EMILIA   How if fair and foolish?

IAGO   She never yet was foolish that was fair,
For even her folly helped her to an heir.   135

DESDEMONA   These are old fond paradoxes to make fools
laugh i'th'alehouse. What miserable praise hast
thou for her that's foul and foolish?

IAGO   There's none so foul, and foolish thereunto,
But does foul pranks which fair and wise ones do.   140

DESDEMONA   O heavy ignorance. Thou praisest the worst best.
But what praise couldst thou bestow on a
deserving woman indeed – one that in the
authority of her merit did justly put on the
vouch of very malice itself?   145

IAGO   She that was ever fair, and never proud;
Had tongue at will, and yet was never loud;
Never lacked gold, and yet went never gay;
Fled from her wish, and yet said 'Now I may';
She that being angered, her revenge being nigh,   150
Bade her wrong stay, and her displeasure fly;
She that in wisdom never was so frail
To change the cod's head for the salmon's tail;
She that could think, and nev'r disclose her mind;
See suitors following, and not look behind: 155
She was a wight (if ever such wights were) –

DESDEMONA   To do what?

IAGO   To suckle fools and chronicle small beer.

DESDEMONA   O most lame and impotent conclusion. Do not
learn of him, Emilia, though he be thy husband.   160
How say you, Cassio? Is he not a most profane
and liberal counsellor?

CASSIO   He speaks home, madam. You may relish him

Iago comments on Cassio's conversation with Desdemona, and Othello arrives

165 **well said** well done *(usually referring to actions in Shakespeare, not speech)*

168 **gyve...courtship** ensnare and fetter you with your own courtly behaviour

172–173 **you are most apt...sir in** you like to do, when playing the fine gentleman

175 **clyster pipes** syringes for injecting enemas

186 **labouring bark** struggling ship

187 **Olympus** *the mountain home of the gods*

188 **If it were now to die** if I were to die now

192 **Succeeds...fate** can follow in the unknown future that is planned for us

Cassio in performance

165–176 If we accept Iago's commentary here, the actor playing Cassio has to continue with the *manners* referred to earlier (98), smiling at Desdemona, talking animatedly and kissing his fingers (a common gesture with Italian courtiers).

Desdemona

165–176 Some people consider Desdemona's behaviour with Cassio to be strangely flirtatious; it does depend on how it is performed. However we interpret her behaviour, it is enough for Iago to convince Roderigo that she is a typical Venetian woman.

Iago's language

175 *clyster pipes:* It is typical of Iago to descend to the nastiest reference he can find.

Dramatic irony

188 *If it were now to die...*There cannot be many clearer examples of dramatic irony than this: we know, but Othello cannot, that he is speaking the literal truth.

more in the soldier than in the scholar. [*They
converse apart*]

IAGO   [*Aside*] He takes her by the palm. Ay, well said,   165
              whisper! With as little a web as this will I ensnare
              as great a fly as Cassio. Ay, smile upon her, do! I
              will gyve thee in thine own courtship. – You say
              true; 'tis so, indeed! – If such tricks as these
              strip you out of your lieutenantry, it had been   170
              better you had not kissed your three fingers so
              oft – which now again you are most apt to play the
              sir in. Very good! Well kissed! An excellent
              courtesy! 'Tis so, indeed. Yet again your fingers to
              your lips? Would they were clyster pipes for   175
              your sake! [*Trumpets within*] – The Moor! I know
              his trumpet.

CASSIO   'Tis truly so.

DESDEMONA Let's meet him and receive him.

CASSIO   Lo, where he comes.   180

              Enter OTHELLO and ATTENDANTS.

OTHELLO   O my fair warrior!

DESDEMONA   My dear Othello.

OTHELLO   It gives me wonder great as my content
              To see you here before me. O my soul's joy,
              If after every tempest come such calms,
              May the winds blow till they have wakened death,   185
              And let the labouring bark climb hills of seas
              Olympus-high, and duck again as low
              As hell's from heaven. If it were now to die,
              'Twere now to be most happy; for I fear
              My soul hath her content so absolute   190
              That not another comfort like to this
              Succeeds in unknown fate.

DESDEMONA   The heavens forbid
              But that our loves and comforts should increase
              Even as our days do grow.

2.1 *Left alone with Roderigo, Iago informs him that Desdemona and Cassio are in love*

194 **Amen...sweet powers!** May the gods grant that it should be so!

197 **And this...** *in most productions, Othello kisses Desdemona*

199 **set down the pegs** loosen the tuning pegs; slacken the strings *(to make discordant music)*

202 **acquaintance** friends

203 **well desired** very popular; well liked

205 **prattle out of fashion** chatter inappropriately

dote behave over-affectionately

207 **disembark my coffers** unload my chests

208 **master** ship's captain

citadel fortress

210 **challenge** demand

212 **presently** immediately

217 **watches...court of guard** is on duty in the guardhouse

218 **directly** definitely

222 **Mark me** remember

Iago (Ian McKellen) looks on as Othello (Willard White) embraces Desdemona (Imogen Stubbs) (RSC, 1989)

Iago in performance

198 *O, you are well tuned now:* 'Iago is witnessing something beautiful, something he cannot bear to watch...I believe that underneath the obvious surface comedy of the line lies pain and cynicism' (David Suchet; Iago in 1985).

OTHELLO   Amen to that, sweet powers!
I cannot speak enough of this content;   195
It stops me here [*touches his breast*]; it is too much of
    joy.
And this, and this, the greatest discords be
That e'er our hearts shall make!

They kiss.

IAGO   [*Aside*] O, you are well tuned now;
But I'll set down the pegs that make this music,
As honest as I am.

OTHELLO   Come, let us to the castle.   200
News, friends! Our wars are done; the Turks are
    drowned.
How does my old acquaintance of this isle?
Honey, you shall be well desired in Cyprus;
I have found great love amongst them. O my sweet,
I prattle out of fashion, and I dote   205
In mine own comforts. I prithee, good Iago,
Go to the bay and disembark my coffers.
Bring thou the master to the citadel;
He is a good one, and his worthiness
Does challenge much respect. Come,
    Desdemona,   210
Once more well met at Cyprus.

Exeunt OTHELLO and DESDEMONA.

IAGO   [*To an* ATTENDANT] Do thou meet me presently at
the harbour. [*To* RODERIGO] Come hither. If thou
be'st valiant – as they say base men being in love
have then a nobility in their natures more than is   215
native to them – list me. The lieutenant tonight
watches on the court of guard. First, I must tell
thee this: Desdemona is directly in love with
him.

RODERIGO   With him? Why, 'tis not possible.   220

IAGO   Lay thy finger thus [*puts his finger to his lips*], and
let thy soul be instructed. Mark me with what
violence she first loved the Moor but for bragging

225   **prating** talking *(with the idea of empty, boastful talk)*

227   **devil** *another racial slur (see 1.1.88)*

227–228   **When the blood...sport** when her desires have been blunted by sex

229–230   **to give satiety...appetite** to renew the appetite after her desires have been satisfied

230   **favour** appearance

sympathy agreement; similarity

233   **conveniences** (1) desirable qualities; (2) points of compatibility

234   **heave the gorge** throw up; vomit

235   **disrelish and abhor** lose the taste for and hate

very nature natural instincts *(because her marriage, according to Iago, is 'unnatural')*

238   **pregnant...position** a plausible viewpoint full of good arguments

239   **eminent** highly placed

240   **voluble** smooth-talking

240–244   **no further conscionable... affection** with no more conscience than to adopt the outward appearance of polite, courteous behaviour, the better to achieve his lecherous (**salt**), secret, immoral desires

244–245   **slipper and subtle** slippery and cunning

245   **a finder of occasions** someone who takes advantage of opportunities

246–247   **can stamp...itself** can create opportunities for himself if none arise

249   **requisites** necessary qualities

250   **green minds look after** inexperienced people look for (find attractive)

pestilent 'plague-ridden'; poisonous

251   **found him** identified his true qualities; knows what he is after

254   **condition** character

255–256   **The wine...grapes** she is just like everybody else; all women are the same

258   **paddle with** stroke; fondle

260   **courtesy** good manners

261   **Lechery, by this hand!** Lust, I swear it!

261–262   **index...prologue** contents page and disguised introduction *(i.e. an indicator of their lust)*

262   **history** story *(continuing the images drawn from books)*

Iago's language

'Iago goes into perhaps the darkest areas of twisted, bitter and sexual language that the play contains' (David Suchet).

and telling her fantastical lies. To love him still
for prating? Let not thy discreet heart think it. 225
Her eye must be fed. And what delight shall she
have to look on the devil? When the blood is
made dull with the act of sport, there should be a
game to inflame it and to give satiety a fresh
appetite, loveliness in favour, sympathy in 230
years, manners, and beauties; all which the Moor
is defective in. Now for want of these required
conveniences, her delicate tenderness will find
itself abused, begin to heave the gorge,
disrelish and abhor the Moor; very nature will 235
instruct her in it and compel her to some second
choice. Now sir, this granted – as it is a most
pregnant and unforced position – who stands so
eminent in the degree of this fortune as Cassio
does? A knave very voluble; no further 240
conscionable than in putting on the mere form
of civil and humane seeming for the better
compass of his salt and most hidden loose
affection. Why, none, why, none! A slipper and
subtle knave, a finder of occasions, that has an 245
eye can stamp and counterfeit advantages,
though true advantage never present itself. A
devilish knave. Besides, the knave is handsome,
young, and hath all those requisites in him that
folly and green minds look after. A pestilent 250
complete knave, and the woman hath found him
already.

RODERIGO   I cannot believe that in her; she's full of most
blessed condition.

IAGO   Blessed fig's-end! The wine she drinks is made 255
of grapes. If she had been blessed, she would never
have loved the Moor. Blessed pudding! Didst thou
not see her paddle with the palm of his hand?
Didst not mark that?

RODERIGO   Yes, that I did; but that was but courtesy. 260

IAGO   Lechery, by this hand! An index and obscure
prologue to the history of lust and foul thoughts.

2.1

Having instructed Roderigo to pick a quarrel with Cassio later that evening, Iago mulls over his plans

265	**When these mutualities...way** when these intimacies show the way
265–266	**hard at hand** right behind; close by
266	**exercise** act *(i.e. the sexual act)*
267	**th'incorporate conclusion** the physical result
269–270	**Watch you...upon you** keep watch tonight – I will give you your orders
271	**Do you...occasion** find an opportunity
272–273	**tainting his discipline** sneering at his ability as a soldier
274	**minister** provide
276	**choler** anger
277	**haply** perhaps
277–278	**that he may** so that he does

279–281	**whose qualification...Cassio** who will not then be satisfied until Cassio has been dismissed *(to 'qualify' the* **taste** = *to dilute or change it)*
283	**prefer** promote; advance
	impediment obstacle
285	**prosperity** success
287	**warrant** assure
	by and by very soon
291	**apt...credit** likely and very believable
292	**howbeit that** although
296	**not...lust** not purely out of lust
	peradventure perhaps
297	**accountant** accountable; responsible
298	**diet** feed

They met so near with their lips that their breaths
embraced together. Villainous thoughts, Roderigo.
When these mutualities so marshal the way, hard   265
at hand comes the master and main exercise,
th'incorporate conclusion: Pish! But, sir, be you
ruled by me. I have brought you from Venice.
Watch you tonight; for the command, I'll lay't
upon you. Cassio knows you not. I'll not be far   270
from you. Do you find some occasion to anger
Cassio, either by speaking too loud, or tainting his
discipline, or from what other course you please
which the time shall more favourably minister.

RODERIGO   Well.   275

IAGO   Sir, he's rash and very sudden in choler, and ~~anger~~
haply may strike at you. Provoke him that he
may; for even out of that will I cause these of
Cyprus to mutiny, whose qualification shall
come into no true taste again but by the   280
displanting of Cassio. So shall you have a shorter
journey to your desires by the means I shall then
have to prefer them; and the impediment most
profitably removed without the which there were
no expectation of our prosperity.   285

RODERIGO   I will do this if you can bring it to any opportunity.

IAGO   I warrant thee. Meet me by and by at the citadel. I
must fetch his necessaries ashore. Farewell.

RODERIGO   Adieu.

                    soliloquay   *Exit.*

IAGO   That Cassio loves her, I do well believe't;   290
That she loves him, 'tis apt and of great credit.
The Moor, howbeit that I endure him not,
Is of a constant, loving, noble nature,
And I dare think he'll prove to Desdemona
A most dear husband. Now I do love her too;   295
Not out of absolute lust, though peradventure
I stand accountant for as great a sin,
But partly led to diet my revenge,

2.2 *Iago explains his plans to destroy Othello with jealousy. A herald announces the festivities in celebration of the Turkish defeat*

299 **lusty** lecherous; lustful

300 **leaped...seat** taken my place in bed with my wife *(literally 'jumped into my saddle')*

301 **inwards** insides

307 **trash** rubbish

trace follow *(a hunting term)*

308 **the putting on** being 'wound up'; being incited

309 **on the hip** at my mercy; where I want him

310 **Abuse...garb** slander him grossly before Othello; *or possibly*, slanderously inform Othello that Cassio is a lecher

313 **egregiously** outstandingly

314 **practising upon** plotting against

2 **certain tidings** sure reports

3 **importing** giving news of

mere perdition total loss

4 **triumph** victory celebrations

6 **addiction** inclination

8 **nuptial** marriage

9 **offices** *kitchens and cellars for supplying food and drink*

11 **told** 'counted'; struck

Iago

'In this second soliloquy the emphasis has changed. Iago is now plotting for revenge, and the motive advanced is no longer anger at missed promotion, but plain sexual jealousy' (M R Ridley). How much of this does Iago actually believe, however? That Cassio and Desdemona are in love? That his wife Emilia has had a sexual relationship with Othello? And with Cassio too?

311 Iago's sexual jealousy now extends to Cassio – conveniently, as Cassio has to be central to Iago's plans. At this point Iago has not got his design fully worked out – it is still *confused*; but the final line demonstrates his confidence that suitable opportunities will arise and that he will not be slow to exploit them.

(handwritten note: suspects him for sleeping with Emilia)

For that I do suspect the lusty Moor
Hath leaped into my seat; the thought whereof   300
Doth, like a poisonous mineral, gnaw my inwards;
And nothing can or shall content my soul
Till I am evened with him, wife for wife.
Or failing so, yet that I put the Moor
At least into a jealousy so strong   305
That judgment cannot cure. Which thing to do,
If this poor trash of Venice, whom I trace
For his quick hunting, stand the putting on,
I'll have our Michael Cassio on the hip,
Abuse him to the Moor in the rank garb   310
(For I fear Cassio with my nightcap too),
Make the Moor thank me, love me, and reward me
For making him egregiously an ass
And practising upon his peace and quiet,
Even to madness. 'Tis here, [*taps his head*] but yet
    confused: 315
Knavery's plain face is never seen till used.

Exit.

(handwritten note: thinks Cassio have done something with Emilia)

Scene 2

A street.

Enter OTHELLO's HERALD, with a proclamation.

HERALD   It is Othello's pleasure, our noble and valiant
general, that upon certain tidings now arrived
importing the mere perdition of the Turkish
fleet, every man put himself into triumph. Some
to dance, some to make bonfires, each man to   5
what sport and revels his addiction leads him.
For, besides these beneficial news, it is the
celebration of his nuptial. So much was his
pleasure should be proclaimed. All offices are
open, and there is full liberty of feasting from this   10
present hour of five till the bell have told eleven.
Bless the isle of Cyprus and our noble general
Othello!

Exit.

1	**look you to** take charge of	14	**cast** dismissed
2	**stop** restraint	19	**full of game** sexually responsive
3	**outsport discretion** celebrate to excess	21–22	**it sounds...provocation** her voice arouses lustful thoughts *(as a trumpet in war is used to give a signal)*
6	**honest** reliable *(see the note below)*	23	**methinks right modest** totally chaste, it seems to me
9	**the fruits are to ensue** the enjoyment is yet to come *(they have not yet consummated their marriage)*	24	**alarum** trumpet-call to arms
13	**Not this hour** not for an hour yet		

Othello

9–10 Despite Othello's earlier protestations about his sexual appetite, he seems to be eagerly looking forward to the consummation of their marriage.

Language

6 *honest:* In Othello's first public reference to Iago, he describes him as *A man...of honesty and trust* (1.3.280). Many critics, but notably William Empson in a famous essay called 'Honest in *Othello*', have pointed to the widespread use of this word and its variant forms throughout the play. It had a range of connected meanings in Shakespeare's time, from our modern usage (law-abiding, trustworthy) to 'sexually chaste', and it is particularly interesting how many people seem to attach it unthinkingly to Iago.

Iago's language

16–18 Jove, king of the gods, was famous for his sexual appetite; linking his name with Desdemona's in this way implies that she is equally lustful. Iago's insinuating references to Desdemona's sexual nature *(full of game...a parley to provocation...etc)* are quietly but firmly rebutted by Cassio, whose admiration for her is expressed in sincere but polite terms *(She's a most exquisite lady...).*

Scene 3

The citadel of Cyprus.

Enter OTHELLO, DESDEMONA, CASSIO, and ATTENDANTS.

OTHELLO   Good Michael, look you to the guard tonight.
Let's teach ourselves that honourable stop,
Not to outsport discretion.

CASSIO   Iago hath direction what to do;
But notwithstanding, with my personal eye   5
Will I look to't.

OTHELLO   Iago is most honest.
Michael, good night. Tomorrow with your earliest
Let me have speech with you. [*To DESDEMONA*] Come,
      my dear love,
The purchase made, the fruits are to ensue,
That profit's yet to come 'tween me and you.   10
[*To CASSIO*] Good night.

Exit OTHELLO with DESDEMONA and ATTENDANTS.

Enter IAGO.

CASSIO   Welcome, Iago. We must to the watch.

IAGO   Not this hour, lieutenant; 'tis not yet ten o'th'
clock. Our general cast us thus early for the love
of his Desdemona; who let us not therefore   15
blame. He hath not yet made wanton the night
with her, and she is sport for Jove.

CASSIO   She's a most exquisite lady.

IAGO   And, I'll warrant her, full of game.

CASSIO   Indeed, she's a most fresh and delicate creature.   20

IAGO   What an eye she has! Methinks it sounds a parley
to provocation.

CASSIO   An inviting eye; and yet methinks right modest.

IAGO   And when she speaks, is it not an alarum to love?

2.3 *Knowing that Cassio gets drunk very easily, Iago persuades him to have a drink*

27 **stoup** a half-gallon (2 litre) tankard

without outside

28 **brace** pair

28–29 **gallants...measure** young gentlemen who would gladly drink a toast

30–31 **I have very...drinking** *Cassio gets drunk very easily and quickly.*

34–35 **But one...for you** Just have one cup. I'll drink your share after that.

37 **craftily qualified** cleverly mixed with water

38 **innovation** disturbing new feelings

44 **it dislikes me** I don't like it

47 **offence** readiness to take offence

48 **my...dog** any young girl's pet dog

50–51 **caroused...pottle-deep** drunk toasts to the bottom of the tankard

51 **he's to watch** he's to be part of the guard

52 **Three else** three others

swelling arrogant

53 **That hold...distance** who are quick to take offence at any insult to their honour

54 **very elements** typical of the types who make up this island; 'the very lifeblood of the island'

55 **flustered** befuddled

Iago

26–44 Knowing exactly which of Cassio's weaknesses to exploit (the fact that he gets drunk easily and readily takes offence when he is drunk), Iago uses all his skills at playing the bluff, good-natured mate. His persuasive techniques – just one more drink...you'll offend the others if you don't – can be heard in any pub today.

Cassio in performance

How does Cassio behave here? In 1964 Derek Jacobi was confident and educated; Sean Baker in 1989 played him as tense and insecure as he begins his responsibilities for the watch.

CASSIO	She is indeed perfection. 25
IAGO	Well, happiness to their sheets! Come, lieutenant, I have a stoup of wine, and here without are a brace of Cyprus gallants that would fain have a measure to the health of black Othello.
CASSIO	Not tonight, good Iago. I have very poor and 30 unhappy brains for drinking; I could well wish courtesy would invent some other custom of entertainment.
IAGO	O, they are our friends. But one cup! I'll drink for you. 35
CASSIO	I have drunk but one cup tonight, and that was craftily qualified too; and behold what innovation it makes here. [*Taps his head*] I am unfortunate in the infirmity and dare not task my weakness with any more. 40
IAGO	What, man! 'Tis a night of revels, the gallants desire it.
CASSIO	Where are they?
IAGO	Here, at the door. I pray you call them in.
CASSIO	I'll do't, but it dislikes me.

Soliloquay · *Exit.*

IAGO	If I can fasten but one cup upon him 45
	With that which he hath drunk tonight already,
	He'll be as full of quarrel and offence
	As my young mistress' dog. Now, my sick fool Roderigo,
	Whom love hath turned almost the wrong side out,
	To Desdemona hath tonight caroused 50
	Potations pottle-deep; and he's to watch.
	Three else of Cyprus, noble swelling spirits,
	That hold their honours in a wary distance,
	The very elements of this warlike isle,
	Have I tonight flustered with flowing cups, 55
	And they watch too. Now, 'mongst this flock of drunkards

59 **If consequence...dream** if the outcome is what I hope for

61 **rouse** large drink

65 **canakin** small can

68 **span** short time *(literally the breadth of a hand)*

73 **potent in potting** good at drinking

Your Dane Danes generally

74 **swag-bellied Hollander** Dutchman with a hanging belly

76 **exquisite** excellent

78–79 **he sweats...Almain** he doesn't have to exert himself to overcome a German

82 **do you justice** match you (in drinking)

84 **was and** *'and' is often added in folk songs to help the rhythm*

87 **lown** loon; lout; cheat

88 **wight** person

<blockquote>
Am I to put our Cassio in some action
That may offend the isle. But here they come.
</blockquote>

Enter CASSIO, MONTANO, and GENTLEMEN.

<blockquote>
If consequence do but approve my dream,
My boat sails freely, both with wind and stream.   60
</blockquote>

CASSIO   'Fore God, they have given me a rouse already.

MONTANO   Good faith, a little one; not past a pint, as I am a
soldier.

IAGO   Some wine, ho!
[*Sings*] And let me the canakin clink, clink;   65
And let me the canakin clink.
A soldier's a man;
A man's life but a span,
Why then, let a soldier drink.
Some wine, boys!   70

CASSIO   'Fore God, an excellent song!

IAGO   I learned it in England, where indeed they are
most potent in potting. Your Dane, your
German, and your swag-bellied Hollander –
Drink, ho! – are nothing to your English.   75

CASSIO   Is your Englishman so exquisite in his drinking?

IAGO   Why, he drinks you with facility your Dane dead
drunk; he sweats not to overthrow your
Almain; he gives your Hollander a vomit ere the
next pottle can be filled.   80

CASSIO   To the health of our general!

MONTANO   I am for it, lieutenant, and I'll do you justice.

IAGO   O sweet England!
[*Sings*] King Stephen was and a worthy peer;
His breeches cost him but a crown;   85
He held them sixpence all too dear,
With that he called the tailor lown.
He was a wight of high renown,

91	**auld** old		115–116	**set the watch** mount guard
101	**general** Othello *(Cassio apologises for putting himself above his superiors in the list of people who are to be 'saved')*		120	**just equinox** exact equivalent *(the 'night' of his vice is precisely as long as the 'day' of his virtues)*
115	**platform** gun ramparts			

Cassio in performance

Actors playing Cassio exploit the language to convey his increasing drunkenness: *exquisite* (76 and 93) is a tricky word to say clearly if your speech is becoming slurred, and Shakespeare has observed accurately that, when a man starts proving that he is sober (*This is my ancient...*109–111), it is a sure sign that he is drunk. Some Cassios have had trouble distinguishing their right hand from their left; others have felt that the simple need to make such a distinction is sufficient indication of drunkenness without any added 'business'.

Iago and Cassio

104–105 Cassio's drunken and comic assertion that *The lieutenant is to be saved before the ancient* doesn't carry any particular significance unless to goad Iago even further with the reminder that he is below Cassio, not merely in military rank (something that can – and will – change), but, more importantly, in social class.

	And thou art but of low degree:	
	'Tis pride that pulls the country down;	90
	And take thine auld cloak about thee.	
	Some wine, ho!	

CASSIO   'Fore God, this is a more exquisite song than the
other.

IAGO   Will you hear't again?   95

CASSIO   No, for I hold him to be unworthy of his place that
does those things. Well, God's above all; and there
be souls must be saved, and there be souls must
not be saved.

IAGO   It's true, good lieutenant.   100

CASSIO   For mine own part – no offence to the general,
nor any man of quality – I hope to be saved.

IAGO   And so do I too, lieutenant.

CASSIO   Ay, but by your leave, not before me. The
lieutenant is to be saved before the ancient. Let's   105
have no more of this; let's to our affairs. – God
forgive us our sins! – Gentlemen, let's look to our
business. Do not think, gentlemen, I am drunk.
This is my ancient; this is my right hand, and this
is my left. I am not drunk now. I can stand well   110
enough, and I speak well enough.

GENTLEMEN   Excellent well!

CASSIO   Why, very well then. You must not think then that
I am drunk.

Exit.

MONTANO   To th' platform, masters. Come, let's set the   115
watch.

IAGO   You see this fellow that is gone before.
He's a soldier fit to stand by Caesar
And give direction; and do but see his vice.
'Tis to his virtue a just equinox,   120

2.3 *As Iago maliciously informs Montano that Cassio is a heavy drinker, Cassio re-enters, angrily pursuing Roderigo*

123 **some odd...infirmity** a chance occasion when he is drunk

125 **evermore his prologue** always the introduction

126 **watch...set** stay awake twice round the clock (24 hours)

135 **hazard...second** risk a position like second-in-command

136 **ingraft infirmity** deeply rooted weakness

141 **Zounds...!** God's wounds!

144 **twiggen** covered in wickerwork *(Cassio will either [1] make a wickerwork pattern with his sword on Roderigo's skin or [2] chase him through the holes in the wickerwork)*

Iago

138 *Not I...:* Once again, Iago masks his duplicity by seeming to be the loyal, faithful friend.

The one as long as th'other. 'Tis pity of him.
I fear the trust Othello puts him in,
On some odd time of his infirmity,
Will shake this island.

MONTANO   But is he often thus?

IAGO   'Tis evermore his prologue to his sleep: 125
He'll watch the horologe a double set
If drink rock not his cradle.

MONTANO   It were well
The general were put in mind of it.
Perhaps he sees it not, or his good nature
Prizes the virtue that appears in Cassio   130
And looks not on his evils. Is not this true?

Enter RODERIGO.

IAGO   [*Aside*] How now, Roderigo?
I pray you after the lieutenant, go!

                                        Exit RODERIGO.

MONTANO   And 'tis great pity that the noble Moor
Should hazard such a place as his own second   135
With one of an ingraft infirmity.
It were an honest action to say so
To the Moor.

IAGO   Not I, for this fair island!
I do love Cassio well and would do much
To cure him of this evil. [*Within* Help! Help!]
                        But hark? What noise?   140

Enter CASSIO, pursuing RODERIGO.

CASSIO   Zounds, you rogue! You rascal!

MONTANO   What's the matter, lieutenant?

CASSIO   A knave teach me my duty? I'll beat the knave into
a twiggen bottle.

RODERIGO   Beat me?   145

2.3 *In the ensuing fight, Cassio wounds Montano, as Roderigo slips out to sound the alarm*

146 **prate** talk rubbish; complain

148 **mazzard** *slang for 'head'; actually a drinking-bowl (skull-shaped)*

152 **mutiny** riot

156 **Diablo, ho!** By the devil!

158 **ashamed** put to shame; dishonoured

160 **He dies** I'll kill him!

Ray Fearon as Othello (RSC, 1999)

Iago

151–152 Iago cannot have known exactly how Roderigo's provocation of Cassio would turn out; but, typically, he is making the most of it, inflaming what could have been contained as a private brawl into a full-scale riot which will awake the island.

CASSIO	Dost thou prate, rogue?

Beats RODERIGO.

MONTANO	Nay, good lieutenant! I pray you, sir, hold your hand.

Restrains him.

CASSIO	Let me go, sir, or I'll knock you o'er the mazzard.
MONTANO	Come, come, you're drunk!
CASSIO	Drunk? **150**

They fight.

IAGO	[*Aside to* RODERIGO] Away, I say! Go out and cry a mutiny!

Exit RODERIGO.

Nay, good lieutenant. God's will, gentlemen!
Help, ho! Lieutenant. Sir. Montano.
Help, masters! Here's a goodly watch indeed! **155**

A bell rung.

Who's that which rings the bell? Diablo, ho!
The town will rise. God's will, lieutenant,
You'll be ashamed for ever.

Enter OTHELLO and ATTENDANTS.

OTHELLO	What is the matter here?
MONTANO	Zounds, I bleed still. I am hurt to the death. He dies. **160**

Attacks CASSIO again.

OTHELLO	Hold for your lives!
IAGO	Hold, ho! Lieutenant. Sir. Montano. Gentlemen! Have you forgot all sense of place and duty? Hold! The general speaks to you. Hold, for shame!
OTHELLO	Why, how now, ho? From whence ariseth this? **165**

166–167 **and to ourselves...Ottomites?** and kill ourselves, something which God prevented the Turks from doing *(by sending the storm which destroyed the Turkish fleet)*

169 **carve for...rage** *either* (1) take action to satisfy his anger *(like carving for yourself at table)*; *or* (2) cut people up as his fury prompts him

170 **Holds...light** does not put much value on his life

171 **dreadful** frightening

172 **propriety** usual ordered state

174 **love** *this often means 'friendship' or 'loyalty' in Shakespeare*

charge order

175 **even now** only a moment ago

176 **In quarter...terms** in their conduct and relationship

177 **Devesting** getting undressed

178 **unwitted men** bereft them of their wits *(astrologers believed that planets coming too close to Earth could cause madness)*

180–181 **I cannot...odds** I cannot explain how this stupid quarrel started

182 **would** wish

action battle

184 **you are thus forgot?** you have forgotten yourself like this?

186 **were wont to be civil** are usually well-mannered (civilised)

187 **gravity and stillness** seriousness and sober behaviour

189 **censure** judgement

190–192 **unlace...spend...** *The image is of Montano loosening the strings of a purse which contains his good name and spending it all, exchanging it for the reputation of a drunken fighter.*

193 **hurt to danger** mortally wounded

195 **offends me** is painful for me

196 **aught** anything

198 **self-charity** looking after yourself

201 **blood** passion; temper

Iago

176–177 Is Iago cleverly reminding Othello of the pleasure that has been interrupted by Cassio?

Iago in performance

173 A good example of those occasions at which Shakespeare includes in the dialogue what is effectively a stage direction: the actor playing Iago has to appear grief-stricken.

Are we turned Turks, and to ourselves do that
Which heaven hath forbid the Ottomites?
For Christian shame put by this barbarous brawl!
He that stirs next to carve for his own rage
Holds his soul light; he dies upon his motion.   170
Silence that dreadful bell. It frights the isle
From her propriety. What is the matter, masters?
Honest Iago, that looks dead with grieving,
Speak. Who began this? On thy love, I charge thee.

IAGO   I do not know. Friends all, but now, even now,   175
In quarter and in terms like bride and groom
Devesting them for bed; and then, but now –
As if some planet had unwitted men –
Swords out, and tilting one at other's breasts
In opposition bloody. I cannot speak   180
Any beginning to this peevish odds,
And would in action glorious I had lost
Those legs that brought me to a part of it!

OTHELLO   How comes it, Michael, you are thus forgot?

CASSIO   I pray you pardon me, I cannot speak.   185

OTHELLO   Worthy Montano, you were wont to be civil;
The gravity and stillness of your youth
The world hath noted, and your name is great
In mouths of wisest censure. What's the matter
That you unlace your reputation thus   190
And spend your rich opinion for the name
Of a night-brawler? Give me answer to it.

MONTANO   Worthy Othello, I am hurt to danger.
Your officer, Iago, can inform you,
While I spare speech, which something now offends
        me,   195
Of all that I do know; nor know I aught
By me that's said or done amiss this night,
Unless self-charity be sometimes a vice,
And to defend ourselves it be a sin
When violence assails us.

OTHELLO   Now, by heaven,   200
My blood begins my safer guides to rule,

202 **collied** muddied; blackened

203 **Assays** attempts

205 **sink in my rebuke** suffer from my disciplinary action

206 **foul rout** shameful brawl

207 **approved in** found guilty of

209 **lose me** *i.e. as a friend*

211 **manage** carry on

212 **court...safety** at the headquarters of the guard, and on duty

214 **partially affined** influenced by friendship

leagued in office connected because of your jobs

216 **Touch...near** don't remind me of things which are so important to me *(his honour as a soldier)*

219–220 **I persuade...him** I am sure that telling the truth will not harm him in any way

224 **this gentleman** Montano

225 **entreats his pause** pleads with him to stop

229 **the rather** earlier than I had intended; all the sooner

230 **For that** because

231 **high in oath** swearing violently

237 **forget** forget themselves

Othello's language

201–213 Othello claims that his temper is beginning to get the better of him. But his language throughout this play is a sure guide to the degree of control that he is capable of exercising at a given moment, and here the language remains measured and dignified – he is every inch the general *(the best of you Shall sink in my rebuke)*. Later, when Iago's poison takes effect, his decline and loss of control are clearly reflected in the language. Despite that, Iago must be pleased to see that Othello becomes particularly infuriated when he fails to get a straight answer to a straight question. He will use this weakness later.

Iago

216–242 In this speech Iago vividly demonstrates his skill with words and his ability to imply much by apparently saying little. Here he has to persuade both Cassio and Othello that he is trying to cover for the lieutenant, while convincing Montano that he is giving a fair and impartial account, all the time painting a picture for Othello which will show up Cassio in the worst light possible. He succeeds on all fronts.

226–231 Iago does not often tell a direct lie, presumably because he knows that it can be checked. Here, though, he changes the facts, but in such a way that no one could challenge his version.

And passion, having my best judgment collied,
Assays to lead the way. If I once stir
Or do but lift this arm, the best of you
Shall sink in my rebuke. Give me to know   205
How this foul rout began, who set it on;
And he that is approved in this offence,
Though he had twinned with me, both at a birth,
Shall lose me. What? In a town of war
Yet wild, the people's hearts brimful of fear,   210
To manage private and domestic quarrel?
In night, and on the court and guard of safety?
'Tis monstrous. Iago, who began't?

MONTANO   If partially affined, or leagued in office,
             Thou dost deliver more or less than truth,   215
             Thou art no soldier.

IAGO   Touch me not so near.
             I had rather have this tongue cut from my mouth
             Than it should do offence to Michael Cassio.
             Yet I persuade myself to speak the truth
             Shall nothing wrong him. This it is, general.   220
             Montano and myself being in speech,
             There comes a fellow crying out for help,
             And Cassio following him with determined sword
             To execute upon him. Sir, this gentleman
             Steps in to Cassio and entreats his pause.   225
             Myself the crying fellow did pursue,
             Lest by his clamour – as it so fell out –
             The town might fall in fright. He, swift of foot,
             Outran my purpose; and I returned the rather
             For that I heard the clink and fall of swords,   230
             And Cassio high in oath; which till tonight
             I ne'er might say before. When I came back –
             For this was brief – I found them close together
             At blow and thrust, even as again they were
             When you yourself did part them.   235
             More of this matter cannot I report;
             But men are men; the best sometimes forget.
             Though Cassio did some little wrong to him,
             As men in rage strike those that wish them best,
             Yet surely Cassio I believe received   240

241	**strange indignity** unknown insult	263	**sense** (1) reason; (2) physical sensation
242	**patience...pass** could not be tolerated	265	**imposition** something laid upon us by other people

Language

243 *honesty:* Here the word seems to mean a desire to tell the truth, but, combined with *love*, may also imply 'friendship and loyalty'.

Othello in performance

246–247 Many actors have performed these two lines in such a way as to imply that Othello's decision to make an example of Cassio is spurred by anger that Desdemona has been disturbed.

Desdemona in performance

Shakespeare gives Desdemona only half a line of dialogue here; what does the actor do? In 1985, while Ben Kingsley's Othello angrily gripped the hilt of his scimitar, Desdemona, played by Niamh Cusack, 'appeared framed in the doorway and seemed unaware of the transparency of her pale blue robe or of her own sensuality' (Keith Parsons and Pamela Mason). (See photograph on page 60.)

Iago

264–268 Iago's disparaging words about reputation are a good example of the way in which he is capable of offering completely contrary views on the same subject, to suit the listener or the context. This comment contrasts starkly with the opinions he will express to Othello later (3.3.155–161).

DECEIT

Act 2 Scene 3

From him that fled some strange indignity,
Which patience could not pass.

OTHELLO   I know, Iago,
Thy honesty and love doth mince this matter,
Making it light to Cassio. Cassio, I love thee,
But never more be officer of mine.   245

Enter DESDEMONA, with ATTENDANTS.

Look if my gentle love be not raised up.
[*To* CASSIO] I'll make thee an example.

DESDEMONA   What is the matter, dear?

OTHELLO   All's well, sweeting; come away to bed.
[*To* MONTANO] Sir, for your hurts, myself will be your
    surgeon.
Lead him off.   250

MONTANO is led off.

Iago, look with care about the town
And silence those whom this vile brawl distracted.
Come, Desdemona: 'tis the soldiers' life
To have their balmy slumbers waked with strife.

Exit with DESDEMONA and ATTENDANTS.

IAGO   What, are you hurt, lieutenant?   255

CASSIO   Ay, past all surgery.

IAGO   Marry, God forbid!

CASSIO   Reputation, reputation, reputation! O, I have lost
my reputation! I have lost the immortal part of
myself, and what remains is bestial. My   260
reputation, Iago, my reputation!

IAGO   As I am an honest man, I had thought you had
received some bodily wound. There is more sense
in that than in reputation. Reputation is an idle
most false imposition, oft got without merit   265
and lost without deserving. You have lost no

2.3 *Iago innocently questions Cassio, who is distraught at having lost his reputation*

269–270 **cast in his mood** dismissed temporarily, because of the way he feels at the moment

270 **in policy** *He had to dismiss Cassio as a public demonstration of his discipline and an example to others.*

272 **Sue to** plead with

276 **speak parrot** utter words without meaning

277–278 **discourse fustian** talk bombastic nonsense

294 **wrath** anger

296 **moraller** moraliser *(condemning himself)*

301 **Hydra** *the many-headed snake killed by Hercules*

Language

293–294 It is interesting how often the devil has so far been invoked in this play, not least in Brabantio's association of Othello's blackness with the devil and his allegations of witchcraft. Now Cassio finds the concept an apt one for describing the moods that have 'possessed' him.

reputation at all unless you repute yourself such a
loser. What, man, there are more ways to recover
the general again. You are but now cast in his
mood – a punishment more in policy than in   270
malice – even so as one would beat his offenceless
dog to affright an imperious lion. Sue to him
again, and he's yours.

CASSIO   I will rather sue to be despised than to deceive so
good a commander with so slight, so drunken, and 275
so indiscreet an officer. Drunk! And speak parrot!
And squabble! Swagger! Swear! And discourse
fustian with one's own shadow! O thou invisible
spirit of wine, if thou hast no name to be known
by, let us call thee devil!   280

IAGO   What was he that you followed with your sword?
What had he done to you?

CASSIO   I know not.

IAGO   Is't possible?

CASSIO   I remember a mass of things, but nothing   285
distinctly: a quarrel, but nothing wherefore. O
God, that men should put an enemy in their
mouths to steal away their brains! that we
should with joy, pleasance, revel, and applause
transform ourselves into beasts!   290

IAGO   Why, but you are now well enough. How came you
thus recovered?

CASSIO   It hath pleased the devil drunkenness to give
place to the devil wrath. One unperfectness shows
me another, to make me frankly despise myself.   295

IAGO   Come, you are too severe a moraller. As the time,
the place, and the condition of this country
stands, I could heartily wish this had not befall'n;
but since it is as it is, mend it for your own good.

CASSIO   I will ask him for my place again: he shall tell me I 300
am a drunkard. Had I as many mouths as Hydra,
such an answer would stop them all. To be now a

Iago advises Cassio to approach Desdemona and enlist her help in regaining his position as Othello's lieutenant

304 **inordinate** excessive

305 **ingredient** contents

306 **familiar** (1) friendly; (2) *a witch's 'familiar' was her attendant spirit; perhaps Iago is picking up the 'devil' language*

310 **approved** proved

316 **denotement of her parts** observation of her qualities

317 **importune** urgently ask

322 **splinter** repair with splints

322–323 **and my fortunes...** and I'll wager everything I have against any reasonable stake (**lay**)

327 **think it freely** believe it unreservedly

betimes early

328 **undertake** take up the matter

329–330 **desperate...check me** I am in despair if this fails

335 **free** open

336 **Probal** reasonable *(it can be proved to be sound)*

Iago

308–309 Iago's line *I think you think I love you* is typical of (a) his love of sentence constructions that need to be unpicked; and (b) his confidence that other people view him as a loyal and trustworthy friend.

312 By refusing to appeal to Othello directly (300–301), Cassio has played into Iago's hands. Opportunist that he is, Iago takes advantage of Cassio's reluctance and suggests an approach to Desdemona which will inevitably bring them together. He expands on this part of the plan in the soliloquy which follows (337–360).

318–321 Also typical is his understanding of other people's characters and his readiness to exploit their greatest virtues – in Desdemona's case, her willingness to go out of her way to help others (see 359).

326 Here Iago applies *honest* to himself within a sentence laden with trust words: *sincerity, love...kindness.*

331–332 *I must to the watch:* Is Iago rubbing salt in Cassio's wounds by subtly reminding him (a) that he has lost his lieutenantship; and (b) that he, Iago, is now in charge of the guard?

	sensible man, by and by a fool, and presently a	
	beast! O strange! Every inordinate cup is unblest,	
	and the ingredient is a devil.	305
IAGO	Come, come, good wine is a good familiar	
	creature if it be well used; exclaim no more	
	against it. And, good lieutenant, I think you think	
	I love you.	
CASSIO	I have well approved it, sir. I drunk?	310
IAGO	You or any man living may be drunk at a time,	
	man. I tell you what you shall do. Our general's	
	wife is now the general. I may say so in this	
	respect, for that he hath devoted and given up	
	himself to the contemplation, mark, and	315
	denotement of her parts and graces. Confess	
	yourself freely to her; importune her help to put	
	you in your place again. She is of so free, so kind,	
	so apt, so blessed a disposition she holds it a vice	
	in her goodness not to do more than she is	320
	requested. This broken joint between you and her	
	husband entreat her to splinter; and my	
	fortunes against any lay worth naming, this crack	
	of your love shall grow stronger than it was before.	
CASSIO	You advise me well.	325
IAGO	I protest, in the sincerity of love and honest kindness.	
CASSIO	I think it freely; and betimes in the morning I	
	will beseech the virtuous Desdemona to undertake	
	for me. I am desperate of my fortunes if they check	
	me.	330
IAGO	You are in the right. Good night, lieutenant; I must	
	to the watch.	
CASSIO	Good night, honest Iago.	

Exit CASSIO.

IAGO	And what's he then that says I play the villain,	
	When this advice is free I give, and honest,	335
	Probal to thinking, and indeed the course	
	To win the Moor again? For 'tis most easy	

Iago plans to use Desdemona's pleas on Cassio's behalf to make Othello jealous

338–339 **Th'inclining...suit** to persuade the good-natured Desdemona, if the business is honest

339–340 **she's framed...elements** in her make-up she is as generous as unrestrained nature

341 **were't to...baptism** even if it were to persuade him to cease being a Christian

342 **All seals...sin** all the signs of the religion that has saved him from damnation

344 **list** wants

345–346 **Even as...function** simply because his desire for her totally controls his weakened actions and faculties

347 **parallel** *in line with his plot*

348 **Directly to** in complete accord with

349 **put on** encourage; incite

350 **suggest...shows** tempt people first by appearing as virtuous as an angel

352 **Plies** solicits

354 **pestilence** plague; poison

355 **repeals him** asks for him to be reinstated

356–357 **And by how...Moor** and the more she tries to help Cassio, the more she will destroy Othello's trust in her

362 **fills up the cry** is there to help the noise; makes up the number

364 **cudgelled** beaten up

366 **wit** sense

371 **dilatory** causing delay

373 **cashiered** dismissed from service

Iago

348 *Divinity of hell!:* Iago explodes the hypocrisy of his own argument: this, he says, is the kind of moral teaching you would expect from the devil!

351–360 Iago's plan, hitherto *confused*, has now become clear to him – at least in its opening phases.

374–375 Iago seems to be saying: although some things look good for other people, Cassio's dismissal means that you will soon enjoy Desdemona. But this is another example of his proverbial sayings which look straightforward, but don't stand close examination.

Performance

In his 1952 film, Orson Welles reflected the world in which Iago's plots can *enmesh them all* by creating light and shadow patterns of latticed windows; his was a Cyprus of 'cramped arches, low ceilings and claustrophobic interiors' (Keith Parsons and Pamela Mason).

Th'inclining Desdemona to subdue
In any honest suit; she's framed as fruitful
As the free elements. And then for her   340
To win the Moor – were't to renounce his baptism,
All seals and symbols of redeemèd sin –
His soul is so enfettered to her love
That she may make, unmake, do what she list,
Even as her appetite shall play the god   345
With his weak function. How am I then a villain
To counsel Cassio to this parallel course,
Directly to his good? Divinity of hell!
When devils will the blackest sins put on,
They do suggest at first with heavenly shows,   350
As I do now. For whiles this honest fool
Plies Desdemona to repair his fortune,
And she for him pleads strongly to the Moor,
I'll pour this pestilence into his ear:
That she repeals him for her body's lust;   355
And by how much she strives to do him good,
She shall undo her credit with the Moor.
So will I turn her virtue into pitch,
And out of her own goodness make the net
That shall enmesh them all. – How now,
    Roderigo?   360

Enter RODERIGO.

RODERIGO   I do follow here in the chase, not like a hound that
hunts, but one that fills up the cry. My money is
almost spent; I have been tonight exceedingly well
cudgelled; and I think the issue will be, I shall have
so much experience for my pains; and so, with no   365
money at all, and a little more wit, return again
to Venice.

IAGO   How poor are they that have not patience!
What wound did ever heal but by degrees?
Thou know'st we work by wit, and not by
    witchcraft;   370
And wit depends on dilatory time.
Does't not go well? Cassio hath beaten thee,
And thou by that small hurt hast cashiered Cassio.
Though other things grow fair against the sun,

2.3 *Having persuaded the disgruntled Roderigo that everything is going according to plan, Iago plots his next moves*

378	**billeted** lodged		384	**jump** exactly
383	**awhile** meanwhile		386	**Dull not device...delay** Don't weaken the plot by lack of energy and delay.

Structure: the time scheme

376 *'tis morning!:* Iago's comment lets us know that the events we have witnessed have taken place in a single night. It is now dawn – the morning on which Cassio has promised to approach Desdemona.

Yet fruits that blossom first will first be ripe.   375
Content thyself awhile. By the mass, 'tis morning!
Pleasure and action make the hours seem short.
Retire thee; go where thou art billeted.
Away, I say! Thou shalt know more hereafter.
Nay, get thee gone!

Exit RODERIGO.

      Two things are to be done: 380
My wife must move for Cassio to her mistress;
I'll set her on;
Myself awhile to draw the Moor apart
And bring him jump when he may Cassio find
Soliciting his wife. Ay, that's the way!   385
Dull not device by coldness and delay.

Exit.

Exam practice

Extracts

1. It has often been said that 2.3 is the last time we see Othello in control. What are the nature and extent of the control that we see Othello exercising in this Act? In your answer you should:
   - discuss the language he employs in this scene and the emotions he seems to be displaying
   - express your own view of the extent of Othello's control here and the kinds of influence that Iago is already exercising over him
   - show an understanding of attitudes to military discipline, duty, reputation and honour, current in Shakespeare's time.

2. Reread 2.1.267–316 ('But, sir...till used'). What do Iago's speeches to Roderigo reveal about his methods at this point in the play? In your answer you should:
   - outline the methods he uses
   - make detailed references to the persuasive language Iago uses which helps to influence Roderigo, and examine the nature of Iago's forward-planning
   - express your own reaction to Iago as well as suggesting how other audiences might respond to him in this scene
   - show some awareness of the use of soliloquy.

3. Reread 2.3.158–254 ('What is the matter...waked with strife'). What does this extract reveal about the features of Othello's make-up which will contribute to his downfall? In your answer you should:
   - make detailed reference to Othello's language and the ways in which it reflects his changing emotions
   - express your own response to his behaviour here, and in particular his reactions to Iago's and Montano's explanations
   - show some awareness of the differences in rank between Othello, Montano, Iago and Cassio and the effect that those differences have on the proceedings.

Extended writing

4. What does Act 2 add to our understanding of Desdemona? In your answer you should:
   - discuss what is revealed about her in her conversations with Iago and Cassio (in 2.1)
   - express your own responses to her in this Act

- show an understanding of the position of a woman like Desdemona in the society depicted in the play.

5. Look again at 2.3. By a careful examination of this scene, consider the importance of Shakespeare's presentation of the military context in which the action is set to your understanding of the play as a whole.

Performance

6. In threes, reread 2.1.159–176. To gain an idea of the kind of behaviour in Cassio that Iago is scorning, act out the scene, using Iago's description as a guide to Cassio's gestures and mannerisms. Then discuss why Iago might find Cassio's manners so irritating. (It will help to read the notes on pages 56 and 62.)

7. Look back at the scene in which Cassio becomes progressively drunk and then bitterly regrets his rash behaviour (2.3.93–114 and 255 onwards). In pairs create two freeze-frames which demonstrate clearly the ways in which Iago and Cassio might behave at the following moments: line 109 ('. . .this is my right hand. . .') and lines 260–261 ('My reputation, Iago...!'). Try to reflect something of each character's thoughts and feelings at these two moments.

3.1 *A Clown dismisses the musicians who have been paid by Cassio to play for Othello*

1 **content your pains** pay you for your trouble

4 **speak...nose** *The inhabitants of Naples had a nasal accent; there is probably also a reference to syphilis, which affected the nose.*

7 **marry, are they** they certainly are

8 **thereby hangs a tale** there's a story about that

10 **a wind instrument** *The clown plays on the word* **tale***; 'tail' is a slang term for the penis (which hangs near a* **wind instrument***, the anus).*

13 **for love's sake** (1) as an act of friendship; (2) so that he can concentrate on love

15 **may not** cannot

16 **to't** set to it *(i.e. play)*

Clown's language

The Clown's wordplay rarely raises a laugh these days – indeed, in most productions his appearance with the musicians is cut altogether. The jokes about venereal disease and the bawdy innuendo concerning 'tails' are found in other plays from this period.

100

Act 3

Scene 1

Outside the citadel.

Enter CASSIO with MUSICIANS.

CASSIO   Masters, play here; I will content your pains.
Something that's brief; and bid 'Good morrow,
general.'

They play.

Enter CLOWN. — mirror themes in plot
— proverbs though through humour - pleas + pun
on thoughts
- does thought we

CLOWN   Why, masters, have your instruments been in
Naples that they speak i'th'nose thus?

MUSICIAN   How, sir, how?   5

CLOWN   Are these, I pray you, wind instruments?

MUSICIAN   Ay, marry, are they, sir.

CLOWN   O, thereby hangs a tale.

MUSICIAN   Whereby hangs a tale, sir?

CLOWN   Marry, sir, by many a wind instrument that I   10
know. But masters, here's money for you; and the
general so likes your music that he desires you,
for love's sake, to make no more noise with it.

MUSICIAN   Well sir, we will not.

CLOWN   If you have any music that may not be heard,   15
to't again. But, as they say, to hear music the
general does not greatly care.

MUSICIAN   We have none such, sir.

CLOWN   Then put up your pipes in your bag, for I'll away.
Go, vanish into air, away!   20

Exeunt MUSICIANS.

CASSIO   Dost thou hear me, mine honest friend?

CLOWN   No. I hear not your honest friend. I hear you.

Cassio enlists the aid of Emilia, Iago's wife, in arranging a meeting with Desdemona

23 **keep up thy quillets** enough of your puns

26 **entreats** begs

29 **seem...her** arrange for her to be told *(perhaps he is mocking Cassio's high-flown speech)*

30 **In happy time** well met; you've arrived at an opportune moment

34 **presently** at once

39 **...A Florentine...** *Cassio is from Florence; Iago isn't. He means:* I have never met such a kind man – not even among my own countrymen.

41 **your displeasure** the fact that you are out of favour

43 **stoutly** wholeheartedly; with determination

44 **he you hurt** Montano

44–45 **of great...affinity** very famous and related to important people ('well connected')

45 **in wholesome wisdom** as sensible self-preservation

46 **might not but** cannot do anything but

Structure: the time scheme

31 It is worth noting here that, if we follow certain pointers in the text, the events on Cyprus all take place within a very short space of time. We know, for example, that Othello landed after the destruction of the Turkish fleet only the previous day (at the beginning of 2.1). We know this because, shortly afterwards, Iago explains the plot against Cassio to Roderigo (*Watch you tonight* 269), a herald announces celebrations *from this present hour of five till the bell hath told eleven* (2.2.10–11) and then we see Cassio's drunken brawl and dismissal in 2.3, which clearly takes place that same night. Then, following Iago's suggestion, Cassio determines to see Desdemona *betimes* [early] *in the morning* (2.3.327); and shortly afterwards, Iago says, *By the mass, 'tis morning!* (376). When they meet again in this scene, Cassio confirms that *the day had broke before we parted* (31). If we call their arrival at Cyprus Day 1, then we are now only at the beginning of Day 2.

| CASSIO | Prithee keep up thy quillets. There's a poor piece of gold for thee. If the gentlewoman that attends the general's wife be stirring, tell her there's one 25 Cassio entreats her a little favour of speech. Wilt thou do this? |

| CLOWN | She is stirring, sir. If she will stir hither, I shall seem to notify unto her. |

Exit CLOWN.

Enter IAGO.

| CASSIO | In happy time, Iago. |

| IAGO | You have not been abed then? 30 |

| CASSIO | Why no; the day had broke before we parted. I have made bold, Iago, to send in to your wife; My suit to her is that she will to virtuous Desdemona Procure me some access. |

| IAGO | I'll send her to you presently, And I'll devise a mean to draw the Moor 35 Out of the way, that your converse and business May be more free. |

| CASSIO | I humbly thank you for't. |

Exit IAGO.

I never knew
A Florentine more kind and honest.

Enter EMILIA.

| EMILIA | Good morrow, good lieutenant. I am sorry 40 For your displeasure; but all will sure be well. The general and his wife are talking of it, And she speaks for you stoutly. The Moor replies That he you hurt is of great fame in Cyprus And great affinity, and that in wholesome wisdom 45 He might not but refuse you. But he protests he loves you, |

103

3.3   *As Othello begins a tour of the fortifications, Desdemona meets Cassio*

48   **take...front** eagerly snatch the first opportunity

51   **discourse** conversation

54   **bosom** private thoughts and feelings

2   **do my duties** pay my respects

3   **works** fortifications

4   **Repair** return

2   **All my abilities** my best

Imogen Stubbs as Desdemona (RSC, 1989)

And needs no other suitor but his likings
To take the safest occasion by the front
To bring you in again.

CASSIO   Yet I beseech you,
If you think fit, or that it may be done,   50
Give me advantage of some brief discourse
With Desdemona alone.

EMILIA   Pray you, come in.
I will bestow you where you shall have time
To speak your bosom freely.

CASSIO   I am much bound to you.

Exeunt.

Scene 2

The citadel.

Enter OTHELLO, IAGO and GENTLEMEN.

OTHELLO   These letters give, Iago, to the pilot
And by him do my duties to the Senate.
That done, I will be walking on the works;
Repair there to me.

IAGO   Well, my good lord, I'll do't.

OTHELLO   This fortification, gentlemen, shall we see't?   5

GENTLEMEN   We'll wait upon your lordship.

Exeunt.

Scene 3

The citadel.

Enter DESDEMONA, CASSIO, and EMILIA.

DESDEMONA   Be thou assured, good Cassio, I will do
All my abilities in thy behalf.

3   **warrant** assure you

12   **strangeness** estrangement; unfriendly distance

13   **politic** caused by policy (necessary official behaviour)

15   **nice** thin; insubstantial

16   **breed...circumstances** grow because of day-to-day happenings

17   **supplied** filled

18   **...will forget...** *because Cassio will have been out of the picture and someone else will have been doing his job*

19   **doubt** fear

20   **warrant** guarantee

22   **article** detail

23   **watch him tame** keep him awake until he does what I want *(a method of training young hawks)*

24   **his board a shrift** his meal table a place where confession is heard *(because Othello will have to 'do penance')*

27   **solicitor** advocate *(someone who argues on your behalf)*

28   **give thy cause away** give up your case

Dramatic irony

5   *honest:* Desdemona's use of the word is heavy with dramatic irony: within minutes Iago's wickedness will have begun to destroy her.

Act 3 Scene 3

we see
O unrued
– duties
+ unmarriage

EMILIA	Good madam, do. I warrant it grieves my husband
	As if the cause were his.
DESDEMONA	O, that's an honest fellow. Do not doubt, Cassio, 5
	But I will have my lord and you again
	As friendly as you were.
CASSIO	Bounteous madam,
	Whatever shall become of Michael Cassio,
	He's never anything but your true servant.
DESDEMONA	I know't; I thank you. You do love my lord, 10
	You have known him long, and be you well assured
	He shall in strangeness stand no farther off
	Than in a politic distance.
CASSIO	Ay, but, lady,
	That policy may either last so long,
	Or feed upon such nice and waterish diet, 15
	Or breed itself so out of circumstances,
	That I being absent, and my place supplied,
	My general will forget my love and service.
DESDEMONA	Do not doubt that; before Emilia here
	I give thee warrant of thy place. Assure thee, 20
	If I do vow a friendship, I'll perform it
	To the last article. My lord shall never rest;
	I'll watch him tame and talk him out of patience;
	His bed shall seem a school, his board a shrift;
	I'll intermingle everything he does 25
	With Cassio's suit. Therefore be merry, Cassio,
	For thy solicitor shall rather die
	Than give thy cause away.

Enter OTHELLO and IAGO at a distance.

EMILIA	Madam, here comes my lord.	
CASSIO	Madam, I'll take my leave.	30
DESDEMONA	Why stay, and hear me speak.	
CASSIO	Madam, not now. I am very ill at ease,	
	Unfit for mine own purposes.	

3.3 *Re-entering with Othello, Iago comments on Cassio's sudden parting from Desdemona*

34 **do your discretion** do whatever seems right and proper

43 **languishes** wastes away

46 **grace** favour in your eyes

47 **present** immediate

52 **I'sooth** truly

Iago

35 *Ha! I like not that:* 'This innocent-seeming half-line is the first poisonous drop in the hellish brew concocted by Iago' (G Salgado). Although it fails in its immediate purpose because of Desdemona's openness (42), it has a longer-term effect, lodging in Othello's consciousness to be recalled a moment or two later (109–110).

Othello in performance

In the 1989 production, Willard White's Othello sat calmly attending to paperwork as this scene began – a stark contrast to the emotional turmoil which was to follow. Olivier (1964) started very differently, reacting instantly to Frank Finlay's half-muttered *Ha! I like not that.*

Act 3 Scene 3

DESDEMONA   Well, do your discretion.

Exit CASSIO.

IAGO   Ha! I like not that.

OTHELLO   What dost thou say?   35

IAGO   Nothing, my lord; or if – I know not what.

OTHELLO   Was not that Cassio parted from my wife?

IAGO   Cassio, my lord? No, sure, I cannot think it,
That he would steal away so guilty-like,
Seeing you coming.

OTHELLO   I do believe 'twas he.   40

DESDEMONA   [*Coming to them*] How now, my lord?
I have been talking with a suitor here,
A man that languishes in your displeasure.

OTHELLO   Who is't you mean?

DESDEMONA   Why, your lieutenant, Cassio. Good my lord,   45
If I have any grace or power to move you,
His present reconciliation take.
For if he be not one that truly loves you,
That errs in ignorance, and not in cunning,
I have no judgment in an honest face.   50
I prithee call him back.

OTHELLO   Went he hence now?

DESDEMONA   I'sooth so humbled
That he hath left part of his grief with me
To suffer with him. Good love, call him back.

OTHELLO   Not now, sweet Desdemon; some other time.   55

DESDEMONA   But shall't be shortly?

OTHELLO   The sooner, sweet, for you.

DESDEMONA   Shall't be tonight at supper?

OTHELLO   No, not tonight.

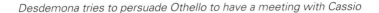

63   **he's penitent** he regrets what he has done

64–67   **And yet his trespass...check** yet his offence – were it not that in wartime you have to make an example of even the best people – would normally warrant no more than a reprimand in private

70   **mamm'ring on** hesitating

74   **bring him in** reinstate him *(as lieutenant)*

       By'r Lady by Our Lady (the Virgin Mary)

76   **boon** favour

79–80   **Or sue...person** or plead with you to do something to your own personal advantage

80   **suit** request

82   **of poise and difficult weight** serious and hard to make a decision about

84   **Whereon...** and, having agreed that, I have something to ask you

88   **fancies** whims

Iago

70–71 *Michael Cassio, That came awooing with you...:* Few things could more effectively fuel Iago's envy of Cassio than this knowledge – that Othello trusted Cassio, rather than Iago, in his most personal affairs. (This idea of Cassio acting as a go-between doesn't fit Othello's account in 1.3; but the inconsistency is never noticed in performance.)

Act 3 Scene 3

DESDEMONA Tomorrow dinner then?

OTHELLO   I shall not dine at home;
I meet the captains at the citadel.

DESDEMONA Why then, tomorrow night, on Tuesday morn,   60
On Tuesday noon, or night, on Wednesday morn.
I prithee name the time, but let it not
Exceed three days. In faith, he's penitent;
And yet his trespass, in our common reason
(Save that they say the wars must make example   65
Out of her best), is not almost a fault
T'incur a private check. When shall he come?
Tell me, Othello. I wonder in my soul
What you would ask me that I should deny,
Or stand so mamm'ring on. What? Michael
    Cassio,   70
That came awooing with you, and so many a time,
When I have spoke of you dispraisingly,
Hath ta'en your part – to have so much to do
To bring him in? By'r Lady, I could do much –

OTHELLO Prithee no more. Let him come when he will;   75
I will deny thee nothing.

DESDEMONA   Why, this is not a boon;
'Tis as I should entreat you wear your gloves,
Or feed on nourishing dishes, or keep you warm,
Or sue to you to do a peculiar profit
To your own person. Nay, when I have a suit   80
Wherein I mean to touch your love indeed,
It shall be full of poise and difficult weight,
And fearful to be granted.

OTHELLO   I will deny thee nothing!
Whereon I do beseech thee, grant me this,
To leave me but a little to myself.   85

DESDEMONA Shall I deny you? No. Farewell, my lord.

OTHELLO Farewell, my Desdemona; I'll come to thee straight.

DESDEMONA Emilia, come. [*To* OTHELLO] Be as your fancies teach you;
Whate'er you be, I am obedient.

Exit with EMILIA.

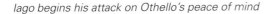

90–92 **Perdition...again** May my soul be
damned if I do not love you! And, if ever
the time comes when I do not love you,
it will be the end of the world.

102 **Discern'st thou aught** do you see
anything

111 **of my counsel** in my confidence;
trusted with my secrets

113 **contract...brow** frown

Othello

90–92 *Perdition catch my soul...:* 'These poignant words are Othello's last complete
affirmation of his love for Desdemona, and with their hint of loss and destruction presage the
tragedy to come' (G Salgado). Like his greeting to Desdemona when she arrives in Cyprus (*If
it were now to die...*2.1.188–192), the statement might suggest that he is in the power of
feelings that he cannot control.

Iago's methods

93 *My noble lord –:* After his initial attempt (35), this is where Iago's 'temptation' of Othello
really begins, and it is important to recognise the wide variety of techniques that he employs:

- He starts off with a question which apparently has little importance (*Did Michael Cassio...?*
  94–95), but which is deliberately given heavy significance by Iago's reaction to the reply:
  Indeed? (101).
- His second ploy is to feign reluctance to give a straight answer, which he does by
  irritatingly echoing Othello's questions: *Honest, my lord?...Think, my lord?* (103, 105). We
  have seen from Othello's reactions at 2.3.200 onwards how much he hates evasions.
- He selects his words very carefully: *No further harm* (98), for example, might imply that
  there must be some 'harm' to begin with.
- He also gives deliberately non-committal answers, such as *for aught I know* (104).
- All this has the desired effect of suggesting to Othello that there is a *monster* in Iago's
  thought *Too hideous to be shown* (107–108).

Iago in performance

113 Shakespeare often gives the actor stage directions through the dialogue (see also note to
2.3.173). Here we can see how the actor playing Iago might have reacted at line 101.

OTHELLO	Excellent wretch! Perdition catch my soul	90
	But I do love thee! And when I love thee not,	
	Chaos is come again.	

IAGO   My noble lord –

OTHELLO   What dost thou say, Iago?

IAGO   Did Michael Cassio, when you wooed my lady,
        Know of your love?   95

OTHELLO He did, from first to last. Why dost thou ask?

IAGO   But for a satisfaction of my thought –
        No further harm.

OTHELLO   Why of thy thought, Iago?

IAGO   I did not think he had been acquainted with her.

OTHELLO Oh, yes, and went between us very oft.   100

IAGO   Indeed?

OTHELLO Indeed? Ay, indeed! Discern'st thou aught in that?
        Is he not honest?

IAGO   Honest, my lord?

OTHELLO   Honest? Ay, honest.

IAGO   My lord, for aught I know.

OTHELLO What dost thou think?

IAGO   Think, my lord?

OTHELLO   Think, my lord? 105
        By heaven, thou echoest me,
        As if there were some monster in thy thought
        Too hideous to be shown. Thou dost mean something.
        I heard thee say even now, thou lik'st not that,
        When Cassio left my wife. What didst not like?   110
        And when I told thee he was of my counsel
        Of my whole course of wooing, thou cried'st 'Indeed?'
        And didst contract and purse thy brow together,

3.3 *Having raised the subject of Cassio's integrity, Iago refuses to tell Othello what is on his mind*

115 **conceit** idea; conception

120 **stops** hesitations

122 **of custom** habitual; customary

just honest

123 **close dilations** delays that you cannot control *(you expect deceitful people to hesitate for effect; but when honest people pause in their speech, it's a sign that they are unsuccessfully trying to suppress their true feelings)*

127 **Or those...none** or, if people are not what they appear to be, they should not have the shape of human beings

131–132 **speak...ruminate** tell me what is in your mind, what you are thinking over

135 **to that** to that thing which

137 **As where's** for example, where is

139 **uncleanly apprehensions** foul thoughts

140–141 **Keep leets...lawful?** *an image taken from the law courts, where, however honest the magistrates might be, they are sometimes joined on the bench* (**in sessions**) *by wicked men; i.e. even the purest-minded person sometimes has foul thoughts*

140 **leets** local courts of justice

Language

118 Again (as with Cassio at 3.1.39 and Desdemona at 3.3.5), Iago's *honesty* is invoked at a point where he is at his most deceitful and treacherous.

Iago's language

Notice how Iago gives the impression of having reservations and doubts through the repetition of the phrase *I think* (125, 129), which Othello picks up (126).

	As if thou then hadst shut up in thy brain
	Some horrible conceit. If thou dost love me, 115
	Show me thy thought.

IAGO   My lord, you know I love you.

OTHELLO   I think thou dost;
And, for I know thou'rt full of love and honesty
And weigh'st thy words before thou giv'st them breath,
Therefore these stops of thine fright me the
        more;   120
For such things in a false disloyal knave
Are tricks of custom; but in a man that's just
They're close dilations, working from the heart,
That passion cannot rule.

IAGO   For Michael Cassio,
I dare be sworn, I think that he is honest.   125

OTHELLO I think so too.

IAGO   Men should be what they seem;
Or those that be not, would they might seem none!

OTHELLO Certain, men should be what they seem.

IAGO   Why then, I think Cassio's an honest man.

OTHELLO Nay, yet there's more in this.   130
I prithee speak to me as to thy thinkings,
As thou dost ruminate, and give thy worst of thoughts
The worst of words.

IAGO   Good my lord, pardon me;
Though I am bound to every act of duty,
I am not bound to that all slaves are free to.   135
Utter my thoughts? Why, say they are vile and false,
As where's that palace whereinto foul things
Sometimes intrude not? Who has that breast so pure
But some uncleanly apprehensions
Keep leets and law days, and in sessions sit   140
With meditations lawful?

OTHELLO Thou dost conspire against thy friend, Iago,
If thou but think'st him wronged, and mak'st his ear

115

3.3 *Iago introduces the concept of a man's reputation and warns Othello to beware of jealously*

147 **jealousy** suspicious nature

148 **Shape...not** imagine faults which do not really exist

149 **imperfectly conceits** imagines things mistakenly

151 **scattering** random; incoherent

152 **quiet...good** peace of mind...welfare

156 **immediate jewel** most precious personal part

163 **if** even if

166 **mock** *because a jealous man is mocked*

167 **cuckold** a man whose wife has been unfaithful

169 **tells** counts

173 **fineless** unbounded; limitless

Richard McCabe as Iago and Ray Fearon as Othello (RSC, 1999)

Iago's language

Iago cleverly makes his statements sound hesitant and reluctantly expressed by speaking in long, complex sentences. For example, lines 144–151 are all one sentence, the main point of which is a simple request that Othello should not take too much notice of Iago's comments. But he extends it and delays its conclusion by adding several clauses – *Though I...; As I confess...; and...Shape faults...; ...that so imperfectly conceits...; nor build yourself...* – so that the overall effect is of a man trying to avoid having to say something unpleasant.

155–161 Iago's statement (*Good name in man and woman...*) is, on the face of it, simply a proverbial comment about reputation. But, by calling it a *jewel* – a word then commonly applied to virginity or chastity – and referring specifically to 'man *and* woman', he cunningly implies a reference to sexual 'reputation' and the mockery that a cuckold has to endure (see the note to 167).

155–167 Notice how quickly Iago raises the stakes. Within a few lines he has moved Othello on from thinking about 'good name', to jealousy (165), to being a cuckold (167). But, all this time, he has made no direct accusations.

A stranger to thy thoughts.

IAGO   I do beseech you –
Though I perchance am vicious in my guess   145
(As I confess it is my nature's plague
To spy into abuses, and of my jealousy
Shape faults that are not) – that your wisdom
From one that so imperfectly conceits
Would take no notice, nor build yourself a trouble   150
Out of his scattering and unsure observance.
It were not for your quiet nor your good,
Nor for my manhood, honesty, and wisdom,
To let you know my thoughts.

OTHELLO   What dost thou mean?

IAGO   Good name in man and woman, dear my lord,   155
Is the immediate jewel of their souls.
Who steals my purse steals trash; 'tis something,
    nothing;
'Twas mine, 'tis his, and has been slave to thousands;
But he that filches from me my good name
Robs me of that which not enriches him   160
And makes me poor indeed.

OTHELLO   By heaven, I'll know thy thoughts!

IAGO   You cannot, if my heart were in your hand;
Nor shall not whilst 'tis in my custody.

OTHELLO   Ha!

IAGO   O beware, my lord, of jealousy!   165
It is the green-eyed monster, which doth mock
The meat it feeds on. That cuckold lives in bliss
Who, certain of his fate, loves not his wronger;
But O, what damnèd minutes tells he o'er
Who dotes, yet doubts – suspects, yet strongly
    loves!   170

OTHELLO   O misery!

IAGO   Poor and content is rich, and rich enough;
But riches fineless is as poor as winter

3.3 *Pretending to be reassured by Othello's declaration that he would never let jealousy take hold of him, Iago tells Othello to watch Desdemona and Cassio closely*

178 **still** continually

182–183 **such exsufflicate...inference** exaggerated and inflated assumptions of the kind which would tie in with your hints

187–188 **Nor from...revolt** nor will I suspect for one moment that she might be unfaithful to me because I am so lacking in attractive qualities

195 **as I am bound** since it is my duty *(to tell him everything)*

198 **Wear your eyes...secure** keep a wary eye – neither oversuspicious, nor too relaxed

199 **free** generous

200 **self-bounty** natural, innate generosity *(in the way he views other people)*

201 **country disposition** the character and behaviour of people in our country *(Venice); perhaps also: the way women behave sexually*

203 **their best conscience** their highest idea of moral behaviour

Othello in performance

171 *O misery!*: Some actors play this as though Othello were simply reacting to the general condition described by Iago – the fact that there are men in the world who suffer in this way. Other actors see in this exclamation a sign that Othello is already applying the comments to himself. This second interpretation is harder to sustain, given the long and apparently controlled statement which follows (176–192). His declarations *To be once in doubt...* (179–180) and *I'll see before...*(190) show that he considers himself to be a man who, once his suspicions have been aroused, would take immediate practical steps to find out the truth and act instantly.

Iago's language

196 The word *yet* is cleverly inserted to imply that, although there is no actual proof at the moment, there will be. In *Look to your wife*, Iago shows that he now feels confident enough to go a stage further, moving from generalisations to a specific and explicit suggestion about Desdemona and Cassio.

201 This comment is designed to create a sense of insecurity in Othello; Iago is effectively saying, 'You are an alien; you don't understand the ways of our Venetian women.' There might also be a sexual allusion in *country* – compare Hamlet's 'Do you think I meant country matters?' (3.2)

Venice

201–204 Iago capitalises on the reputation of Venetian women for their sophistication and sensuality.

To him that ever fears he shall be poor.
Good God the souls of all my tribe defend   175
From jealousy!

OTHELLO   Why? Why is this?
Think'st thou I'd make a life of jealousy,
To follow still the changes of the moon
With fresh suspicions? No! To be once in doubt
Is once to be resolved. Exchange me for a goat   180
When I shall turn the business of my soul
To such exsufflicate and blown surmises,
Matching thy inference. 'Tis not to make me jealous
To say my wife is fair, feeds well, loves company,
Is free of speech, sings, plays, and dances;   185
Where virtue is, these are more virtuous.
Nor from mine own weak merits will I draw
The smallest fear or doubt of her revolt,
For she had eyes, and chose me. No, Iago.
I'll see before I doubt; when I doubt, prove;   190
And on the proof there is no more but this:
Away at once with love or jealousy!

IAGO   I am glad of this; for now I shall have reason
To show the love and duty that I bear you
With franker spirit. Therefore, as I am bound,   195
Receive it from me. I speak not yet of proof.
Look to your wife; observe her well with Cassio;
Wear your eyes thus: not jealous nor secure.
I would not have your free and noble nature
Out of self-bounty be abused. Look to't.   200
I know our country disposition well:
In Venice they do let heaven see the pranks
They dare not show their husbands; their best
    conscience
Is not to leave't undone, but keep't unknown.

OTHELLO   Dost thou say so?   205

IAGO   She did deceive her father, marrying you;
And when she seemed to shake and fear your looks,
She loved them most.

OTHELLO   And so she did.

119

208   **go to then** there you are, then

210   **seel** close up *(a term taken from hawking: the bird's eyelids were sometimes sewn together while it was being trained)*

close as oak as tightly as the grain in oak

218   **strain** exaggerate

219   **To grosser issues** (1) to more definite conclusions; (2) to conclusions to do with sex

222–223   **My speech...not at** my words would have evil consequences that I did not intend

225   **I do not...honest** I have no reason to believe that Desdemona is anything but chaste.

229   **affect** be attracted by

232   **Foh!** *an expression of disgust*

a will most rank (1) a most corrupt intention; (2) a most lecherous sexual desire

233   **Foul disproportion** disgusting perversion

234–235   **I do not...her** I am not referring specifically to her

---

Performance

211 *But I am much to blame....:* What makes Iago suddenly draw back here? In some productions he reacts to a changed response in Othello at this point, perhaps feeling that he has gone too far. A similar acting cue can be taken from line 224: *My lord, I see y'are moved.*

Dramatic irony

213 Othello's *I am bound to thee for ever* is truer than he can know. He presumably means 'indebted'; but from this point on Othello will be *bound* by Iago's power over him.

Iago's language

218–220 This is one of several instances where Iago urges Othello not to take a particular course of action in the sure knowledge that he is putting the idea firmly into his head.

226 *to think so:* The second half of this line is a devastating insinuation that Othello is being a credulous fool for believing in his wife's faithfulness.

228 Iago seems to have been waiting for this moment and pounces upon Othello's thought before he has a chance to complete it.

230 Iago highlights three aspects of Desdemona likely to make Othello feel alien and inferior: her European origins; her *complexion* (which can mean both 'skin colour' and 'personality'); and her social class (she is a senator's daughter). That things of this kind are troubling Othello is clear from the description of himself he then provides, to explain why a beautiful young Venetian girl might reject him in favour of a smooth young Florentine like Cassio: *Haply for I am black...*(262–265).

234 Again Iago covers himself, apparently drawing back from a direct accusation. Up to this point, he can always say 'Sorry, I was wrong.'

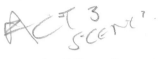 
IAGO	Why, go to then!
	She that so young could give out such a seeming
	To seel her father's eyes up close as oak – 210
	He thought 'twas witchcraft. But I am much to
	blame.
	I humbly do beseech you of your pardon
	For too much loving you.
OTHELLO	I am bound to thee for ever.
IAGO	I see this hath a little dashed your spirits.
OTHELLO	Not a jot, not a jot.
IAGO	Trust me, I fear it has. 215
	I hope you will consider what is spoke
	Comes from my love. But I do see y'are moved.
	I am to pray you not to strain my speech
	To grosser issues, nor to larger reach
	Than to suspicion. 220
OTHELLO	I will not.
IAGO	Should you do so, my lord,
	My speech should fall into such vile success
	Which my thoughts aimed not at. Cassio's my worthy
	friend –
	My lord, I see y'are moved.
OTHELLO	No, not much moved.
	I do not think but Desdemona's honest. 225
IAGO	Long live she so. And long live you to think so.
OTHELLO	And yet, how nature erring from itself –
IAGO	Ay, there's the point; as (to be bold with you)
	Not to affect many proposed matches
	Of her own clime, complexion, and degree, 230
	Whereto we see in all things nature tends –
	Foh! one may smell in such a will most rank,
	Foul disproportion, thoughts unnatural.
	But pardon me, I do not in position
	Distinctly speak of her; though I may fear 235
	Her will, recoiling to her better judgment,

Iago leaves, advising Othello that any pleading by Desdemona on Cassio's behalf will be suspicious

237 **May fall...forms** might come to compare you with the way her countrymen look

238 **happily repent** perhaps regret it *(her marriage)*

244 **I would...entreat...** I wish I could persuade you

249 **means** methods *(to get his job back, or to carry on an affair with Desdemona?)*

250 **strain his entertainment** begs you to employ him again

251 **vehement importunity** powerfully expressed pleading

253 **too busy in my fears** oversuspicious

255 **hold her free** think of her as innocent

259–261 **If I do...** *Othello adopts the language of falconry: a* **haggard** *is a wild hawk, held by leather straps (***jesses***); to set an untameable hawk free, the falconer would release it in the direction the wind is blowing.*

262 **prey at fortune** fend for herself

Haply for perhaps because

263–264 **soft parts...have** attractive social skills possessed by courtiers (*or* men who hang around bedrooms)

266 **abused** deceived (and disgraced)

Iago's language

237 ...country forms: Iago seems to have perceived Othello's insecurity concerning his origins and colour; again he slyly exploits these feelings by reminding Othello that Desdemona must be constantly making comparisons with white-skinned Venetians.

244–245 A further example of Iago urging one course of action with the intention that Othello will do the opposite. He does the same shortly afterwards (252–255).

Othello

240 Set on thy wife....: Othello has sunk very low very quickly.

258–259 knows all...dealings: Comments like this help to explain why Othello is so willing to believe Iago: the ancient is not only considered 'honest', but also experienced in the ways of the world – especially Venetian society – whereas Othello, an outsider and a soldier since childhood, is not.

sunk v. low
v. quickly

May fall to match you with her country forms,
And happily repent.

OTHELLO   Farewell, farewell.
If more thou dost perceive, let me know more.
Set on thy wife to observe. Leave me, Iago.   240

IAGO   My lord, I take my leave.

Going.

OTHELLO   Why did I marry? This honest creature doubtless
Sees and knows more, much more, than he unfolds.

IAGO   [*Returns*] My lord, I would I might entreat your
                honour
To scan this thing no farther. Leave it to time.   245
Although 'tis fit that Cassio have his place,
For sure he fills it up with great ability,
Yet, if you please to hold him off awhile,
You shall by that perceive him and his means.
Note if your lady strain his entertainment   250
With any strong or vehement importunity;
Much will be seen in that. In the meantime
Let me be thought too busy in my fears
(As worthy cause I have to fear I am)
And hold her free, I do beseech your honour.   255

OTHELLO   Fear not my government.

IAGO   I once more take my leave.

Exit.

OTHELLO   This fellow's of exceeding honesty,
And knows all qualities, with a learnèd spirit
Of human dealings. If I do prove her haggard,
Though that her jesses were my dear heartstrings,   260
I'd whistle her off and let her down the wind
To prey at fortune. Haply for I am black
And have not those soft parts of conversation
That chamberers have, or for I am declined
Into the vale of years – yet that's not much –   265
She's gone. I am abused, and my relief
Must be to loathe her. O curse of marriage,

Now prey to insecurity, Othello responds despondently when Desdemona enters to accompany him to dinner; and Emilia picks up Desdemona's handkerchief, inadvertently dropped

273 **Prerogatived...base** they are less privileged than common people *(Othello is perhaps saying that, when famous people become cuckolds, their shame is greater as it is more public)*

275 **forkèd plague** *It was a common belief that a cuckold grew horns which everybody but himself could see.*

276 **do quicken** are born

280 **attend** wait for

283 **a pain** *Othello might be referring to the growing cuckold's horns (see line 275).*

284 **watching** staying awake; not getting enough sleep

286 **napkin** handkerchief

290 **remembrance** gift; keepsake

291 **wayward** unaccountable; perverse *(the word implies that Iago does odd illogical things)*

293 **conjured her** made her solemnly promise

294 **reserves** keeps

Ray Fearon as Othello (RSC, 1999)

can't be used of

like token

control

v. jealousy

That we can call these delicate creatures ours,
And not their appetites! I had rather be a toad
And live upon the vapour of a dungeon ——— 270
Than keep a corner in the thing I love
For others' uses. Yet 'tis the plague of great ones;
Prerogatived are they less than the base.
'Tis destiny unshunnable, like death.
Even then this forkèd plague is fated to us 275
When we do quicken. Look where she comes.

Enter DESDEMONA and EMILIA.

If she be false, O then heaven mocks itself!
I'll not believe't.

DESDEMONA   How now, my dear Othello?
Your dinner, and the generous islanders
By you invited, do attend your presence. 280

OTHELLO   I am to blame.

DESDEMONA   Why do you speak so faintly?
Are you not well?

OTHELLO   I have a pain upon my forehead, here.

DESDEMONA   Why, that's with watching; 'twill away again.
Let me but bind it hard, within this hour 285
It will be well.

OTHELLO   Your napkin is too little;

He brushes her handkerchief aside, and it falls.

Let it alone. Come, I'll go in with you.

DESDEMONA   I am very sorry that you are not well.

Exit with OTHELLO.

EMILIA   I am glad I have found this napkin;
This was her first remembrance from the Moor. 290
My wayward husband hath a hundred times
Wooed me to steal it; but she so loves the token
(For he conjured her she should ever keep it)
That she reserves it evermore about her

125

295 **I'll have the work ta'en out** I'll have the embroidery copied

298 **I nothing...fantasy** my only concern is to satisfy his whims

300–301 **thing** *'thing' often meant the female sexual organ;* **common thing** *insultingly implies 'available to everyone'*

311 **to th'advantage** opportunely; luck being on my side

315 **import** importance

Emilia

301–302 Emilia's reactions to *It is a common thing – (Ha!...O, is that all?)* possibly indicate that she thinks at first that Iago is going to raise her alleged infidelity again.

To kiss and talk to. I'll have the work ta'en out 295
And give't Iago.
What he'll do with it, Heaven knows, not I;
I nothing but to please his fantasy.

Enter IAGO.

IAGO	How now? What do you here alone?
EMILIA	Do not you chide; I have a thing for you. 300
IAGO	You have a thing for me? It is a common thing –
EMILIA	Ha!
IAGO	To have a foolish wife.
EMILIA	O, is that all? What will you give me now For that same handkerchief?
IAGO	What handkerchief? 305
EMILIA	What handkerchief? Why, that the Moor first gave to Desdemona, That which so often you did bid me steal.
IAGO	Hast stol'n it from her?
EMILIA	No, but she let it drop by negligence, 310 And to th'advantage, I, being here, took't up. Look, here't is.
IAGO	A good wench; give it me.
EMILIA	What will you do with't, that you have been so earnest To have me filch it?
IAGO	Why, what is that to you?

Snatches it.

EMILIA	If it be not for some purpose of import, 315 Give't me again. Poor lady, she'll run mad When she shall lack it.

3.3 *Having explained his plan to deposit the handkerchief in Cassio's lodgings, Iago is faced by an emotional Othello*

317 **Be not acknown on't** *either* (1) say you
know nothing about it; *or* (2) the less you
know about it, the better

324 **conceits** imaginings; fantasies

325 **to distaste** to taste unpleasant

327 **mines of sulphur** *either actual mines, or
the pits of hell*

328 **mandragora** *a narcotic*

329 **drowsy** soporific; sleep-inducing

331 **owedst** owned; possessed

333 **Avaunt** go away

the rack an instrument of torture

340 **wanting** missing

344 **Pioneers** *the lowest-ranking soldiers
whose job was to dig trenches*

345 **So I...known** so long as I had known
nothing about it

346 **the tranquil mind** peace of mind

Performance

327 If Iago spots Othello entering after *...sulphur*, his comment *I did say so* can have the force of 'See what I mean?' Othello has been offstage only a short while, but most actors use the absence and re-entrance here to indicate the great physical and emotional change that he has undergone.

Iago's language

328–331 'This "incantation of the high priest of evil" presents the actor with a problem...Is he to try to keep it in character by delivering it with a malignant and almost snarling triumph or is he to give it as a piece of superb and rounded poetry, which Shakespeare has put incongruously into Iago's mouth?' (M R Ridley)

Othello's language

345–355 *O now, for ever Farewell....:* 'The heavy weight of the repeated "Farewell" falls like a drumbeat of doom' (G Salgado). This speech contains some of Othello's grandest language. He creates a picture of all the magnificence and glory that he is destined never again to enjoy; and, significantly, it is all associated with his career as a soldier. This is what he was really good at, and he knows it. Nowhere in these lines does he talk of his private life: the tragedy for him at this point is that *Othello's occupation's gone.*

| IAGO | Be not acknown on't. |
| | I have use for it. Go, leave me. |

Exit EMILIA.

	I will in Cassio's lodging lose this napkin	
	And let him find it. Trifles light as air	320
	Are to the jealous confirmations strong	
	As proofs of Holy Writ. This may do something.	
	The Moor already changes with my poison:	
	Dangerous conceits are in their natures poisons,	
	Which at the first are scarce found to distaste,	325
	But with a little act upon the blood,	
	Burn like the mines of sulphur. I did say so.	

Enter OTHELLO.

	Look where he comes! Not poppy nor mandragora,	
	Nor all the drowsy syrups of the world,	
	Shall ever medicine thee to that sweet sleep	330
	Which thou owedst yesterday.	

| OTHELLO | Ha, ha! False to me? |

| IAGO | Why how now, general? No more of that. |

OTHELLO	Avaunt, be gone! Thou hast set me on the rack.
	I swear 'tis better to be much abused
	Than but to know't a little.

| IAGO | How now, my lord? | 335 |

OTHELLO	What sense had I of her stol'n hours of lust?	
	I saw't not, thought it not, it harmed not me;	
	I slept the next night well, fed well, was free and merry;	
	I found not Cassio's kisses on her lips.	
	He that is robbed, not wanting what is stol'n,	340
	Let him not know't, and he's not robbed at all.	

| IAGO | I am sorry to hear this. |

OTHELLO	I had been happy if the general camp,	
	Pioneers and all, had tasted her sweet body,	
	So I had nothing known. O now, for ever	345
	Farewell the tranquil mind! Farewell content!	

In turmoil at the thought of Desdemona's infidelity, Othello angrily threatens Iago, who feigns injured innocence

348	**That makes...virtue** which make it a noble thing to be ambitious		363	**probation** proof
349	**trump** trumpet		373	**God b'wi'you** goodbye (God be with you)
352	**Pride, pomp** proud displays			**Take mine office** take back my job *(as your ensign)*
	circumstance ceremonies; pageantry		374	**to make...vice** to be so honest that it injures you *(Iago addresses himself)*
353	**mortal engines** deadly cannons		377	**profit** profitable lesson
	rude rough		378	**sith** since
354	**Th'immortal...counterfeits** imitate the terrifying noises of immortal Jupiter *(the thunderclaps of the king of the gods)*			**breeds such offence** has such harmful effects
355	**occupation** vocation			
358	**ocular** visible			

Othello's language

357 Three aspects of this line show a development in Othello's thinking: the first, that he now uses the crudest and most brutal language to describe Desdemona's alleged behaviour; the second, that he now makes a specific demand of Iago to give him proof; the third, that he now depends totally upon Iago to give him *ocular proof*, while cursing him for having put him on the rack. The qualities which served him well as a soldier – decisiveness, acting upon proof – are now his undoing.

366 Othello exactly describes his deceiver's actions here; but the possibility that this is what Iago is actually doing never seems to become a reality to him. He struggles to describe how damnable such an act would be *(Never pray more...)*, but it only takes Iago's expression of wounded loyalty *(O grace!...)* to muddy his thoughts once again.

Othello in performance

Olivier (1964) hurled Iago to the ground on *Villain, be sure...* and held a stiletto blade, sprung out of his bracelet, to Iago's throat. It was with this blade that he would later take his own life. Ben Kingsley's Othello (1985) similarly showed here that he was a man who, as the actor himself described it, 'if provoked at a primal level, would react with the violence of a psychopath'.

Language

377–378 A couplet often signals the end of a scene; here it indicates that Iago is about to leave.

379–380 *Thou shouldst* means 'you probably are'; Iago plays upon the verb with *I should* ('I ought to be').

Farewell the plumèd troops, and the big wars
That makes ambition virtue! O, farewell!
Farewell the neighing steed and the shrill trump,
The spirit-stirring drum, th'ear-piercing fife,   350
The royal banner, and all quality,
Pride, pomp, and circumstance of glorious war!
And O you mortal engines whose rude throats
Th'immortal Jove's dread clamours counterfeit,
Farewell! Othello's occupation's gone!   355

IAGO   Is't possible, my lord?

OTHELLO   Villain, be sure thou prove my love a whore!
              Be sure of it; give me the ocular proof;
              Or by the worth of mine eternal soul,
              Thou hadst been better have been born a dog   360
              Than answer my waked wrath!

IAGO   Is't come to this?

OTHELLO   Make me to see't; or at the least so prove it
              That the probation bear no hinge nor loop
              To hang a doubt on – or woe upon thy life!

IAGO   My noble lord –   365

OTHELLO   If thou dost slander her and torture me,
              Never pray more; abandon all remorse;
              On horror's head horrors accumulate;
              Do deeds to make heaven weep, all earth amazed;
              For nothing canst thou to damnation add   370
              Greater than that.

IAGO   O grace! O heaven forgive me!
              Are you a man? Have you a soul or sense?
              God b'wi'you! Take mine office. O wretched fool,
              That lov'st to make thine honesty a vice!
              O monstrous world! Take note, take note,
                  O world,   375
              To be direct and honest is not safe.
              I thank you for this profit, and from hence
              I'll love no friend, sith love breeds such offence.

OTHELLO   Nay stay. Thou shouldst be honest.

3.3   *Iago, with pretended reluctance, agrees to give Othello the evidence that he has demanded*

381   **that** what; that which

385   **Dian's visage** the face of Diana, goddess of chastity

386   **cords** ropes *(to hang or strangle himself with)*

388   **Would I were satisfied!** *This has the sense of 'I wish I had proof!'*

393   **supervisor** onlooker

      gape on watch open-mouthed

394   **topped** *a variation of tupped – see 1.1.86*

397–398   **bolster...own** sleep on any pillow other than their own

401   **prime** sexually excited

      hot lecherous

402   **salt** lustful

      in pride 'on heat'

404   **imputation...circumstances** opinion founded on strong circumstantial evidence

407   **living** strong

408   **office** job

409   **entered in this cause** become involved in this matter

410   **Pricked** spurred on

Iago in performance

David Suchet (Iago in 1985) said: 'I played the next section [from *O grace!* (371)] very aggressively and very hurt. How could he, Othello, even think of treating me like that! From then on I played Iago on the attack right up until line [424: *...gave thee to the Moor!*].'

Othello

386–387 Othello lists the methods by which he might commit suicide.

Iago's language

389–406 In contrast to Othello's passionate outbursts, Iago at first seems quite deliberately to keep his language matter-of-fact, with expressions such as *How satisfied, my lord?* and *It were a tedious difficulty, I think....* Then, to torment Othello further, he makes explicit and crude references which force him to visualise Desdemona and Cassio in the sexual act, *as prime as goats, as hot as monkeys....*

IAGO	I should be wise; for honesty's a fool	380
	And loses that it works for.	

OTHELLO   By the world,
I think my wife be honest, and think she is not;
I think that thou art just, and think thou art not.
I'll have some proof. My name, that was as fresh
As Dian's visage, is now begrimed and black   385
As mine own face. If there be cords, or knives,
Poison, or fire, or suffocating streams,
I'll not endure it. Would I were satisfied!

IAGO   I see you are eaten up with passion.
I do repent me that I put it to you.   390
You would be satisfied?

OTHELLO   Would? Nay, and I will.

IAGO   And may; but how? How satisfied, my lord?
Would you, the supervisor, grossly gape on?
Behold her topped?

OTHELLO   Death and damnation! O!

IAGO   It were a tedious difficulty, I think,   395
To bring them to that prospect. Damn them then,
If ever mortal eyes do see them bolster
More than their own! What then? How then?
What shall I say? Where's satisfaction?
It is impossible you should see this,   400
Were they as prime as goats, as hot as monkeys,
As salt as wolves in pride, and fools as gross
As ignorance made drunk. But yet, I say,
If imputation and strong circumstances
Which lead directly to the door of truth   405
Will give you satisfaction, you might have't.

OTHELLO   Give me a living reason she's disloyal.

IAGO   I do not like the office.
But sith I am entered in this cause so far,
Pricked to't by foolish honesty and love,   410
I will go on. I lay with Cassio lately,
And being troubled with a raging tooth,

3.3 *Iago claims that Cassio has recently cried out Desdemona's name in his sleep, and then declares that he has seen Desdemona's handkerchief in Cassio's possession*

414 **loose of soul** loose-tongued about their secret thoughts and feelings

426 **denoted...conclusion** was evidence that something had already happened between them

427 **'Tis a shrewd doubt** it's a strong suspicion; 'it's a fair bet' *(this line is given to Iago in some editions)*

433 **Spotted with** embroidered with a pattern of

440 **the slave** Cassio

443 **fond** foolish

Iago's language

417–424 *'Sweet Desdemona...!'*: Iago's sudden switch to direct speech adds conviction to his story, and he ensures that the description is a graphic one. To an outsider, it is a comic scene that he conjures up – Cassio kissing him hard and laying his leg over his thigh – but it has its desired effects of both convincing and tormenting Othello.

425 *Nay...*: This is another example of Iago's 'reverse-intention' tactics: he claims to be minimising the significance of the dream in the knowledge that Othello will think 'He's trying to play it down – but I know it's true and important!' Possibly he has another motive too: if Othello were to confront Cassio, Iago could always say 'Well, I told you it was only a dream.'

430 *Nay, yet be wise*: Iago restrains Othello: he doesn't want him rushing off before he has totally convinced him; there is still the handkerchief...

439 Iago cleverly slips this in: there are no *other proofs*; nothing whatever has been proved yet.

I could not sleep.
There are a kind of men so loose of soul
That in their sleeps will mutter their affairs.   415
One of this kind is Cassio.
In sleep I heard him say, 'Sweet Desdemona,
Let us be wary, let us hide our loves!'
And then, sir, would he gripe and wring my hand,
Cry 'O sweet creature!' Then kiss me hard,   420
As if he plucked up kisses by the roots
That grew upon my lips; laid his leg o'er my thigh,
And sigh, and kiss, and then cry, 'Cursèd fate
That gave thee to the Moor!'

OTHELLO   O monstrous! monstrous!

IAGO   Nay, this was but his dream.   425

OTHELLO   But this denoted a foregone conclusion,
'Tis a shrewd doubt, though it be but a dream.

IAGO   And this may help to thicken other proofs
That do demonstrate thinly.

OTHELLO   I'll tear her all to pieces!

IAGO   Nay, yet be wise. Yet we see nothing done;   430
She may be honest yet. Tell me but this:
Have you not sometimes seen a handkerchief
Spotted with strawberries in your wife's hand?

OTHELLO   I gave her such a one; 'twas my first gift.

IAGO   I know not that; but such a handkerchief –   435
I am sure it was your wife's – did I today
See Cassio wipe his beard with.

OTHELLO   If it be that –

IAGO   If it be that, or any that was hers,
It speaks against her with the other proofs.

OTHELLO   O, that the slave had forty thousand lives!   440
One is too poor, too weak for my revenge.
Now do I see 'tis true. Look here, Iago:
All my fond love thus do I blow to heaven.

3.3 *Iago pledges his dedicated service to assist Othello in fulfilling his vowed revenge*

446 **hearted** located in the heart

447 **fraught** burden; freight

448 **aspics'** asps' *(poisonous snakes)*

content patient

451–454 **Pontic Sea...Propontic...Hellespont** *Shakespeare might be drawing upon a translation of a work by the Roman Pliny, who stated that the Black (***Pontic***) Sea always flows into the Sea of Marmara (***Propontic***) through the Dardanelles (***Hellespont***), but never ebbs back again (***Ne'er keeps retiring ebb***).*

452 **compulsive** irresistible

457 **capable** ample; all-embracing

458 **marble** *mottled with light and shade; but possibly also hard and unyielding, like Othello's determination*

460 **engage** pledge

462 **clip** embrace

464 **execution** practical application

wit intelligence

466–467 **to obey...business ever** whatever bloody deed you command me to perform, I will do because of the pity I feel for you

469 **to't** to the proof; to the test

Othello in performance

458 To show his utter rejection of the civilisation, culture and religion he had adopted, Olivier's Othello (1964) tore off his crucifix on *by yond marble heaven* and then crouched down, his forehead to the ground, to make his *sacred vow.*

Performance

460 *Do not rise yet:* This is a powerful moment on stage, as Iago joins Othello in kneeling; we see the parody of a pious act: two men praying, but for the furtherance of evil.

Act 3 Scene 3

3.3

OTHELLO 'Tis gone. *seriously driving this home*
all the way
Arise, black vengeance, from the hollow hell! 445
Yield up, O Love, thy crown and hearted throne
To tyrannous hate! Swell, bosom, with thy fraught,
For 'tis of aspics' tongues.

IAGO   Yet be content – *— enjoying*
his inner
turmoil.

OTHELLO O, blood, blood, blood!

IAGO Patience, I say. Your mind may change. 450

OTHELLO Never, Iago. Like to the Pontic Sea,
Whose icy current and compulsive course
Ne'er keeps retiring ebb, but keeps due on
To the Propontic and the Hellespont,
Even so my bloody thoughts, with violent pace, 455
Shall ne'er look back, ne'er ebb to humble love,
Till that a capable and wide revenge
Swallow them up. [*He kneels*] Now, by yond marble
    heaven, *→ subservient*
In the due reverence of a sacred vow *epitomises*
I here engage my words. *his complete control*

IAGO   Do not rise yet. 460

IAGO kneels. *Subtext*
— THEATRE
going down
to his level.

our
dramatic

Witness, you ever-burning lights above,
You elements that clip us round about,
Witness that here Iago doth give up
The execution of his wit, hands, heart
To wronged Othello's service. Let him command, 465
And to obey shall be in me remorse, *twisting the knife*
What bloody business ever.

They rise. *together*
in harmony.
gay love?

OTHELLO   I greet thy love,
Not with vain thanks but with acceptance bounteous,
And will upon the instant put thee to't.
Within these three days let me hear thee say 470
That Cassio's not alive. *total trust*
— will serve him.

137

Wakeu'o

473 **lewd minx** lecherous animal

1 **sirrah** *a term of address used to people of lower status, such as servants*

lies is staying; is lodging *(the clown plays on the other meaning – tells a lie – in lines 2 and 4)*

4–5 **for me...'tis stabbing** any soldier would stab me if I called him a liar

7 **is to tell you...lie** would be for me to tell a lie *(because he doesn't know where Cassio is lodging)*

11 **lie in mine own throat** tell a bare-faced lie

12 **be edified** learn

13 **catechize** go through a question-and-answer routine *(catechism is a method of instruction used by the Church)*

16 **moved** attempted to persuade

Iago

473 *But let her live:* More 'reverse intention' from Iago: Othello has nowhere suggested that Desdemona should die (unless we count the intemperate exclamation at line 429); it is Iago who here puts the thought into his head.

477 Iago has now achieved both aims from his original *double knavery* (1.3.387–388): to get Cassio's position as lieutenant, and to exercise his power over Othello.

478 Othello will take this to mean 'I am your loyal servant'; this is, of course, exactly the reverse of the truth. Iago's statement might more accurately be interpreted as 'you have become possessed with my spirit'.

Performance

1–19 The exchange between Desdemona and the Clown, with its feeble wordplay, is, like the Clown's conversation with the musicians at the beginning of 3.1, often cut in performance. If left in, it can provide a break in the intensity of the preceding and following scenes.

Language

1–19 Like all Shakespeare's clowns, this one is, in Feste's description from *Twelfth Night*, a 'corrupter of words' (3.1). After the Clown's punning on *lie*, Desdemona herself tries to match his wordplay with her own extravagant use of language (12), but he has the last word (18–19).

central, pivotal Act of play
central + important action!

IAGO	My friend is dead. 'Tis done at your request. But let her live.

such change? to early man fault neither nature.

OTHELLO	Damn her, lewd minx! O, damn her! Damn her! Come, go with me apart. I will withdraw 475 To furnish me with some swift means of death For the fair devil. Now art thou my lieutenant.

IAGO	I am your own for ever.

juxtaposition while block.

not really by M   manipulative Othello

Exeunt.

Scene 4

A street.

Enter DESDEMONA, EMILIA, and CLOWN.

DESDEMONA	Do you know, sirrah, where Lieutenant Cassio lies?

CLOWN	I dare not say he lies anywhere.

DESDEMONA	Why, man?

CLOWN	He's a soldier, and for me to say a soldier lies, 'tis stabbing. 5

DESDEMONA	Go to. Where lodges he?

CLOWN	To tell you where he lodges is to tell you where I lie.

DESDEMONA	Can anything be made of this?

CLOWN	I know not where he lodges, and for me to devise a lodging, and say he lies here or he lies there, 10 were to lie in mine own throat.

DESDEMONA	Can you enquire him out, and be edified by report?

CLOWN	I will catechize the world for him; that is, make questions, and by them answer.

DESDEMONA	Seek him, bid him come hither. Tell him I have 15 moved my lord on his behalf and hope all will be well.

18 **compass** scope; range of ability

23 **crusadoes** *Portuguese gold coins, bearing a cross*

but if it were not for the fact that

25 **were** would be

28 **humours** *the bodily fluids believed to control people's temperament; jealousy was thought to be caused by an excess of black bile*

31 **O, hardness to dissemble!** *Othello could be referring to himself (it is hard for me to keep up a pretence), or to Desdemona (she must have a hard nature to be able to deceive me like this).*

33 **moist** *Some people (including Othello here) believed that a moist palm was a sign of a lustful nature; others (including Desdemona – see line 34) saw it as simply an indication of youth.*

35 **fruitfulness** (1) generosity; (2) an amorous character; (3) fertility

liberal generous and free *(with the possible implication of 'a bit too free')*

37 **sequester** restraint; imprisonment

38 **castigation** correction through discipline

41 **frank** open and honest; too free

Emilia in performance

People often ask: if Emilia is Desdemona's friend, why doesn't she tell her where the handkerchief is? Zoë Wanamaker (1989) answered this question by creating an Emilia who was jealous of the loving relationship that Desdemona had and who was prepared to see Desdemona experience some of the marital disharmony which was her daily lot.

Othello's language

1–48 Throughout this exchange with Desdemona, Othello's dissembling (31) shows itself in his use of words which have more than one layer of meaning – *fruitfulness; liberal; moist; frank; salt* – all of which can hint at sexual excess if interpreted in a certain way; and obscure references that Desdemona cannot understand *(The hearts of old gave hands...).*

Act 3 Scene 4

CLOWN	To do this is within the compass of man's wit, and therefore I will attempt the doing it.

Exit CLOWN.

DESDEMONA	Where should I lose the handkerchief, Emilia?	20

EMILIA   I know not, madam.

DESDEMONA	Believe me, I had rather have lost my purse
	Full of crusadoes. And but my noble Moor
	Is true of mind, and made of no such baseness
	As jealous creatures are, it were enough	25
	To put him to ill thinking.

EMILIA   Is he not jealous?

DESDEMONA	Who, he? I think the sun where he was born
	Drew all such humours from him.

EMILIA   Look where he comes.

Enter OTHELLO.

DESDEMONA	I will not leave him now till Cassio
	Be called to him. How is't with you, my lord?	30

OTHELLO	Well, my good lady. [*Aside*] O, hardness to
	dissemble! –
	How do you, Desdemona?

DESDEMONA   Well, my good lord.

OTHELLO   Give me your hand. This hand is moist, my lady.

DESDEMONA   It hath felt no age nor known no sorrow.

OTHELLO	This argues fruitfulness and liberal heart.	35
	Hot, hot and moist. This hand of yours requires
	A sequester from liberty; fasting and prayer,
	Much castigation, exercise devout;
	For here's a young and sweating devil here
	That commonly rebels. 'Tis a good hand,	40
	A frank one.

3.4 *Othello questions Desdemona about the whereabouts of the handkerchief, describing its special powers*

43–44 **The hearts of old...not hearts** *Othello imagines emblems on a coat of arms (**heraldry**): in the old days, he says, people gave their hearts when they gave their hands in marriage; these days, they give only their hands.*

46 **chuck** *a term of affection*

48 **salt and sorry rheum** a nasty running cold in the nose *(but **salt** could also mean 'lecherous')*

55 **charmer** enchantress

57 **amiable** lovable

59–60 **my father's...loathèd** she would become hated in my father's sight

60 **spirits** emotions

61 **fancies** loves

64 **darling** precious object

65 **perdition** damnation; destruction *(a term he used when envisaging the loss of Desdemona's love in 3.3.90–92)*

67 **web** weaving

Imogen Stubbs as Desdemona and Willard White as Othello (RSC, 1989)

DESDEMONA　　　　　　　　You may, indeed, say so;
　　　　　　　　For 'twas that hand that gave away my heart.

OTHELLO　　A liberal hand! The hearts of old gave hands,
　　　　　　But our new heraldry is hands, not hearts.

DESDEMONA　I cannot speak of this. Come now, your promise.　　**45**

OTHELLO　　What promise, chuck?

DESDEMONA　I have sent to bid Cassio come speak with you.

OTHELLO　　I have a salt and sorry rheum offends me.
　　　　　　Lend me thy handkerchief.

DESDEMONA　　　　　　　　　　　　Here, my lord.

OTHELLO　　That which I gave you.

DESDEMONA　　　　　　　　　　I have it not about me.　　**50**

OTHELLO　　Not?

DESDEMONA　No, indeed my lord.

OTHELLO　　　　　　　　　That's a fault.
　　　　　　That handkerchief
　　　　　　Did an Egyptian to my mother give.
　　　　　　She was a charmer, and could almost read　　**55**
　　　　　　The thoughts of people. She told her, while she kept it
　　　　　　'Twould make her amiable and subdue my father
　　　　　　Entirely to her love; but if she lost it
　　　　　　Or made a gift of it, my father's eye
　　　　　　Should hold her loathèd, and his spirits should
　　　　　　　　hunt　　**60**
　　　　　　After new fancies. She, dying, gave it me,
　　　　　　And bid me, when my fate would have me wive
　　　　　　To give it her. I did so; and take heed on't;
　　　　　　Make it a darling like your precious eye.
　　　　　　To lose't or give't away were such perdition　　**65**
　　　　　　As nothing else could match.

DESDEMONA　　　　　　　　　　Is't possible?

OTHELLO　　'Tis true. There's magic in the web of it.

Desdemona struggles in the face of Othello's increasingly emotional interrogation

68 **sibyl** prophetess

69 **to course...compasses** to go two hundred times round the Earth

70 **prophetic fury** prophetess's frenzy of inspiration

work embroidered pattern

72 **mummy** *a substance derived from embalmed bodies and supposed to possess magical properties*

72–73 **the skilful...hearts** trained people prepared it as a drug made from the hearts of virgins

77 **startingly and rash** disjointedly and excitedly

78 **out o'th'way** lost; mislaid

81 **an if** if

86 **suit** request

88 **My mind misgives** I don't like the sound of this

90 **sufficient** capable

92 **your love** affection for you

Desdemona

81–85 Why does Desdemona fail to answer Othello's question about the handkerchief directly (line 50) and then persist in lying (line 81 onwards)? Perhaps, despite her avowed faith in Othello's lack of jealousy (23–26), she does doubt his reaction.

Othello's language

76–96 Othello's increasing loss of control is reflected in the sequence of short, abrupt sentences *(Say you?...How?...)* and his obsessive references to the handkerchief: 'the word handkerchief flutters ominously like a storm signal. Othello calls for it three times in succession, as if the handkerchief would, like a magical object, automatically guarantee Desdemona's innocence' (G Salgado).

Emilia in performance

50–96 What does Emilia do during Othello's inquisition about the handkerchief? She knows exactly where it is and must be aware of Desdemona's discomfort; yet she remains silent.

A sibyl that had numbered in the world
The sun to course two hundred compasses,
In her prophetic fury sewed the work;   70
The worms were hallowed that did breed the silk,
And it was dyed in mummy which the skilful
Conserved of maidens' hearts.

DESDEMONA   Indeed? Is't true?

OTHELLO   Most veritable. Therefore look to't well.

DESDEMONA   Then would to God that I had never seen't!   75

OTHELLO   Ha? Wherefore?

DESDEMONA   Why do you speak so startingly and rash?

OTHELLO   Is't lost? Is't gone? Speak, is it out o'th' way?

DESDEMONA   Heaven bless us!

OTHELLO   Say you?   80

DESDEMONA   It is not lost. But what an if it were?

OTHELLO   How?

DESDEMONA   I say it is not lost.

OTHELLO   Fetch't, let me see't!

DESDEMONA   Why, so I can; but I will not now.   85
This is a trick to put me from my suit:
Pray you let Cassio be received again.

OTHELLO   Fetch me the handkerchief! My mind misgives.

DESDEMONA   Come, come!
You'll never meet a more sufficient man –   90

OTHELLO   The handkerchief!

DESDEMONA   A man that all his time
Hath founded his good fortunes on your love,
Shared dangers with you –

100   **unhappy in** (1) miserable about; (2) unfortunate in

101   **'Tis not a year...man** even a year or two won't show us what a man is really like

105–106   **There...happiness!** *As they enter, Iago is reminding Cassio that his only chance of regaining Othello's favour is through Desdemona; 'What a stroke of luck!'* (**lo the happiness**), *he says: here she is.*

106   **importune her** make your request of her

111   **Whom I** the man whom I

     office duty; loyal service

113   **mortal** serious enough to kill off friendship

114   **nor my** neither my

115   **purposed...futurity** the good things I propose to do in the future

116   **ransom me** buy my way back

117   **But...benefit** then I will benefit even by knowing only that (because I will know the worst)

118–120   **So shall...alms** If that is the case, I will force myself to be happy, and restrict myself to some other way of life, accepting whatever gifts fortune can spare me.

121   **advocation** skill at pleading a case

Emilia in performance

101–104 These bitter sentiments cause some actresses to play all the scenes between Iago and Emilia as though their relationship has for some time been soured by Iago's selfish and *wayward* behaviour (3.3.291). Zoë Wanamaker's Emilia, for example (RSC, 1989), is clearly attempting to win back her husband's affection; but Ian McKellen's Iago constantly exploits and humiliates her. Emilia's coarse expressions (particularly the imagery to do with stomachs and belching) reveal a hard-headed, down-to-earth attitude towards love and marriage which is in stark contrast with Desdemona's innocent idealism.

OTHELLO   The handkerchief!

DESDEMONA I'faith, you are to blame.   95

OTHELLO   Away!

Exit OTHELLO.

EMILIA   Is not this man jealous?

DESDEMONA I ne'er saw this before.
           Sure there's some wonder in this handkerchief;
           I am most unhappy in the loss of it.   100

EMILIA   'Tis not a year or two shows us a man.
           They are all but stomachs, and we all but food;
           They eat us hungerly, and when they are full,
           They belch us.

Enter IAGO and CASSIO.

           Look you, Cassio and my husband.

IAGO   There is no other way; 'tis she must do't.   105
           And lo the happiness! Go and importune her.

DESDEMONA How now, good Cassio? What's the news with you?

CASSIO   Madam, my former suit. I do beseech you
           That by your virtuous means I may again
           Exist, and be a member of his love   110
           Whom I with all the office of my heart
           Entirely honour. I would not be delayed.
           If my offence be of such mortal kind
           That nor my service past, nor present sorrows,
           Nor purposed merit in futurity,   115
           Can ransom me into his love again,
           But to know so must be my benefit.
           So shall I clothe me in a forced content,
           And shut myself up in some other course
           To fortune's alms.

DESDEMONA   Alas, thrice-gentle Cassio,   120
           My advocation is not now in tune.
           My lord is not my lord; nor should I know him

147

123 **Were he...altered** if he were as much changed in his appearance as he is in his mood

124–125 **So help...As I have** I swear by all the blessed spirits that I have

126 **stood...displeasure** have been a target for his anger

136 **of moment** of great importance

137 **There's matter in't indeed** it must be really serious

138 **Something sure of state** it must certainly be something to do with state affairs

139 **unhatched practice** a plot, discovered before it can be accomplished

140 **Made demonstrable** come to light; discovered

141 **puddled** muddied

142 **wrangle with** argue about

144 **endues** leads; draws

147–148 **Nor of them...bridal** nor expect the same kind, affectionate attention (**observancy**) from them that they give us on our wedding day

148 **Beshrew me much** *a mild oath implying 'I am greatly to blame'*

150 **Arraigning** accusing *(the first in a series of legal terms used here by Desdemona)*

151 **suborned** influenced (in order to give false evidence)

152 **indicted** charged; accused

153 **conception** fantasy; silly idea

154 **toy** whim; idea with no basis in reality

Desdemona

149 Desdemona's criticism of herself as an *unhandsome warrior* – one who has failed to live up to the name of 'soldier' – is possibly called to mind by recollection of Othello's earlier loving compliment: *O my fair warrior!* (2.1.181).

Were he in favour as in humour altered.
So help me every spirit sanctified,
As I have spoken for you all my best,   125
And stood within the blank of his displeasure
For my free speech. You must awhile be patient.
What I can do I will; and more I will
Than for myself I dare. Let that suffice you.

IAGO   Is my lord angry?

EMILIA   He went hence but now,   130
And certainly in strange unquietness.

IAGO   Can he be angry? I have seen the cannon   *cause the trebles*
When it hath blown his ranks into the air
And, like the devil, from his very arm
Puffed his own brother. And is he angry?   135
Something of moment then. I will go meet him.
There's matter in't indeed if he be angry.

DESDEMONA   I prithee do so.

                                                Exit IAGO.

                          Something sure of state,
Either from Venice or some unhatched practice
Made demonstrable here in Cyprus to him,   140
Hath puddled his clear spirit; and in such cases
Men's natures wrangle with inferior things,
Though great ones are their object. 'Tis even so.
For let our finger ache, and it endues
Our other, healthful members even to a sense   145
Of pain. Nay, we must think men are not gods,
Nor of them look for such observancy
As fits the bridal. Beshrew me much, Emilia,
I was, unhandsome warrior as I am,
Arraigning his unkindness with my soul;   150
But now I find I had suborned the witness,
And he's indicted falsely.

EMILIA   Pray heaven it be
State matters, as you think, and no conception
Nor no jealous toy concerning you.

157 **for the cause** for a reason

158 **for** because

163 **If I do...suit** if I find him in a receptive mood, I will plead your case

166 **Save you** God save you *(a common greeting)*

What make...home? What are you doing away from home?

171 **Eightscore eight** eight score plus eight (168 hours)

174 **with leaden...pressed** *Cassio uses an image taken from a form of torture in which the victim is crushed to death with heavy weights.*

175 **continuate** uninterrupted

176 **Strike off this score** settle the debt I owe

177 **Take me this work out** make a copy of this embroidery for me

178 **friend** mistress

179 **To the...cause** I now see the reason for your absence.

Emilia

156–159 Like Iago, Emilia conceives of jealousy as being a self-creating monster (compare 3.3.165–167). Her definition of jealousy and the ways in which it affects people is strikingly accurate as it applies to Othello (and also, of course, to Iago, with his fantasies about Emilia's supposed unfaithfulness). It is a further example of the contrast between the worldly-wise Emilia and the sheltered Desdemona.

Structure: the time scheme

170–171 Bianca's question helps to establish the idea that Cassio (and therefore Othello and Desdemona) must have been on Cyprus for some time – at the very least, a period longer than the week that Bianca complains about. If we check the scenes so far, however, it becomes clear that this scene takes place the day following their arrival (see the note to 2.3.376). This is an example of the 'double time scheme' of *Othello*, in which the events seem to happen in 'short time', in order to heighten the intensity of the drama and give an impression of the headlong nature of the tragedy; while a longer background time is established to add plausibility to the idea that a reasonable period has elapsed during which an affair might have taken place and Othello's jealousy evolved.

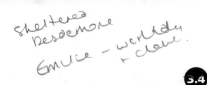
malicious
+ jealous
character

sheltered
Desdemona
Emilia — worldly
+ clever.

| DESDEMONA | Alas the day, I never gave him cause. | 155 |

EMILIA	But jealous souls will not be answered so;
	They are not ever jealous for the cause,
	But jealous for they're jealous. It is a monster
	Begot upon itself, born on itself.

self-creating
monster

she bred + hmm.

| DESDEMONA | Heaven keep the monster from Othello's mind! | 160 |

| EMILIA | Lady, amen. |

DESDEMONA	I will go seek him. Cassio, walk here about.
	If I do find him fit, I'll move your suit
	And seek to effect it to my uttermost.

| CASSIO | I humbly thank your ladyship. | 165 |

Exit DESDEMONA with EMILIA.

Enter BIANCA.

| BIANCA | Save you, friend Cassio! |

CASSIO	What make you from home?
	How is't with you, my most fair Bianca?
	I'faith, sweet love, I was coming to your house.

BIANCA	And I was going to your lodging, Cassio.
	What, keep a week away? Seven days and nights?	170
	Eightscore eight hours? And lovers' absent hours
	More tedious than the dial eightscore times?
	O weary reck'ning!

passionate
+ open

established
relationship

CASSIO	Pardon me, Bianca.
	I have this while with leaden thoughts been
	pressed,
	But I shall in a more continuate time	175
	Strike off this score of absence. Sweet Bianca,

polite
respectful

wife? of rank

malicious
character

Gives her DESDEMONA's handkerchief.

want to make it up.   *he cares*
for her.

Take me this work out.

BIANCA	O Cassio, whence came this?
	This is some token from a newer friend.
	To the felt absence now I feel a cause.

151

[handwritten annotation: his honour is more important to him than anything else.]

[handwritten annotation: give handkerchief to copy.]

3.4 *Bianca is jealous when Cassio produces the handkerchief and asks her to copy the embroidery*

180 **Go to...!** Don't be ridiculous!

186–187 **ere it be demanded...will** before somebody asks for it back, as they probably will

191–192 **no addition...womaned** not to my credit (it will look bad) if Othello sees me with a woman

194 **bring** accompany

197 **I attend** I have to wait

198 **I must be circumstanced** I'll have to give way to circumstances; I'll put up with the way things are

Marsha Hunt as Bianca and Sean Baker as Cassio (RSC, 1989)

Bianca

177–180 By her assumptions about the origins of the handkerchief, Bianca adds to the theme of jealousy.

Iago

185 Cassio's explanation about finding the handkerchief shows how quickly and efficiently Iago has put into practice the plan he devised at 3.3.319.

*established
relationship*

Is't come to this? Well, well.

CASSIO Go to, woman! 180
Throw your vile guesses in the devil's teeth,
From whence you have them. You are jealous now
That this is from some mistress, some remembrance. *sexual*
No, by my faith, Bianca. *JEALOUSY*

BIANCA Why, whose is it?

CASSIO I know not neither; I found it in my chamber. 185
I like the work well; ere it be demanded,
As like enough it will, I would have it copied.
Take it and do't, and leave me for this time.

BIANCA Leave you? Wherefore? *HONESTY OPENNESS*

CASSIO I do attend here on the general 190
And think it no addition, nor my wish,
To have him see me womaned.

BIANCA Why, I pray you?

CASSIO Not that I love you not.

BIANCA But that you do not love me!
I pray you bring me on the way a little,
And say if I shall see you soon at night. 195

CASSIO 'Tis but a little way that I can bring you,
For I attend here; but I'll see you soon.

BIANCA 'Tis very good; I must be circumstanced.

Exeunt OMNES.

153

Exam practice

Extracts

1. Reread 3.3.93–170 ('My noble lord. . .strongly loves!'). In what ways does this dialogue develop your understanding of the methods Iago uses to deceive Othello? In your answer you should:
   - outline the methods he seems to be using
   - make detailed reference to the ways in which he plants thoughts in Othello's mind and to the language Iago uses
   - express your own reaction to Iago's methods, as well as suggesting how other audiences might respond to them
   - show some awareness of contemporary attitudes to sexual infidelity and cuckolds.

2. Reread 3.3.331–388 ('Ha, ha! False. . .Would I were satisfied!'). What does Othello's language reveal about the kind of person he is and his present state of mind? In your answer you should:
   - show in detail how characterisation is revealed through Shakespeare's choice of language
   - express your own thoughts and feelings about the scene at this point in the play, as well as suggesting how audiences might respond to it
   - show an understanding of Shakespearean verse.

3. Reread 3.4.29–96 ('I will not leave...Away!'). What might the thoughts and feelings of an audience be as they watch this part of the scene? In your answer you should:
   - show in detail how characterisation and dramatic tension are created by Shakespeare's choice of language
   - express your own thoughts and feelings about the scene at this point in the play, as well as suggesting how other audiences might respond to it
   - show some awareness of dramatic conflict and Shakespearean tragedy.

Extended writing

4. David Suchet, who played Iago in the 1985 RSC production, said that 3.3 was 'a scene which must be played dangerously, i.e. moment by moment, thought by thought, as much improvised as possible. . .If it is played in any way calculatingly, by Iago gleefully observing Othello's grabbing the bait, it becomes comic and makes Othello look really foolish.' Discuss the ways in which this statement helps you to understand Iago's methods and behaviour in 3.3.

154

Performance

5. In pairs, reread 3.3.93–117 ('My noble lord...know I love you'). Act out the exchange, using Othello's description of Iago's behaviour (111–115) as a guide to the way in which Iago might behave during this sequence. Then discuss how an actor playing Iago ought to perform this scene in order to seem credible, both to the audience and to Othello.

6. Look back at 3.3.356–361 ('Is't possible...Is't come to this?') and read the note on page 130 on 'Villain, be sure...'. In pairs, create three or four different freeze-frames to represent this moment. Compare your versions with other people's and then discuss how you think the moment ought to be acted on stage. For example, should Othello threaten Iago physically?

Ben Kingsley as Othello (right) and David Suchet as Iago (RSC, 1985)

Iago intensifies Othello's belief in Desdemona's adultery and reminds him about the handkerchief

2 **unauthorized** illicit *(because adulterous)*

3 **friend** lover

6 **hypocrisy against the devil** *Anyone committing an evil act under the pretence of doing good would be guilty of hypocrisy against God; the opposite – a virtuous act which appeared sinful – is hypocrisy against the devil.*

7 **and yet do so** *i.e. lie naked in bed together*

9 **a venial slip** a minor sin

17 **They have it** they give the appearance of possessing it

21–22 **As doth the raven...to all** *The handkerchief reminds Othello of his misery, just as a raven on a house-top acts as an omen (***Boding***) that there is death or the plague within.*

Dramatic structure

Another scene beginning *in medias res* – in the middle of things (the most obvious example of this technique is the very opening of the play). The entrance of Othello and Iago already in the middle of a conversation helps to maintain dramatic tension: we are left to fill in for ourselves the implied offstage opening of their exchange, in which Iago has presumably been embellishing his story of the affair between Desdemona and Cassio with fabricated details.

Iago

10 Some critics have wondered why Iago takes the risk of reminding Othello of the handkerchief, given that it has presumably already served its purpose as *ocular proof* and could always be checked up on.

Act 4

Scene 1

A court before the citadel.

Enter OTHELLO and IAGO.

IAGO   Will you think so?

OTHELLO   Think so, Iago?

IAGO   What,
To kiss in private?

OTHELLO   An unauthorized kiss?

IAGO   Or to be naked with her friend in bed
An hour or more, not meaning any harm?

OTHELLO   Naked in bed, Iago, and not mean harm?   5
It is hypocrisy against the devil.
They that mean virtuously, and yet do so,
The devil their virtue tempts, and they tempt heaven.

IAGO   If they do nothing, 'tis a venial slip.
But if I give my wife a handkerchief –   10

OTHELLO   What then?

IAGO   Why, then 'tis hers, my lord; and being hers,
She may, I think, bestow't on any man.

OTHELLO   She is protectress of her honour too.
May she give that?   15

IAGO   Her honour is an essence that's not seen;
They have it very oft that have it not.
But for the handkerchief –

OTHELLO   By heaven, I would most gladly have forgot it!
Thou said'st – O, it comes o'er my memory   20
As doth the raven o'er the infected house,
Boding to all – he had my handkerchief.

IAGO   Ay, what of that?

OTHELLO   That's not so good now.

IAGO   What if I had said I had seen him do you wrong?

4.1 *When Iago claims that Cassio has been boasting of his affair with Desdemona, Othello is struck by a seizure*

25–29 **as knaves...must blab** just as there are villains around who, by their own persistent persuading, or a woman's own willing infatuation, have overcome her reluctance (**convincèd**) or satisfied her desires (**supplied them**), and then boast about it

31 **unswear** deny on oath

37 **belie** tell lies about; slander

Zounds God's wounds! *(a strong oath)*

38 **fulsome** foul; disgusting

41–43 **Nature would...instruction** My nature would not let itself be covered (**invest** = *clothe*) by such a dark passion unless there were some basis of fact (**instruction**) in what I have heard.

44 **Pish!** *an exclamation of strong emotion*

47 **credulous** gullible

48 **chaste dames** morally pure women

49 **reproach** shame

Iago's language

34–35 Iago plays upon the different meanings of the word *lie*: (1) tell a lie ('lie on'); (2) physically lie down; (3) have sex. Othello recognises that 'lie on' can mean both 'physically lie upon' and 'tell lies about' (36–37). Typically he fails to see that this is exactly what is happening with Iago's tales concerning Desdemona and Cassio. Iago returns to deliberate wordplay in *Have you not hurt your head?* (61), a phrase calculated to remind Othello that he is a cuckold (64).

Othello's language

36–45 Othello's mental and physical degeneration are represented not only in disjointed utterances *(Handkerchief – confessions – handkerchief)*, illogical statements *(...first to be hanged, and then to confess)* and passionate, obsessive outbursts *(Noses, ears, and lips?)*, but also in a degree of self-awareness that he is falling apart physically *(It is not words that shakes me thus)*.

Performance

Falls in a trance: According to Iago, Othello's seizure is caused by epilepsy (52). It is difficult to know whether we are to believe him when he says that Othello suffered a seizure *yesterday* (53), or when he describes the potential outcome as *savage madness* (57).

emphasis on the word lie.

4.1

	Or heard him say – as knaves be such abroad	25
	Who having, by their own importunate suit,	
	Or voluntary dotage of some mistress,	
	Convincèd or supplied them, cannot choose	
	But they must blab –	

OTHELLO   Hath he said anything?

IAGO   He hath, my lord; but be you well assured,   30
               No more than he'll unswear.

OTHELLO   What hath he said?

IAGO   Why, that he did – I know not what he did.

prelude to know details

OTHELLO   What? What?

IAGO   Lie –

OTHELLO   With her?

crudeness

IAGO   With her, on her; what you will.   35

OTHELLO   Lie with her? Lie on her? – We say lie on her when
               they belie her. – Lie with her! Zounds, that's
               fulsome. – Handkerchief – confessions –
               handkerchief! To confess, and be hanged for his
               labour – first to be hanged, and then to confess!   40
               I tremble at it. Nature would not invest herself in
               such shadowing passion without some
               instruction. It is not words that shakes me thus. –
               Pish! Noses, ears, and lips? Is't possible? –
               Confess? – Handkerchief? – O devil!   45

Iago builds up up

                                    Falls in a trance.

IAGO   Work on,
               My med'cine works! Thus credulous fools are caught,
               And many worthy and chaste dames even thus,
               All guiltless, meet reproach. What ho! My lord!
               My lord, I say! Othello!

Iago manipulates, innocents

               Enter CASSIO.

                             How now, Cassio?   50

4.1 *When Othello regains full consciousness, Iago reminds him how common cuckolding is*

55 **lethargy** fit of unconsciousness

must have...course must be allowed to run its natural course

59 **straight** straightaway

60 **on great occasion** about something very important

61–62 **hurt your head...mock me?** *Othello takes Iago's question to be a reference to the cuckold's horns (see 3.3.283 and the note below).*

63 **Would you would** I wish you would

66 **civil** civilised

68–69 **Think...you** remember that every married man is in the same boat (**draw** = [1] pull, like a yoked ox; [2] join)

70–71 **That nightly...peculiar** who every night lie in beds which they think are exclusively theirs (**peculiar**), but which they are sharing with someone else (**unproper** = not belonging to them exclusively)

72 **arch-mock** greatest act of mockery

73 **lip...couch** kiss a sexually immoral woman (**a wanton**) in bed, while being free from suspicion (**secure**)

77 **Confine...list** keep yourself within the bounds of self-control

Structure: the time scheme

53 Iago's claim that Othello had a similar seizure *yesterday* helps to reinforce the concept of 'long time' established earlier. (See Bianca's complaint to Cassio for having deserted her for a week at 3.4.170–171.)

Iago's language

74–75 Iago delivers another of his cryptic remarks, which are difficult to translate word for word. Here he might mean: 'If I am a cuckold, I want to know; then I will know how to treat my wife'; or possibly 'knowing that I am imperfect, I know she is bound to be imperfect as well'.

CASSIO	What's the matter?

IAGO
My lord is fall'n into an epilepsy. *lie*
This is his second fit; he had one yesterday.

CASSIO
Rub him about the temples.

IAGO
The lethargy must have his quiet course.   55
If not, he foams at mouth, and by and by
Breaks out to savage madness. Look, he stirs.
Do you withdraw yourself a little while.
He will recover straight. When he is gone,
I would on great occasion speak with you.   60

Exit CASSIO.

How is it, general? Have you not hurt your head? *Cuckold*

OTHELLO
Dost thou mock me?

IAGO
                                   I mock you not, by heaven.
Would you would bear your fortune like a man.

OTHELLO
A hornèd man's a monster and a beast.

IAGO
There's many a beast then in a populous city,   *stereotype – myth* 65 *unfaithful*
And many a civil monster.

OTHELLO
Did he confess it?

IAGO
                        Good, sir, be a man.
Think every bearded fellow that's but yoked
May draw with you. There's millions now alive
That nightly lie in those unproper beds   70
Which they dare swear peculiar. Your case is better.
O, 'tis the spite of hell, the fiend's arch-mock,
To lip a wanton in a secure couch,
And to suppose her chaste. No, let me know;
And knowing what I am, I know what she shall
    be.   75

OTHELLO
O, thou art wise. 'Tis certain.

IAGO
                                   Stand you awhile apart;
Confine yourself but in a patient list.
Whilst you were here, o'erwhelmed with your grief –

4.1 *Iago persuades Othello to eavesdrop and overhear Cassio's boasts about his affair with Desdemona*

80 **shifted him away** managed to get rid of him

81 **laid good 'scuse upon** gave a plausible reason for

ecstasy trance

83 **encave** conceal

84 **fleers** sneers

notable scorns blatant mockery

88 **cope** copulate with

90 **all in...spleen** controlled by your temper

93 **That's not amiss** that's the right way to behave

96 **huswife** *pronounced 'huzzif', the word originally meant 'housewife', but had taken on the sense of 'prostitute' (like our modern 'hussy'); Bianca later denies that she is a prostitute (see 5.1.122–123)*

99 **beguile** deceive through charm

103 **unbookish** unlearned

conster interpret

104 **light** light-hearted

106 **addition** title; honour

107 **want** lack

108 **Ply** work on

110 **speed** succeed

Iago's language

87–88 These two lines are made up almost exclusively of crude monosyllables; culminating in *cope your wife*, they force Othello to contemplate the physical and repetitive nature of Desdemona's alleged infidelity.

89–91 Iago can enjoin Othello to be patient and exercise self-control (77) in the knowledge that he can manipulate him as and when he wishes. Othello's self-control is required here so that he can overhear Cassio's supposed confession; by the end of the scene, Iago will be inciting Othello to extreme violence.

103–105 Iago compares Othello to an ill-educated student who mistranslates what he reads – a perfect image for a man who easily misinterprets the behaviour of others through his lack of worldly-wisdom.

Othello in performance

Othello conceals himself...: For many actors, this scene represents one of the lowest points in Othello's decline and degradation, as he humiliatingly hides himself at Iago's instruction and eavesdrops in order to hear another man, as he thinks, describe an affair with his wife.

A passion most unsuiting such a man –
Cassio came hither. I shifted him away   80
And laid good 'scuse upon your ecstasy;
Bade him anon return, and here speak with me;
The which he promised. Do but encave yourself
And mark the fleers, the gibes, and notable scorns
That dwell in every region of his face.   85
For I will make him tell the tale anew:
Where, how, how oft, how long ago, and when
He hath, and is again to cope your wife.
I say, but mark his gesture. Marry patience,
Or I shall say you're all in all in spleen,   90
And nothing of a man.

OTHELLO   Dost thou hear, Iago?
I will be found most cunning in my patience;
But – dost thou hear? – most bloody.

IAGO   That's not amiss;
But yet keep time in all. Will you withdraw?

[OTHELLO conceals himself where he can see but not hear.]

[*Aside*] Now will I question Cassio of Bianca,   95
A huswife that by selling her desires
Buys herself bread and cloth. It is a creature
That dotes on Cassio (as 'tis the strumpet's plague
To beguile many and be beguiled by one).
He, when he hears of her, cannot restrain   100
From the excess of laughter. Here he comes.

Enter CASSIO.

As he shall smile, Othello shall go mad;
And his unbookish jealousy must conster
Poor Cassio's smiles, gestures, and light behaviours
Quite in the wrong. – How do you, lieutenant? –   105

CASSIO   The worser that you give me the addition
Whose want even kills me.

IAGO   Ply Desdemona well, and you are sure on't.
Now, if this suit lay in Bianca's power,
How quickly should you speed!

110 **caitiff** wretch

114 **faintly** without meaning it

     laughs it out laughs it off

115 **importunes** begs; persuades

116 **Go to, well said** Oh, yes, well done *(sarcastically)*

120 **triumph...** gloat *(like a Roman general enjoying a public triumph after a great victory)*

121 **customer** prostitute *(but see 5.1.122–123)*

121–122 **Prithee bear...wit** please, give me credit for some intelligence!

122 **unwholesome** corrupt *(his intelligence)*

124 **They laugh that win** *compare the proverb: He laughs best that laughs last*

125 **cry** rumour

128 **scored me** *the meaning is not clear; possibly:* (1) wounded me; (2) published me (as a cuckold); (3) 'summed me up' *(some editions have 'stored' = produced children for me)*

Structure: the time scheme

134 *the other day:* another example of 'long time' (see note to 3.4.170–171).

CASSIO	Alas, poor caitiff!	110

OTHELLO   Look how he laughs already!

IAGO   I never knew woman love man so.

CASSIO   Alas, poor rogue, I think, i'faith, she loves me.

OTHELLO   Now he denies it faintly, and laughs it out.

IAGO   Do you hear, Cassio?

OTHELLO   Now he importunes him   115
To tell it o'er. Go to, well said, well said!

IAGO   She gives it out that you shall marry her.
Do you intend it?

CASSIO   Ha, ha, ha!

OTHELLO   Do ye triumph, Roman? Do you triumph?   120

CASSIO   I marry? What, a customer? [prostitute] Prithee bear some
charity to my wit; do not think it so unwholesome.
Ha, ha, ha!

OTHELLO   So, so, so, so. They laugh that win.

IAGO   Why, the cry goes that you marry her.   125

CASSIO   Prithee, say true.

IAGO   I am a very villain else.

OTHELLO   Have you scored me? Well.

CASSIO   This is the monkey's [Bianca] own giving out. She is
persuaded I will marry her out of her own love   130
and flattery, not out of my promise.

OTHELLO   Iago beckons me; now he begins the story.

OTHELLO moves closer.

CASSIO   She was here even now; she haunts me in every
place. I was the other day talking on the sea bank

4.1 *Othello overhears Cassio's scornful laughter and disparaging comments about Bianca, believing that he is talking about Desdemona*

135–136	**thither comes the bauble** the plaything comes up to me	150–151	**take out the work** copy the embroidery
136	**falls me...neck** throws her arms round my neck like this	153	**some minx's token** a love-token from some harlot
142–143	**I shall throw it to** *i.e. when he has cut it off*	155	**hobby horse** whore
145	**Before me!** *an exclamation based upon 'before God!'*	157	**How now?** What's the matter?
		158	**should** must
146	**such another fitchew** a polecat, just like all the others *(polecat, an animal known for its lechery, was a slang term for prostitute)*	160	**when you are next prepared for** when I am next ready for you *(she implies: never)*
		162	**rail** kick up a fuss
	perfumed *because: (1) prostitutes wore perfume; (2) polecats were usually noted for their foul smell*		

Iago

148 Bianca's arrival with the handkerchief is an unlooked-for stroke of good fortune for Iago; typically he thinks quickly and exploits it to the full (172).

161 Knowing when to quit while he is ahead, Iago urges Cassio to run after Bianca; he cannot afford to let Cassio say anything which might help Othello to realise that the disparaging comments about a mistress have been about Bianca, not Desdemona.

163 Iago checks Cassio's planned movements for the evening (just as Macbeth does of Banquo – see *Macbeth* 3.1); he will use this information.

Bianca

Most editions of this play describe Bianca as a 'courtesan'. What evidence is there for assuming that Bianca is a courtesan or prostitute? Iago and Cassio certainly declare that she is (see 4.1.96, 121 and 146); but her affronted allegations in this scene concerning *some minx* and *your hobby horse* (153 and 155), together with her spirited denial at 5.1.122–123, are powerful indicators that she is not.

| | with certain Venetians, and thither comes the | 135 |
| | bauble, and falls me thus about my neck – |

OTHELLO   Crying 'O dear Cassio!' as it were. His gesture
           imports it.

CASSIO   So hangs, and lolls and weeps upon me; so shakes
           and pulls me! Ha, ha, ha!   140

OTHELLO   Now he tells how she plucked him to my chamber.
           O, I see that nose of yours, but not that dog I shall
           throw it to.

CASSIO   Well, I must leave her company.

IAGO   Before me! Look where she comes.   145

Enter BIANCA.

CASSIO   'Tis such another fitchew! Marry a perfumed one?
           What do you mean by this haunting of me?

BIANCA   Let the devil and his dam haunt you! What did
           you mean by that same handkerchief you gave me
           even now? I was a fine fool to take it. I must take   150
           out the work? A likely piece of work, that you
           should find it in your chamber and know not who
           left it there! This is some minx's token, and I must
           take out the work? There! [*She throws down the*
           handkerchief.] Give it your hobby horse.   155
           Wheresoever you had it, I'll take out no work on't.

CASSIO   How now, my sweet Bianca? How now? how now?

OTHELLO   By heaven, that should be my handkerchief!

BIANCA   If you'll come to supper tonight, you may; if you
           will not, come when you are next prepared for.   160

                                                       Exit.

IAGO   After her, after her!

CASSIO   Faith, I must; she'll rail in the streets else.

IAGO   Will you sup there?

(margin handwritten note) make / how as / look at / another / woman

4.1 *His beliefs now confirmed by Bianca's appearance with the handkerchief, Othello plans to kill Desdemona*

165–166	**would very fain** would very much like to	184	**that's not your way** that's not the way you should be thinking
174	**by this hand** I swear	189	**invention** imagination
177	**I would...a-killing** I would love to spend nine years killing him	191–192	**so gentle a condition** so amiable in character

Willard White as Othello and Ian McKellen as Iago (RSC, 1989)

Act 4 Scene 1

CASSIO	Yes, I intend so.
IAGO	Well, I may chance to see you, for I would very 165 fain speak with you.
CASSIO	Prithee come. Will you?
IAGO	Go to, say no more.

Exit CASSIO.

OTHELLO	[*Coming forward*] How shall I murder him, Iago?
IAGO	Did you perceive how he laughed at his vice? 170
OTHELLO	O Iago!
IAGO	And did you see the handkerchief?
OTHELLO	Was that mine?
IAGO	Yours, by this hand. And to see how he prizes the foolish woman your wife! She gave it him, and he 175 hath given it his whore.
OTHELLO	I would have him nine years a-killing! – A fine woman, a fair woman, a sweet woman!
IAGO	Nay, you must forget that.
OTHELLO	Ay, let her rot, and perish, and be damned tonight; 180 for she shall not live. No, my heart is turned to stone; I strike it, and it hurts my hand. O, the world hath not a sweeter creature! She might lie by an emperor's side and command him tasks.
IAGO	Nay, that's not your way. 185
OTHELLO	Hang her! I do but say what she is. So delicate with her needle. An admirable musician. O, she will sing the savageness out of a bear! Of so high and plenteous wit and invention –
IAGO	She's the worse for all this. 190
OTHELLO	O, a thousand, a thousand times. And then, of so gentle a condition!

4.1 *Just as Othello has agreed to strangle Desdemona in her bed, Lodovico arrives from Venice*

193 **too gentle** *i.e. she gives in too easily*

196 **fond over her iniquity** foolish and doting about her sinfulness

196–197 **give her patent** permit her officially

197–198 **comes near** affects

199 **messes** pieces of food

204 **expostulate with** explain my grievance to

205 **unprovide my mind** weaken my resolution

209 **let me be his undertaker** let me deal with him

Iago

206 Why does Iago make this suggestion? Does he want Desdemona to suffer a more violent end, or Othello to endure the torment of killing her with his bare hands? Or are his intentions more practical, in that poison can take time to take effect, allowing Desdemona the opportunity to explain her innocence?

Othello

177–205 *A fine woman...unprovide my mind again:* This section illustrates the conflict in Othello between his love for Desdemona and his jealous fury: what the poet Coleridge called 'the struggle not to love her'.

208 From this point onwards, Othello thinks of the approaching murder as an act of justice, and a necessary sacrifice.

[handwritten: D = v. accomplished]

Act 4 Scene 1

4.1

IAGO	Ay, too gentle.
OTHELLO	Nay, that's certain. But yet the pity of it, Iago. O Iago, the pity of it, Iago. 195
IAGO	If you are so fond over her iniquity, give her patent to offend; for if it touch not you, it comes near nobody. *[handwritten: unfaithfulness]*
OTHELLO	I will chop her into messes! Cuckold me! *[handwritten: Iago – so sublte strange]*
IAGO	O, 'tis foul in her. 200
OTHELLO	With mine officer! *[handwritten: s whatanothe]*
IAGO	That's fouler. *[handwritten: slow death slow power not the same]*
OTHELLO	Get me some poison, Iago, this night. I'll not expostulate with her, lest her body and beauty unprovide my mind again. This night, Iago! 205 *[handwritten: caught out also. going escal.]*
IAGO *[handwritten: sadistic]*	Do it not with poison. Strangle her in her bed, even the bed she hath contaminated. *[handwritten: old instinct]*
OTHELLO	Good, good. The justice of it pleases. Very good. *[handwritten: easily manipulated / convinced]*
IAGO	And for Cassio, let me be his undertaker. You shall hear more by midnight. 210 *[handwritten: has total power over him]*
OTHELLO	Excellent good!

A trumpet.

What trumpet is that same?

IAGO	I warrant something from Venice. *[handwritten: represents order / calm + justice.]*

Enter LODOVICO, DESDEMONA, and ATTENDANTS.

'Tis Lodovico.
This comes from the Duke. See, your wife's with him.

LODOVICO	God save you, worthy general.
OTHELLO	With all my heart, sir.

Lodovico assumes that Othello's distracted behaviour has been caused by the contents of a letter recalling him to Venice

216 **the instrument...pleasures** the letter which expresses their wishes

222 **unkind breach** uncharacteristic division

229 **atone them** bring them together; reconcile them

233 **Deputing...government** replacing him in his post by Cassio

4.1

LODOVICO	The Duke and the senators of Venice greet you.	215

Gives him a letter.

OTHELLO I kiss the instrument of their pleasures.

Opens the letter and reads.

DESDEMONA And what's the news, good cousin Lodovico?

IAGO I am very glad to see you, signior.
Welcome to Cyprus.

LODOVICO I thank you. How does Lieutenant Cassio?

IAGO Lives, sir. 220

DESDEMONA Cousin, there's fall'n between him and my lord
An unkind breach; but you shall make all well.

OTHELLO Are you sure of that?

DESDEMONA My lord?

OTHELLO [*Reads*] 'This fail you not to do, as you will –' 225

LODOVICO He did not call; he's busy in the paper.
Is there division 'twixt my lord and Cassio?

DESDEMONA A most unhappy one. I would do much
T'atone them, for the love I bear to Cassio.

OTHELLO Fire and brimstone!

DESDEMONA My lord?

OTHELLO Are you wise? 230

DESDEMONA What, is he angry?

LODOVICO May be th'letter moved him;
For, as I think, they command him home,
Deputing Cassio in his government.

DESDEMONA Trust me, I am glad on't.

OTHELLO Indeed?

235 **I am glad to see you mad** *an obscure line; perhaps Othello is pleased to see Desdemona (as it appears) recklessly expressing her true feelings for Cassio*

239 **'Tis very much** This is outrageous!

242 **crocodile** *Crocodiles were supposed to shed false tears in an attempt to deceive their intended prey; Othello accuses Desdemona of being similarly hypocritical (see line 250).*

248–250 **turn...** *the word often has a sexual connotation*

251 **she's obedient** she will do whatever you want *(again with a sexual connotation)*

252 **Proceed...tears** Carry on crying!

253 **well-painted passion** cleverly feigned emotions

255 **anon** soon

   mandate official order

256 **avaunt!** get away!

Othello

Strikes her: Following his eavesdropping on a man supposedly gloating that he has had sex with his wife – a humiliation enjoyed only by Iago, Othello here shames himself publicly.

Desdemona in performance

Actors can find this a difficult scene to play. On the one hand, Desdemona has the audience's sympathy as we observe her being treated appallingly by the man she loves; on the other hand, her lines seem very passive (*I have not deserved this...I will not stay to offend you...*) and she appears to be merely acted upon and told what to do by the men around her.

Act 4 Scene 1

DESDEMONA   My lord?

OTHELLO   I am glad to see you mad.

DESDEMONA   Why, sweet Othello –   235

OTHELLO   Devil!

only Othello
enjoys this

Strikes her. *Othello*
– everything
confirmed.
he deceived

DESDEMONA   I have not deserved this.

LODOVICO   My lord, this would not be believed in Venice,
Though I should swear I saw't. 'Tis very much.
Make her amends; she weeps.

D is of status
picks

OTHELLO   O devil, devil!   240   *change,*
If that the earth could teem with woman's tears,   *lowered*
Each drop she falls would prove a crocodile.   *he stands*
Out of my sight!

order and calm
+ control.

DESDEMONA   I will not stay to offend you.

Going.

LODOVICO   Truly, an obedient lady.
I do beseech your lordship call her back.   245

OTHELLO   Mistress!

DESDEMONA   My lord?

sex

OTHELLO   What would you with her, sir?

LODOVICO   Who? I, my lord?

OTHELLO   Ay! You did wish that I would make her turn.
Sir, she can turn, and turn, and yet go on
And turn again; and she can weep, sir, weep;   250
And she's obedient; as you say, obedient.
Very obedient. Proceed you in your tears.
Concerning this, sir – O well-painted passion! –
I am commanded home. – Get you away;
I'll send for you anon. – Sir, I obey the mandate   255
And will return to Venice. – Hence, avaunt! –

Exit DESDEMONA. *humiliated*

When Lodovico expresses his profound shock at Othello's behaviour, Iago privately implies that it is typical

261   **all in all sufficient** totally competent

262–264   **Whose solid...pierce** whose steadfast goodness could not be shaken by any unexpected fate or accident *(the image is appropriately from warfare: wild, misdirected cannon-shots and arrows or spears)*

265   **Are his wits...brain?** *Lodovico not unnaturally questions Othello's sanity.*

266   **that** what

     I may not...censure I must not criticise him

267–268   **What he might be...he were!** He might be insane. If he isn't, I wish he were *(as it would offer an excuse for his behaviour – see the note below).*

269   **would I knew** I wish I could believe

270   **use** custom *(i.e. Is he in the habit of striking her?)*

271   **work upon his blood** make him angry

272   **new-create his fault** make him behave badly like this for the first time

275   **courses will denote him so** actions will reveal him in such a way

---

Othello's language

259 *Goats and monkeys!:* This sudden outburst recalls 3.3.401.

Iago's language

267–268 This is one of the best examples of Iago's cryptic utterances (compare, for example, 4.1.74–75). In keeping with *It is as sure as you are Roderigo, Were I the Moor, I would not be Iago* (1.1.53–54) and *I am not what I am* (1.1.62), each of these statements has something to do with people appearing to be something they are not, but none of the utterances yields up a simple word-for-word meaning.

272–274 Exploiting his reputation for 'honesty', Iago manages to appear the loyal and discreet servant, while clearly implying that, yes, Othello *is* in the habit of beating his wife. (Compare his similar 'defence' of Cassio at 2.3.217–218.)

Cassio shall have my place. And, sir, tonight
I do entreat that we may sup together.
You are welcome, sir, to Cyprus. – Goats and
　monkeys!

Exit.

LODOVICO　Is this the noble Moor whom our full Senate　　260
Call all in all sufficient? Is this the nature
Whom passion could not shake? Whose solid virtue
The shot of accident nor dart of chance
Could neither graze nor pierce?

IAGO　　　　　　　　　　　　　　　He is much changed.

LODOVICO　Are his wits safe? Is he not light of brain?　　265

IAGO　He's that he is; I may not breathe my censure.
What he might be (if, what he might, he is not)
I would to heaven he were!

LODOVICO　　　　　　　　　　　What, strike his wife?

IAGO　Faith, that was not so well; yet would I knew
That stroke would prove the worst.

LODOVICO　　　　　　　　　　Is it his use?　　270
Or did the letters work upon his blood
And new-create his fault?

IAGO　　　　　　　　　　　Alas, alas!
It is not honesty in me to speak
What I have seen and known. You shall observe him,
And his own courses will denote him so　　275
That I may save my speech. Do but go after
And mark how he continues.

LODOVICO　I am sorry that I am deceived in him.

Exeunt.

177

5   **made up** gave voice to

12   **durst** dare

     honest chaste; sexually pure

13   **Lay down...stake** wager my soul *(that Desdemona is chaste)*

14   **doth abuse your bosom** deceives your innermost being

16   **serpent's curse** *the curse that God laid upon the serpent for deceiving Eve (see Genesis 3.14); the implication is that such a deception would be a crime worthy of Satan himself*

18   **happy** content that his wife is faithful

20–21 **yet...much** yet even the most simple-minded bawd would be capable of saying what Emilia has said (**bawd** = a person who manages prostitutes; a brothel-keeper)

21   **This** this woman (Desdemona)

     subtle cunning

22   **a closet lock and key** a locker-up; a concealer

Dramatic structure

This is another scene which begins *in medias res* (see note on page 156). Again it is not difficult to recreate the conversation between Othello and Emilia which has preceded their entrance; it quickly becomes clear that he now thinks of Desdemona as a prostitute and Emilia, accordingly, as her bawd.

Othello

Othello's degradation continues. After being forced to suffer the indignity of eavesdropping on the supposed lover of his wife, and then shamefully striking Desdemona in public, Othello now cross-examines Emilia in the hope of discovering incriminating evidence. Moreover, he is now so thoroughly convinced of Desdemona's guilt, that he rejects evidence which might count in her favour: Emilia's testimony and the evidence of his own eyes that Desdemona is a moral and religious woman (23).

Scene 2

The citadel.

finally   afraid → too late

Enter OTHELLO and EMILIA.

OTHELLO	You have seen nothing then?
EMILIA	Nor ever heard, nor ever did suspect.
OTHELLO	Yes, you have seen Cassio and she together.
EMILIA	But then I saw no harm, and then I heard Each syllable that breath made up between them.　5
OTHELLO	What, did they never whisper?
EMILIA	Never, my lord.
OTHELLO	Nor send you out o'th'way?
EMILIA	Never.
OTHELLO	To fetch her fan, her gloves, her mask, nor nothing?
EMILIA	Never, my lord.　　　　　　　　　　　　　　10
OTHELLO	That's strange.

spot on

EMILIA	I durst, my lord, to wager she is honest, Lay down my soul at stake. If you think other, Remove your thought. It doth abuse your bosom. If any wretch have put this in your head,　　　15 Let heaven requite it with the serpent's curse, For if she be not honest, chaste, and true, There's no man happy. The purest of their wives Is foul as slander.
OTHELLO	Bid her come hither. Go.

Exit EMILIA.

She says enough; yet she's a simple bawd　　　20
That cannot say as much. This is a subtle whore,
A closet lock and key of villainous secrets,
And yet she'll kneel and pray; I have seen her do't.

Enter DESDEMONA and EMILIA.

4.2 *Othello dismisses Emilia and accuses Desdemona of infidelity*

24 **chuck** *a term of affection used earlier (at 3.4.46), but possibly here employed sarcastically*

26 **fancy** fantasy

27 **Some of your function** do your job *(i.e. as a bawd)*

28 **procreants** people about to have sex

29 **'hem'** 'ahem' *(the fake clearing of the throat used to alert someone)*

30 **mystery** trade *(like the French* métier*)*

dispatch! hurry up!

31 **what doth...import?** what do your words mean?

35 **being...heaven** because you look like an angel

36 **double-damned** *i.e. by committing adultery and then swearing that she is innocent*

42 **motive of** reason for

43 **haply** perhaps

43–44 **If...calling back** if you perhaps believe that my father has been instrumental in having you recalled to Venice

---

Othello

40 Othello has to fight back the love for Desdemona each time she approaches him. Ray Fearon (who played Othello in 1999) said: 'This man swears allegiance to hate and murder, throws away love – but he takes three Acts to kill Desdemona: he tries to hate her but he can't because, unlike Iago, he's not made like that. Every time he faces Desdemona he crumbles.' (See the note to 4.1.177–205.)

DESDEMONA My lord, what is your will?

term of affection / sarcastic

OTHELLO Pray you, chuck, come hither.

DESDEMONA What is your pleasure?

OTHELLO Let me see your eyes. 25
Look in my face.

DESDEMONA What horrible fancy's this?

OTHELLO [*To EMILIA*] Some of your function, mistress:
Leave procreants alone and shut the door;
Cough or cry 'hem' if anybody come.
Your mystery, your mystery! Nay, dispatch! 30

monastery *Exit EMILIA.* *treating [her] as she is a madam*

DESDEMONA [*kneeling*] Upon my knee, what doth your speech
import? *know angry*
I understand a fury in your words, but not the words.

OTHELLO Why, what art thou?

DESDEMONA Your wife, my lord; your true
And loyal wife.

OTHELLO Come, swear it, damn thyself;
Lest, being like one of heaven, the devils
themselves 35
Should fear to seize thee. Therefore be double-
damned:
Swear thou art honest.

DESDEMONA Heaven doth truly know it.

OTHELLO Heaven truly knows that thou art false as hell.

DESDEMONA To whom, my lord? With whom? How am I false?

OTHELLO Ah, Desdemon! Away! Away! Away! 40

DESDEMONA Alas the heavy day! Why do you weep?
Am I the motive of these tears, my lord?
If haply you my father do suspect
An instrument of this your calling back,

45   **lost him** offended him

48   **sores and shames** *perhaps a reference to the afflictions heaped upon Job in the Bible*

49   **Steeped** drowned

53–54   **The fixèd figure...at** an everlasting figure of fun, always there for people to point mockingly at *(the metaphor is of the dial of a clock, on which the hour hand points so slowly that it seems always to be pointing to the same place)*

56   **garnered** stored

58   **fountain from the which** spring from which

60   **cistern** water-tank; *possibly* cess-pool

61   **knot and gender** writhe and procreate *(copulate)*

   turn thy complexion there turn pale at the thought of it

62   **cherubin** angel

64   **esteems me honest** considers me chaste

65   **shambles** butchers' slaughter-houses

66   **quicken...blowing** come to life immediately the eggs are laid

69   **ignorant** inadvertent; unintentional

   committed *Unfortunately for Desdemona, 'committed' frequently meant 'committed adultery', and Othello pounces on the word to make it the theme of his reply (lines 71–79).*

72   **commoner** prostitute

73–75   **I should...deeds** *Othello imagines that even to speak Desdemona's deeds would cause his cheeks to redden as fiercely as a blacksmith's forge and consume all sense of shame in the flames.*

76   **stops** closes up

   winks shuts its eyes *(the moon was a symbol of chastity)*

77   **bawdy** sexually free

78   **mine** cave

Othello

52–54 As a man for whom reputation has been everything, the prospect of public mockery is a nightmare.

Othello's language

60–61 Othello's language now intermittently descends into the coarse animal imagery heard earlier from Iago. He also imagines Desdemona as a life-giving spring transformed into a cess-pool (58–61); a sweet-smelling weed (66–68); and a defiled book (70–71).

61–63 *turn thy...cherubin....:* These lines have caused some trouble. One possible interpretation is that Othello is challenging Patience (imagined as a beautiful young angel) to try contemplating the horror of Desdemona's infidelity and still retain her pale beauty; Othello, by contrast, will look as grim as hell. (Alternatively, given that 'I' is a common spelling for 'Ay', the final line simply means, 'Yes, Patience will look grim as hell when she contemplates Desdemona's behaviour.')

Lay not your blame on me. If you have lost him,   45
I have lost him too.

OTHELLO   Had it pleased heaven
To try me with affliction, had they rained
All kinds of sores and shames on my bare head,
Steeped me in poverty to the very lips,
Given to captivity me and my utmost hopes,   50
I should have found in some place of my soul
A drop of patience. But alas, to make me
The fixèd figure for the time of scorn   →   *cant*
To point his slow unmoving finger at.   *bear*
Yet could I bear that too, well, very well;   55   *people sneering*
But there where I have garnered up my heart,
Where either I must live or bear no life,
The fountain from the which my current runs
Or else dries up – to be discarded thence,   *sexual animal*
Or keep it as a cistern for foul toads   *imagery*   60
To knot and gender in – turn thy complexion there,
Patience, thou young and rose-lipped cherubin!
I here look grim as hell!   *realise faithfulness truth*

DESDEMONA I hope my noble lord esteems me honest.   *realise*

OTHELLO   O ay, as summer flies are in the shambles,   65
baby   That quicken even with blowing. O thou weed,
not   Who art so lovely fair, and smell'st so sweet,
wanted   That the sense aches at thee, would thou hadst ne'er
                been born!

DESDEMONA Alas, what ignorant sin have I committed?

OTHELLO   Was this fair paper, this most goodly book,   70
Made to write 'whore' upon? What committed?
Committed? O thou public commoner,
I should make very forges of my cheeks
That would to cinders burn up modesty,
Did I but speak thy deeds. What committed?   75
Heaven stops the nose at it, and the moon winks;
The bawdy wind that kisses all it meets
Is hushed within the hollow mine of earth
And will not hear't. What committed?

DESDEMONA By heaven, you do me wrong!   80

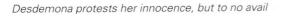

81 **strumpet** whore

82 **this vessel** my body

87 **cry you mercy** beg your pardon

90 **office...Saint Peter** the job *(in hell)* which corresponds with St Peter's *(guarding the gates of heaven)*

92 **done our course** finished our business *(he returns to the idea of Emilia being a brothel-keeper and Desdemona her prostitute)*

93 **keep our counsel** keep our affairs secret

94 **conceive** imagine

96 **half asleep** dazed *(stunned by Othello's outburst)*

Desdemona

96 Although she was at first able to fight back against Othello's accusations (80–85), Desdemona's *half asleep* aptly describes her dazed bewilderment after his departure.

OTHELLO　　Are not you a strumpet?

DESDEMONA　　　　　　　　　　No, as I am a Christian!
If to preserve this vessel for my lord
From any other foul unlawful touch
Be not to be a strumpet, I am none.

OTHELLO　　What, not a whore?

DESDEMONA　　　　　　　　　No, as I shall be saved!　　85

OTHELLO　　Is't possible?

DESDEMONA　　O heaven forgive us!

OTHELLO　　　　　　　　　　I cry you mercy then.
I took you for that cunning whore of Venice
That married with Othello. [*Raising his voice*] You,
　　mistress,

Enter EMILIA.

That have the office opposite to Saint Peter　　90
And keep the gate of hell! You, you, ay, you!
We have done our course; there's money for your
　　pains.

　　　　　　　　　　　　　　Flings her some coins.

I pray you turn the key and keep our counsel.

　　　　　　　　　　　　　　　　Exit.

EMILIA　　Alas, what does this gentleman conceive?
How do you, madam? How do you, my good
　　lady?　　95

DESDEMONA　　Faith, half asleep.

EMILIA　　Good madam, what's the matter with my lord?

DESDEMONA　　With who?

EMILIA　　Why, with my lord, madam.

DESDEMONA　　Who is thy lord?

103   **go by water** be expressed through tears

106   **meet** fitting; appropriate

107–108   **stick...misuse** have the slightest reason to criticise my most insignificant fault

112   **chid** scolded; rebuked

113   **I am a child to chiding** I have no experience of being rebuked

114   **bewhored** called her 'whore'

115   **despite** verbal abuse

120   **laid such terms** used such language

      callet slut

124   **forsook** given up; turned her back on

Desdemona

Desdemona's child-like innocence is effectively conveyed through the echoing phrase *I am a child to chiding* (113) and the awkward circumlocution she devises in order to avoid having to say the word *whore* (118; though she utters it, albeit reluctantly, at 160–161). Emilia's down-to-earth directness – *He called her whore* (119) – acts as a stark contrast.

| EMILIA | He that is yours, sweet lady. | 100 |

DESDEMONA I have none. Do not talk to me, Emilia.
I cannot weep, nor answers have I none
But what should go by water. Prithee tonight
Lay on my bed my wedding sheets, remember. –
And call thy husband hither.

| EMILIA | Here's a change indeed! | 105 |

Exit.

DESDEMONA 'Tis meet I should be used so, very meet.
How have I been behaved, that he might stick
The small'st opinion on my least misuse?

Enter IAGO and EMILIA.

IAGO   What is your pleasure, madam? How is't with you?

DESDEMONA I cannot tell. Those that do teach young babes   110
Do it with gentle means and easy tasks.
He might have chid me so; for, in good faith,
I am a child to chiding.

IAGO   What is the matter, lady?

EMILIA   Alas, Iago, my lord hath so bewhored her,
Thrown such despite and heavy terms upon her   115
That true hearts cannot bear it.

DESDEMONA Am I that name, Iago?

IAGO   What name, fair lady?

DESDEMONA Such as she said my lord did say I was. *can't even say 'whore'*
repulsed by idea

EMILIA   He called her whore. A beggar in his drink
Could not have laid such terms upon his callet.   120

IAGO   Why did he so?

DESDEMONA I do not know; I am sure I am none such. *Prelude*
trying to comfort

IAGO   Do not weep, do not weep. Alas the day!

EMILIA   Hath she forsook so many noble matches,

187

When Iago enters, Emilia angrily expresses her suspicions that someone has poisoned Othello's mind

127 **Beshrew** curse

128 **trick** delusion; misconception

130 **busy** interfering *(as in 'busybody')*

insinuating wheedling his way into favour

131 **cogging, cozening** *both words mean 'cheating', 'deceiving'*

135 **halter** hangman's noose

140 **O heavens...unfold** I pray heaven would expose villains like that

143 **within door** more quietly

144 **squire** *like 'companions' (line 140), used as a term of contempt*

145 **turned...without** turned your common sense the wrong side out

147 **Go to** be quiet

152 **discourse of thought** thinking processes

Emilia

129–132 These speculations by Emilia that some deceiving villain has spread slander against Desdemona in order to *get some office* are often cited as a perfect example of dramatic irony – we know that (a) her deductions are spot on; and that (b) the man with whom she is sharing her theory is the culprit himself. It often strikes audiences as odd, however, that Emilia could suddenly get so close to the truth here, but not actually make the final deductive step and realise that the only person who stands to gain by Cassio's downfall is her husband. After all, Othello has just named Cassio specifically as Desdemona's supposed lover (3), and there is only one person who would gain (indeed, has already gained) by Cassio's disgrace, and that is Iago. Some actresses have delivered these lines very pointedly, as though Emilia knows what Iago has done. They reason that, although Emilia's reactions in Act 5 (2.140–180) seem to show that she has been ignorant of Iago's plots, she has earlier delivered up Desdemona's handkerchief to him, knowing that when Desdemona misses it *she'll run mad* (3.3.289–318), and has remained silent even in the face of her mistress's obvious distress (3.4.20–104).

144–146 This shows that Iago has at some time accused Emilia with the jealous fantasies he expresses at 1.3.380–382.

	Her father and her country, and her friends,	125
	To be called whore? Would it not make one weep?	

DESDEMONA   It is my wretched fortune.

IAGO   Beshrew him for't!
How comes this trick upon him?

DESDEMONA   Nay, heaven doth know.

EMILIA   I will be hanged if some eternal villain,
Some busy and insinuating rogue,   130
Some cogging, cozening slave, to get some office,
Have not devised this slander. I will be hanged else.

IAGO   Fie, there is no such man! It is impossible.

DESDEMONA   If any such there be, heaven pardon him.

EMILIA   A halter pardon him! And hell gnaw his bones!   135
Why should he call her whore? Who keeps her
      company?
What place? What time? What form? What likelihood?
The Moor's abused by some most villainous knave,
Some base notorious knave, some scurvy fellow.
O heavens, that such companions thou'dst
      unfold,   140
And put in every honest hand a whip
To lash the rascals naked through the world
Even from the east to th'west!

IAGO   Speak within door.

EMILIA   O fie upon them! Some such squire he was
That turned your wit the seamy side without   145
And made you to suspect me with the Moor.

IAGO   You are a fool. Go to.

DESDEMONA   Alas, Iago,
What shall I do to win my lord again?
Good friend, go to him, for, by this light of heaven,
I know not how I lost him. Here I kneel: 150
If e'er my will did trespass' gainst his love
Either in discourse of thought or actual deed,

4.2 *Having offered comforting words to Desdemona, Iago is faced by an angry and frustrated Roderigo*

153 **Or that** or if

154 **Delighted them** took delight

158 **forswear** disown; abandon

159 **defeat** destroy

161 **does abhor me** disgusts me; fills me with abhorrence *(playing on the word 'whore')*

162–163 **To do...make me** all the luxuries in the world (**the world's mass of vanity**) could not make me commit the deed which would earn me the title (**addition**) of 'whore'

164 **humour** mood

165 **does him offence** is irritating him

166 **If 'twere no other!** I wish it was nothing but that!

but so, I warrant nothing else, I promise you

168 **stay the meat** are waiting for their meal

173 **thou daff'st...device** you put me off with some excuse

174–175 **keep'st...conveniency** deny me opportunities

177–178 **put up in peace** patiently put up with

180–181 **your words...together** your deeds do not match your words

Or that mine eyes, mine ears, or any sense
Delighted them in any other form;
Or that I do not yet, and ever did,   155
And ever will (though he do shake me off
To beggarly divorcement) love him dearly,
Comfort forswear me. Unkindness may do much,
And his unkindness may defeat my life,
But never taint my love. I cannot say 'whore'.   160
It does abhor me now I speak the word;
To do the act that might the addition earn
Not the world's mass of vanity could make me.

IAGO   I pray you be content. 'Tis but his humour.
              The business of the state does him offence.   165

DESDEMONA If 'twere no other!

IAGO   It is but so, I warrant.

Trumpets within.

Hark how these instruments summon to supper.
The messengers of Venice stay the meat.
Go in, and weep not; all things shall be well.

Exeunt DESDEMONA and EMILIA.

Enter RODERIGO.

How now, Roderigo?   170

RODERIGO I do not find that thou deal'st justly with me.

IAGO   What in the contrary?

RODERIGO Every day thou daff'st me with some device,
              Iago, and rather, as it seems to me now, keep'st
              from me all conveniency than suppliest me with   175
              the least advantage of hope. I will indeed no longer
              endure it; nor am I yet persuaded to put up in
              peace what already I have foolishly suffered.

IAGO   Will you hear me, Roderigo?

RODERIGO I have heard too much, and your words and   180
              performances are no kin together.

4.2 *Roderigo threatens to approach Desdemona personally and demand the return of his gifts*

183–184   **wasted...means** spent all I had

186   **votarist** nun

190–191   **go to...** *Iago uses the expression in a general dismissive sense ('OK, be quiet'); Roderigo interprets it as 'have sex' – and complains that that's his problem: he can't.*

193   **fopped** duped; cheated

197   **suit** request; application

198   **solicitation** wooing

199   **seek satisfaction** *by demanding his jewels and money back or challenging him to a duel*

201–202   **protest intendment** declare the intention

203   **mettle** spirit; courage; 'backbone'

206–207   **taken...exception** objected reasonably to my behaviour

207   **protest** assure you

209   **It...appeared** That's not the way it has looked to me.

Roderigo

According to the play's 'long time', Iago has been stringing Roderigo along for some while (*Every day thou daff'st me...*173). His complaint is that Iago has taken jewels (184), promising to pass them on to Desdemona as gifts from Roderigo, in return encouraging him to expect her immediate favour (*sudden respect* 188) and acquaintanceship. The reality is that Roderigo has not even met Desdemona in Cyprus, let alone enjoyed her sexually.

Iago

It is interesting to observe how Iago modifies his behaviour and adapts his tactics to suit Roderigo's changing moods and responses. At first he seems content to bluff his way out of Roderigo's accusations, dismissively replying with *go to* and *Very well* (190–194). The turning point comes when Roderigo threatens to reveal all to Desdemona; realising that he has to head off a course of action which would expose him, Iago switches to flattery (*Why, now I see there's mettle in thee* 203) and injured innocence (206–208). In due course he will resort to direct lies (*he goes into Mauritania* 223) and a kind of bustling urgency (238–242).

4.2

IAGO	You charge me most unjustly.
RODERIGO	With naught but truth. I have wasted myself out of my means. The jewels you have had from me to deliver to Desdemona would half have corrupted 185 a votarist. You have told me she hath received them, and returned me expectations and comforts of sudden respect and acquaintance; but I find none.
IAGO	Well, go to; very well. 190
RODERIGO	Very well? Go to? I cannot go to, man; nor 'tis not very well. Nay, I think it is scurvy, and begin to find myself fopped in it.
IAGO	Very well.
RODERIGO	I tell you 'tis not very well. I will make myself 195 known to Desdemona. If she will return me my jewels, I will give over my suit and repent my unlawful solicitation. If not, assure yourself I will seek satisfaction of you.
IAGO	You have said now? 200
RODERIGO	Ay, and said nothing but what I protest intendment of doing.
IAGO	Why, now I see there's mettle in thee, and even from this instant do build on thee a better opinion than ever before. Give me thy hand, Roderigo. 205 Thou hast taken against me a most just exception; but yet I protest I have dealt most directly in thy affair.
RODERIGO	It hath not appeared.
IAGO	I grant indeed it hath not appeared, and your 210 suspicion is not without wit and judgment. But Roderigo, if thou hast that in thee indeed which I have greater reason to believe now than ever – I mean purpose, courage, and valour – this night show it. If thou the next night following enjoy not 215

[handwritten annotations: "complements", "hear, flattery"]

4.2 *Iago manages to pacify Roderigo, who agrees to hear Iago's reasons for killing Cassio*

217	**devise engines for** invent plots against	235	**fashion to fall out** arrange to take place
218	**compass** practical possibility	236	**take him at your pleasure** attack him wherever and however suits you
223	**Mauritania** the land of the Moors in North Africa *(presumably Iago invents this fact to prevent Roderigo from thinking that he can approach Desdemona for the return of his jewels on her return to Venice)*	237	**second** back up
		238	**stand not amazed** don't stand there looking bewildered
224–225	**abode be lingered** stay be lengthened	241	**high** fully *(as in 'it's high time we were gone')*
226	**determinate** decisive	242	**grows to waste** is passing *(perhaps with the sense that they are wasting time talking)*
232	**harlotry** whore		**About it** Come on, let's get going.
233–234	**his honourable fortune** *i.e. being made governor of Cyprus when Othello leaves*		

Dramatic irony

215–217 As things turn out, Roderigo does not enjoy Desdemona, and the forces of justice do *devise engines* for Iago's life (5.2.364–366). This is a form of dramatic irony which can only be appreciated **predictively** – if we guess what will happen to the characters; or **retrospectively** – when we actually know the ending.

Desdemona, take me from this world with
treachery and devise engines for my life.

RODERIGO   Well, what is it? Is it within reason and compass?

IAGO   Sir, there is especial commission come from Venice
            to depute Cassio in Othello's place.   220

RODERIGO   Is that true? Why, then Othello and Desdemona
            return again to Venice.

IAGO   O, no; he goes into Mauritania and taketh away
            with him the fair Desdemona, unless his abode be
            lingered here by some accident; wherein none   225
            can be so determinate as the removing of Cassio.

RODERIGO   How do you mean, removing him?

IAGO   Why, by making him uncapable of Othello's place
            – knocking out his brains.

RODERIGO   And that you would have me to do?   230

IAGO   Ay, if you dare do yourself a profit and a right. He
            sups tonight with a harlotry, and thither will I go
            to him. He knows not yet of his honourable
            fortune. If you will watch his going thence, which I
            will fashion to fall out between twelve and one,   235
            you may take him at your pleasure. I will be near
            to second your attempt, and he shall fall between
            us. Come, stand not amazed at it, but go along
            with me. I will show you such a necessity in his
            death that you shall think yourself bound to put   240
            it on him. It is now high supper time, and the
            night grows to waste. About it.

RODERIGO   I will hear further reason for this.

IAGO   And you shall be satisfied.

Exeunt.

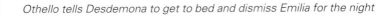

4.3 *Othello tells Desdemona to get to bed and dismiss Emilia for the night*

7–8 on th'instant...forthwith *both expressions (as well as 'incontinent', line 12) mean straightaway*

8 your attendant Emilia

19 So would not I I don't *(wish I had never seen him)*

doth so approve thinks so well of

20 stubbornness rough behaviour

checks rebukes

Performance

21 *Prithee unpin me* is an indication of what the actors are expected to be doing on stage: presumably Emilia is helping Desdemona to get ready for bed.

Scene 3

The citadel.

*Enter OTHELLO, LODOVICO, DESDEMONA, EMILIA and
ATTENDANTS.*

LODOVICO	I do beseech you, sir, trouble yourself no further.	
OTHELLO	O, pardon me; 'twill to me good to walk.	
LODOVICO	Madam, good night. I humbly thank your ladyship.	
DESDEMONA	Your honour is most welcome.	
OTHELLO	Will you walk, sir? O, Desdemona –	5
DESDEMONA	My lord?	
OTHELLO	Get you to bed on th'instant; I will be returned forthwith. Dismiss your attendant there. Look't be done.	
DESDEMONA	I will, my lord.	10

Exit OTHELLO, with LODOVICO and ATTENDANTS.

EMILIA	How goes it now? He looks gentler than he did.	
DESDEMONA	He says he will return incontinent, And hath commanded me to go to bed, And bade me to dismiss you.	
EMILIA	Dismiss me?	
DESDEMONA	It was his bidding; therefore, good Emilia, Give me my nightly wearing, and adieu. We must not now displease him.	15
EMILIA	I would you had never seen him!	
DESDEMONA	So would not I. My love doth so approve him That even his stubbornness, his checks, his frowns – Prithee unpin me – have grace and favour.	20
EMILIA	I have laid those sheets you bade me on the bed.	

23 **All's one** all right

25 **You talk** What nonsense!

26 **Barbary** *a form of the name Barbara; but perhaps it also calls to mind Iago's description of Othello as 'an erring barbarian' (1.3.354).*

28 **forsake** desert

'Willow' *the willow was traditionally associated with forsaken lovers*

31–32 **I have much...my head** it's all I can do to stop myself from hanging my head

33 **dispatch** hurry up

36 **This Ludovico...** *There is no justification for giving this line to Emilia, as one or two editors do, who take the view that it is out of character for Desdemona.*

39–40 **walked barefoot to Palestine** *the kind of thing a religious person might have done as an act of devotion*

40 **nether** lower

51 **hie thee** hurry

anon at once

DESDEMONA All's one. Good faith, how foolish are our minds!
          If I do die before, prithee shroud me
          In one of those same sheets.

EMILIA   Come, come! You talk.   25

DESDEMONA My mother had a maid called Barbary.
          She was in love; and he she loved proved mad
          And did forsake her. She had a song of 'Willow';
          An old thing 'twas, but it expressed her fortune,
          And she died singing it. That song tonight   30
          Will not go from my mind; I have much to do
          But to go hang my head all at one side
          And sing it like poor Barbary. Prithee dispatch.

EMILIA   Shall I go fetch your nightgown?

DESDEMONA No, unpin me here.   35
          This Lodovico is a proper man.

EMILIA   A very handsome man.

DESDEMONA He speaks well.

EMILIA   I know a lady in Venice would have walked
          barefoot to Palestine for a touch of his nether lip.   40

DESDEMONA [Sings]
              'The poor soul sat singing by a sycamore tree,
                  Sing all a green willow;
              Her hand on her bosom, her head on her knee,
                  Sing willow, willow, willow.
              The fresh streams ran by her and murmured her
                  moans;   45
                  Sing willow, willow, willow;
              Her salt tears fell from her, and soft'ned the stones –
                  Sing willow, willow, willow –'
          Lay by these.

                                        Gives EMILIA her clothes.

              'Willow, Willow' –   50
          Prithee hie thee; he'll come anon.
              'Sing all a green willow must be my garland.
                  Let nobody blame him; his scorn I approve' –
          Nay, that's not next. Hark! Who is't that knocks?

58   ***moe*** more

      couch 'go to bed with'; have sex with

60   **Doth that bode** is that a sign of

63   **abuse** deceive

64   **In such gross kind** so obscenely

66–67 **by this heavenly light** *an oath: see
       4.2.149; but Emilia means 'in the light
       of the moon'*

75   **joint-ring** a ring made in two sections

      lawn fine white linen

76–77 **petty exhibition** small gift

79–80 **venture purgatory** risk not going
       straight to heaven

Emilia

67–68 Emilia's bawdy joke (*I might do't as well i'th'dark*) typifies the contrast between her down-to-earth worldly-wisdom and Desdemona's innocent idealism. Throughout her following speeches, there is an undercurrent of bawdy references (91–95: *duties*; *treasures*; *laps*; *having*), giving her complaints about husbands' material meanness a secondary, sexual meaning.

EMILIA	It is the wind.

                                                                                          55

DESDEMONA [*Sings*]
    'I called my love false love; but what said he then?
      Sing willow, willow, willow:
    If I court moe women, you'll couch with moe men.'
    So, get thee gone; good night. Mine eyes do itch.
    Doth that bode weeping?

EMILIA   'Tis neither here nor there. 60

DESDEMONA I have heard it said so. O, these men, these men.
    Dost thou in conscience think, tell me, Emilia,
    That there be women do abuse their husbands
    In such gross kind?

EMILIA   There be some such, no question.

DESDEMONA Wouldst thou do such a deed for all the world?   65

EMILIA   Why, would not you?

DESDEMONA   No, by this heavenly light!

EMILIA   Nor I neither, by this heavenly light.
    I might do't as well i'th'dark.

DESDEMONA Wouldst thou do such a deed for all the world?

EMILIA   The world's a huge thing; it is a great price for a   70
    small vice.

DESDEMONA In troth, I think thou wouldst not.

EMILIA   In troth, I think I should; and undo't when I had
    done. Marry, I would not do such a thing for a
    joint-ring, nor for measures of lawn, nor for   75
    gowns, petticoats, nor caps, nor any petty
    exhibition. But for all the whole world? Why,
    who would not make her husband a cuckold to
    make him a monarch? I should venture
    purgatory for't.   80

DESDEMONA Beshrew me if I would do such a wrong for the
    whole world.

88   **to th'vantage** in addition

89   **store** populate *(presumably by frequent sexual activity – another of Emilia's bawdy comments)*

91   **slack their duties** cease to give their wives' sexual fulfilment

92   **pour our treasures...laps** (1) give jewels, etc which should be ours to other women; (2) have sexual relations outside marriage

93   **peevish** bad-tempered

94   **Throwing...us** limiting our freedom

95   **scant our former having** (1) reduce our allowances; (2) cut down on sexual relations with us

       in despite to spite us

96   **galls** spirit to resent injury

101 **change** exchange

102 **affection** passion *(also line 104)*

103 **frailty...errs** weakness that causes men to behave wrongly

107 **The ills...so** if women behave badly, it is because we have learned from men

108 **uses** habits; ways of behaving

109 **Not to...mend** not to copy bad behaviour, but to learn from it and do better

---

Emilia

90–107 Emilia's plea for women to be given the same emotional rights as men (98–100) and especially her conclusion (107) recall Shylock's famous justification for revenge in *The Merchant of Venice* ('Hath not a Jew eyes...fed with the same food...as a Christian is...The villainy you teach me I will execute...' 3.1).

EMILIA   Why, the wrong is but a wrong i'th'world; and
having the world for your labour, 'tis a wrong in
your own world, and you might quickly make it   85
right.

DESDEMONA   I do not think there is any such woman.

EMILIA   Yes, a dozen; and as many to th'vantage as would
store the world they played for.
But I do think it is their husbands' faults   90
If wives do fall. Say that they slack their duties
And pour our treasures into foreign laps;
Or else break out in peevish jealousies,
Throwing restraint upon us; or say they strike us,
Or scant our former having in despite –   95
Why, we have galls; and though we have some grace,
Yet have we some revenge. Let husbands know
Their wives have sense like them. They see, and smell,
And have their palates both for sweet and sour,
As husbands have. What is it that they do   100
When they change us for others? Is it sport?
I think it is. And doth affection breed it?
I think it doth. Is't frailty that thus errs?
It is so too. And have not we affections?
Desires for sport? and frailty? as men have?   105
Then let them use us well; else let them know,
The ills we do, their ills instruct us so.

DESDEMONA   Good night, good night. [*Exit* EMILIA] Heaven me
     such uses send,
Not to pick bad from bad, but by bad mend.

                             Exit.

Exam practice

Extracts

1. Reread 4.1.95–174 ('Now will I...by this hand'). In what ways does this extract show that Iago's success is due not only to clever planning but also to a measure of good luck? In your answer you should:
   - identify the moments at which we can see Iago (a) benefiting from planning done earlier; and (b) laying the ground for future plots
   - give your own views on the extent to which a successful outcome for Iago seems to depend upon strokes of good fortune
   - show some awareness of the ways in which the staging of this scene in Shakespeare's theatre would have reinforced the idea that Iago is both clever and fortunate.

2. Reread 4.1.211–278 ('What trumpet...deceived in him'). In what ways does this extract illustrate the importance of Venice and the role played by its representative, Lodovico? In your answer you should:
   - refer in detail to all references to Venice and the outside world
   - express your own opinions on Othello's behaviour and Lodovico's responses
   - show some understanding of the significance of Venice in Shakespeare's time.

3. Reread 4.3.61–109 ('O, these men...by bad mend'). In what ways does this extract exemplify the differences between Desdemona and Emilia? In your answer you should:
   - make detailed references to the characters' ideas and language
   - give your own responses to the attitudes expressed by the two women
   - show an awareness of the position of women within marriage, and different views of sexual morality in Shakespeare's time.

Extended writing

4. Many people feel that Othello reaches the depths of degradation and humiliation in Act 4. Which features of his behaviour in Act 4 support this view? In your answer you should:
   - examine in detail his eavesdropping on Cassio, interrogation of Emilia and striking of Desdemona
   - give your own responses to his behaviour at these moments

- show some understanding of the nature of tragedy and the figure of Othello as a Shakespearean tragic hero.

Performance

5. In groups of four, reread 4.1.214–243 and the note on Desdemona on page 174. Act out the scene in such a way as to portray Desdemona in a much less passive light than the lines might at first suggest. Then discuss how you think Desdemona ought to behave here, considering the possible pitfalls in playing her as too passive or too defiant.

6. In pairs reread 4.2.124–147 ('Hath she forsook...Go to') and the note on page 188. Perform it in two ways: first as though it never dawns upon Emilia that Iago might be the 'villainous knave' in question; second as though she has definite suspicions. In each case, consider carefully how Iago ought to react. Then discuss which version (a) seems most interesting and effective at this point in the play; (b) is more consistent with the way Emilia behaves in Act 5 when the truth is revealed (5.2.136–191).

Willard White as Othello and Ian McKellen as Iago (RSC, 1989)

Iago has persuaded Roderigo to kill Cassio, and tells us that he hopes both will die

1	**bulk** a projecting part of a building	15	**calls me to** will call me to account for
	straight straightaway		**restitution large** giving back a large amount
2	**Wear...rapier bear** have your sword already drawn *(unsheathed)*	16	**bobbed** swindled
	put it home thrust your sword into him	21	**unfold** expose
4	**mars** ruins	23	**gait** footstep
6	**miscarry in't** make a mistake	24	**had** would have
8	**devotion to** enthusiasm for	25	**But that** were it not for the fact that
11	**quat** boil *(which can be irritated until it is raw – **to the sense** – by rubbing)*		**coat** *possibly a soldier's reinforced leather undercoat*
14	**makes my gain** makes me the winner	26	**I will make proof of thine** I'll put yours to the test
	Live Roderigo if Roderigo survives		

Performance

1 It has been suggested that the *bulk* behind which Roderigo hides might, on Shakespeare's stage, have been one of the pillars supporting the stage canopy (see photographs on pages vi and 214).

8–22 Now presumably standing on opposite sides of the stage, Roderigo and Iago both speak their thoughts, Roderigo in a brief soliloquy in which he callously concludes *'Tis but a man gone*; Iago in an aside to the audience which explains his practical reasons for the deeds to come as well as some illuminating motivation (18–20; see below).

Iago and Cassio

18–22 Although it is usually unwise to trust Iago to be telling the truth about his motivation, even in soliloquy, it is nonetheless fascinating that he should put envy of Cassio's attractiveness above fear of exposure as a motive for killing him. Cassio's *daily beauty* is not defined; but perhaps Iago is envious of Cassio's popularity with Othello, his easy confidence with women and the fact that he clearly 'belongs' to the officer class in ways that Iago never could. In productions of the play, Cassio is usually played as well-spoken, young and attractive.

Act 5

Scene 1

A street in front of the citadel.

Enter IAGO and RODERIGO.

IAGO	Here, stand behind this bulk; straight will he come.
	Wear thy good rapier bare, and put it home.
	Quick, quick! Fear nothing; I'll be at thy elbow.
	It makes us, or it mars us, think on that,
	And fix most firm thy resolution. 5
RODERIGO	Be near at hand; I may miscarry in't.
IAGO	Here, at thy hand. Be bold, and take thy stand.

Moves to one side.

RODERIGO	I have no great devotion to the deed,
	And yet he hath given me satisfying reasons.
	'Tis but a man gone. Forth my sword! He dies. 10
IAGO	[*Aside*] I have rubbed this young quat almost to the
	sense,
	And he grows angry. Now, whether he kill Cassio,
	Or Cassio him, or each do kill the other,
	Every way makes my gain. Live Roderigo,
	He calls me to a restitution large 15
	Of gold and jewels that I bobbed from him
	As gifts to Desdemona.
	It must not be. If Cassio do remain,
	He hath a daily beauty in his life
	That makes me ugly; and besides, the Moor 20
	May unfold me to him; there stand I in much peril.
	No, he must die. But so, I hear him coming.

Enter CASSIO.

RODERIGO	I know his gait. 'Tis he. Villain, thou diest!

Thrusts at CASSIO.

CASSIO	That thrust had been mine enemy indeed
	But that my coat is better than thou know'st. 25
	I will make proof of thine.

Draws sword; they fight.

31   **brave** noble, excellent *(rather than courageous)*

33   **Minion** darling *(used contemptuously here for Desdemona)*

34   **your unblest fate hies** your damnable fate approaches swiftly

Strumpet whore

35   **Forth...blotted** your charms...are erased from my heart

37   **watch** watchmen

passage passers-by

38   **direful** full of distress

42   **heavy** dark and gloomy

43   **counterfeits** people pretending to be injured *(in order to rob passers-by who come to help)*

44   **come into the cry** (1) approach the source of the cries; (2) join 'the hunt'

Performance

27 The eighteenth-century editor Theobald added a stage direction here which has often been retained: 'Iago wounds Cassio in the leg and exits.' Most performances show Iago wounding Cassio in this way, unseen by his victim.

Enter Othello: In performance, it is important to keep Othello away from the wounded Cassio and Roderigo: he must not realise that neither man is actually dead (see 5.2.113–115). In Shakespeare's theatre he could enter on to the upper stage (the balcony – see photographs on pages vi and 214), but because of the difficulties of staging, Othello's appearance here (27–36) is often cut.

29 Othello's comment *It is even so* can be delivered as though he has mistaken Roderigo's cry for Cassio's, or is simply continuing his previous speech.

Act 5 Scene 1

RODERIGO	O, I am slain!
CASSIO	I am maimed for ever. Help, ho! Murder! Murder!

Enter OTHELLO.

OTHELLO	The voice of Cassio. Iago keeps his word.	
RODERIGO	O villain that I am!	
OTHELLO	It is even so.	
CASSIO	O help, ho! Light! A surgeon!	30
OTHELLO	'Tis he. O brave Iago, honest and just,	
	That hast such noble sense of thy friend's wrong!	
	Thou teachest me. Minion, your dear lies dead,	
	And your unblest fate hies. Strumpet, I come.	
	Forth of my heart those charms, thine eyes, are	
	blotted.	35
	Thy bed, lust-stained, shall with lust's blood be	
	spotted.	

Exit OTHELLO.

Enter LODOVICO and GRATIANO.

CASSIO	What, ho? No watch? No passage? Murder! Murder!	
GRATIANO	'Tis some mischance; the voice is very direful.	
CASSIO	O, help!	
LODOVICO	Hark!	40
RODERIGO	O wretched villain!	
LODOVICO	Two or three groan. 'Tis heavy night.	
	These may be counterfeits. Let's think't unsafe	
	To come into the cry without more help.	
RODERIGO	Nobody come? Then shall I bleed to death.	45
LODOVICO	Hark!	

Enter IAGO with a light.

5.1 *As Gratiano (Desdemona's uncle) and Lodovico arrive on the scene, Iago surreptitiously stabs Roderigo*

47 **Here's one** someone's coming

  in his shirt *i.e. it looks as though he has just got out of bed*

53 **What** who

54 **spoiled** fatally wounded

  undone destroyed

66 **As you...us** *judge us by our actions*

Iago

52 Even in the midst of bloody turmoil, people find the time to comment on Iago's finer qualities: with notable dramatic irony, Lodovico describes a man who is about to treacherously stab his wounded friend as *a very valiant fellow*.

5.1

GRATIANO	Here's one comes in his shirt, with light and weapons.
IAGO	Who's there? Whose noise is this that cries on murder?
LODOVICO	We do not know.
IAGO	Do not you hear a cry?
CASSIO	Here, here! For heaven's sake, help me!
IAGO	What's the matter? 50
GRATIANO	This is Othello's ancient, as I take it.
LODOVICO	The same indeed, a very valiant fellow.
IAGO	What are you here that cry so grievously?
CASSIO	Iago? O, I am spoiled, undone by villains. Give me some help. 55
IAGO	O me, lieutenant! What villains have done this?
CASSIO	I think that one of them is hereabout And cannot make away.
IAGO	O treacherous villains! [*To LODOVICO and GRATIANO*] What are you there? Come in, and give some help.
RODERIGO	O, help me there! 60
CASSIO	That's one of them.
IAGO	O murd'rous slave! O villain!

Stabs RODERIGO.

RODERIGO	O damned Iago! O inhuman dog!
IAGO	Kill men i'th'dark? – Where be these bloody thieves? – How silent is this town! – Ho! Murder! Murder! – [*To LODOVICO and GRATIANO*] What may you be? Are you of good or evil? 65
LODOVICO	As you shall prove us, praise us.

Having heard the noise, Bianca enters and is accused by Iago of being part of the conspiracy to kill Cassio

69 **I cry you mercy** I beg your pardon

75 **Who is't that cried?** *This is possibly a mistake in the text (the printer having repeated the previous speaker's line); alternatively Iago might be mockingly echoing Bianca's question to imply that she knows full well who it was.*

78 **notable** notorious

79 **mangled** wounded

82 **garter** band worn round the leg to keep a stocking up

86 **a party in** party to; implicated in

Iago

From his re-entrance at line 46, Iago stage-manages the whole scene. He cannot have anticipated the arrival of men as important as Lodovico and Gratiano (65), but he exploits their presence as authority figures when Bianca comes out to investigate the cries (74). It is worth recalling that he has planned this incident to take place near Bianca's lodging at a time when he has arranged for Cassio to leave (4.2.234–236). In what is therefore possibly a pre-planned interrogation, he first declares her a whore and *trash* (78, 85), accuses her of being party to the attack (85–86), alleges that her paleness and shock signify guilt (105–110) and finally asks questions designed to incriminate her to which he already knows the answers (117–120).

Iago in performance

82 *So* indicates that Iago ties the garter round the wound (already bound with his shirt – 73).

5.1

IAGO	Signior Lodovico?
LODOVICO	He, sir.
IAGO	I cry you mercy. Here's Cassio hurt by villains.
GRATIANO	Cassio? 70
IAGO	How is't, brother?
CASSIO	My leg is cut in two.
IAGO	Marry, heaven forbid! Light, gentlemen. I'll bind it with my shirt.

Enter BIANCA.

BIANCA	What is the matter, ho? Who is't that cried?
IAGO	Who is't that cried? 75
BIANCA	O my dear Cassio! My sweet Cassio! O Cassio, Cassio, Cassio!
IAGO	O notable strumpet! – Cassio, may you suspect Who they should be that have thus mangled you?
CASSIO	No. 80
GRATIANO	I am sorry to find you thus. I have been to seek you.
IAGO	Lend me a garter. So. O for a chair To bear him easily hence.
BIANCA	Alas, he faints! O Cassio, Cassio, Cassio!
IAGO	Gentlemen all, I do suspect this trash 85 To be a party in this injury. – Patience awhile, good Cassio. – Come , come. Lend me a light. Know we this face or no? Alas, my friend and my dear countryman Roderigo? No. – Yes, sure. – Yes, 'tis Roderigo. 90
GRATIANO	What, of Venice?
IAGO	Even he, sir. Did you know him?

5.1 *Gratiano discovers Roderigo, and Iago continues to accuse Bianca*

98 **well said** well done

100 **For** as for

101 **Save you your labour** spare your efforts; don't trouble yourself by trying to help him

102 **malice** ill feelings; 'bad blood'

104 **bear him out o'th'air** carry him indoors

106 **gastness of** terror in

109–110 **guiltiness will...use** guilt will show itself without the need for words

114 **quite dead** *Iago, as it turns out, is mistaken (see 5.2.324–325).*

The Swan playhouse c. 1596, built near modern Blackfriars Bridge in London. The nearby Globe Theatre (built 1599) – where Othello was performed – may have been similar, with an upper stage or balcony where Brabantio appears in 1.1 and Othello in 5.1 (lines 27–36)

GRATIANO	Know him? Ay.	
IAGO	Signior Gratiano? I cry your gentle pardon. These bloody accidents must excuse my manners That so neglected you.	
GRATIANO	I am glad to see you.	95
IAGO	How do you, Cassio? – O, a chair, a chair!	
GRATIANO	Roderigo?	
IAGO	He, he, 'tis he! [*A chair is brought in*] O, that's well said; the chair. Some good man bear him carefully from hence. I'll fetch the general's surgeon. [*To* BIANCA] For you, mistress, Save you your labour. [*To* CASSIO] He that lies slain here, Cassio, Was my dear friend. What malice was between you?	100
CASSIO	None in the world; nor do I know the man.	
IAGO	What, look you pale? – O bear him out o'th'air.	

CASSIO is carried off.

| | Stay you, good gentlemen. – [*To* BIANCA] Look you pale, mistress? [*To the rest*] Do you perceive the gastness of her eye? Nay, if you stare, we shall hear more anon. Behold her well; I pray you look upon her. Do you see, gentlemen? Nay, guiltiness will speak, Though tongues were out of use. | 105

110 |

Enter EMILIA.

EMILIA	Alas, what is the matter? What is the matter, husband?	
IAGO	Cassio hath here been set on in the dark By Roderigo and fellows that are scaped. He's almost slain, and Roderigo quite dead.	
EMILIA	Alas, good gentleman! Alas, good Cassio!	115
IAGO	This is the fruits of whoring. Prithee, Emilia,	

117 **know of** find out from *(a question designed to incriminate Bianca – see the note below)*

119 **but I therefore shake not** but I'm not shaking through guilt

120 **charge** order

121 **Oh fie...strumpet!** You whore!

123 **Foh!** *an expression of disgust*

124 **see...Cassio dressed** get Cassio's wounds bandaged

125 **tell's** tell us

126 **citadel** fortress

127 **happed** happened

128 **afore** ahead

129 **fordoes me quite** ruins me completely

1 **the cause** the reason for killing her: her unfaithfulness

4 **that whiter...snow** her skin, which is whiter than snow

5 **monumental alabaster** alabaster *(a white stone)* used for tombs and statues

7 **Put out the light...** extinguish the lamp, and then extinguish her life

8 **flaming minister** *i.e. the lamp (a 'provider' of fire)*

Bianca and Emilia

122–123 Given Emilia's part in the loss of Desdemona's handkerchief and her continued silence throughout her mistress's ensuing distress, Bianca's claim to be *as honest As you that thus abuse me* strikes some audiences as more than justified.

Othello

Othello's opening words, *It is the cause...*, have been interpreted in many ways. From his references to justice (4.1.208, 5.2.17 and 138), and a statement he makes to Desdemona (64–65), Othello seems to be regarding what he has to do in the light of a just sacrifice, rather than a revenge murder. Indeed he even seems to believe that he is killing Desdemona for the good of society: *else she'll betray more men* (6). From his reluctance to speak its name to the *chaste stars* (2), *the cause* is most obviously Desdemona's supposed infidelity.

Othello's language

After degenerating into crude, disconnected utterances, such as *Goats and monkeys!* (4.1.259), Othello's language now regains some of its former majesty: phrases like *monumental alabaster* (5), *flaming minister* (8) and *Promethean heat...relume* (12–13) are notable for the high content of Romance (Latin and French origin) vocabulary. This gives the language a measured formality to match Othello's rediscovered calmness and his belief that a solemn sacrifice is about to take place.

Go know of Cassio where he supped tonight.
[*To* BIANCA] What, do you shake at that?

BIANCA   He supped at my house; but I therefore shake not.

IAGO   O, did he so? I charge you go with me.   120

EMILIA   Oh fie upon thee, strumpet!

BIANCA   I am no strumpet, but of life as honest
As you that thus abuse me.

EMILIA   As I? Foh! Fie upon thee!

IAGO   Kind gentlemen, let's go see poor Cassio dressed.
[*To* BIANCA] Come, mistress, you must tell's another
        tale.   125
Emilia, run you to the citadel
And tell my lord and lady what hath happed.

                                        Exit EMILIA.

Will you go on afore?

                                Exeunt all but IAGO.

                    This is the night
That either makes me or fordoes me quite.

                                        Exit.

Scene 2

Desdemona's chamber.

Enter OTHELLO with a light; and DESDEMONA in her bed.

OTHELLO   It is the cause, it is the cause, my soul.
Let me not name it to you, you chaste stars.
It is the cause. Yet I'll not shed her blood,
Nor scar that whiter skin of hers than snow,
And smooth as monumental alabaster.   5
Yet she must die, else she'll betray more men.
Put out the light, and then put out the light.
If I quench thee, thou flaming minister,
I can again thy former light restore,

10 **thy** your *(Desdemona's)*

11 **thou cunning'st...nature** you beautiful creation of nature at its most perfect

12 **Promethean heat** divine fire *(in Greek mythology the Titan Prometheus was the first to give fire to humans)*

13 **relume** relight

14 **vital** enabling it to live

16 **balmy** perfumed and health-giving

17 **break her sword** not carry out the punishment *(Justice is still often represented as a woman holding scales in one hand and a sword – representing punishment – in the other)*

20 **So sweet...fatal** something as sweet as this kiss was never so deadly

26 **bethink yourself of** recall

27 **Unreconciled...grace** that you have not confessed and repented

28 **Solicit** ask *(God for forgiveness)*

    straight at once

29 **Alack** alas *(an expression of sadness or concern)*

31 **unprepared** not ready to go to heaven *(because there are sins which have not been confessed)*

32 **forfend** forbid

Desdemona in performance

In the 1952 Orson Welles film, we see Suzanne Cloutier's frightened Desdemona pretending that she is asleep.

Othello

21–22 *This sorrow's heavenly...:* Again Othello reinforces, perhaps to give himself reassurance, that killing Desdemona will be an action comparable to God punishing those he loves (see the Bible: Hebrews 12.6).

Should I repent me; but once put out thy light,   10
Thou cunning'st pattern of excelling nature,
I know not where is that Promethean heat
That can thy light relume. When I have plucked the
     rose,
I cannot give it vital growth again;
It needs must wither. I'll smell thee on the tree.   15

Kisses her.

O balmy breath, that dost almost persuade
Justice to break her sword. One more, one more!
Be thus when thou art dead, and I will kill thee,
And love thee after. One more, and that's the last.
So sweet was ne'er so fatal. I must weep,   20
But they are cruel tears. This sorrow's heavenly;
It strikes where it doth love. She wakes.

DESDEMONA Who's there? Othello?

OTHELLO   Ay, Desdemona.

DESDEMONA Will you come to bed, my lord?

OTHELLO   Have you prayed tonight, Desdemon?

DESDEMONA   Ay, my lord.   25

OTHELLO   If you bethink yourself of any crime
Unreconciled as yet to heaven and grace,
Solicit for it straight.

DESDEMONA Alack, my lord, what may you mean by that?

OTHELLO   Well, do it, and be brief; I will walk by.   30
I would not kill thy unprepared spirit.
No, heavens forfend, I would not kill thy soul.

DESDEMONA Talk you of killing?

OTHELLO   Ay, I do.

DESDEMONA   Then heaven
Have mercy on me!

OTHELLO   Amen, with all my heart.

37   **fatal** dangerous

40   **They are loves** *She implies that her only sin is in loving Othello more than God.*

43   **nether** lower *(see the note below)*

44   **frame** body

45   **portents** ominous signs

46   **do not point on me** aren't a sign of what will happen to me

51   **perjury** lying on oath

52   **Presently** immediately

53   **freely** without holding anything back

54–56   **to deny...withal** even if you were to take an oath that you were innocent of each one of these sins, it would not take away or wipe out the powerful belief which afflicts me

---

Othello in performance

36 Othello's *Humh* might be interpreted as an unwillingness to give a direct reply. Desdemona's references to Othello's eye-rolling, lip-biting and shaking (38, 43, 44) are sometimes ignored by actors who take the view that the lines were probably inserted to help audiences who could not make out detailed facial expressions, and that they now seem crude and unsubtle.

DESDEMONA	If you say so, I hope you will not kill me. **35**
OTHELLO	Humh.
DESDEMONA	And yet I fear you; for you're fatal then When your eyes roll so. Why I should fear I know not, Since guiltiness I know not; but yet I feel I fear.
OTHELLO	Think on thy sins.
DESDEMONA	They are loves I bear to you. **40**
OTHELLO	Ay, and for that thou diest.
DESDEMONA	That death's unnatural that kills for loving. Alas, why gnaw you so your nether lip? Some bloody passion shakes your very frame. These are portents; but yet I hope, I hope, **45** They do not point on me.
OTHELLO	Peace, and be still.
DESDEMONA	I will so. What's the matter?
OTHELLO	That handkerchief which I so loved and gave thee, Thou gav'st to Cassio.
DESDEMONA	No, by my life and soul! Send for the man and ask him.
OTHELLO	Sweet soul, take heed, **50** Take heed of perjury; thou art on thy deathbed.
DESDEMONA	Ay, but not yet to die.
OTHELLO	Presently. Therefore confess thee freely of thy sin, For to deny each article with oath Cannot remove nor choke the strong conception **55** That I do groan withal. Thou art to die.
DESDEMONA	Then Lord have mercy on me!
OTHELLO	I say, amen.
DESDEMONA	And have you mercy too. I never did

5.2 *Othello informs Desdemona that Cassio has admitted his affair and is now dead*

59	**Offend** sin against
60–61	**general warranty...love** permission from God that we all have to love our fellow creatures
63	**stone** turn to stone
70	**used...Unlawfully** had illicit sexual relations
72	**ta'en order for** arranged

73 **my fear interprets** *she understands what he means – because of her own fear of death and because she fears the worst for Cassio*

74 **Had all...lives** even if he had had as many lives as hairs on his head

75 **stomach** appetite

78 **banish me** send me away

81 **strive** struggle

Othello

62–65 Desdemona's repeated denials concerning the handkerchief seem to inflame Othello: he has hoped to kill her as an act of justice, but now finds that the *sacrifice* is being polluted by thoughts of revenge.

Desdemona in performance

Imogen Stubbs (1989) was determined to reject the interpretation of Desdemona as a passive and willing sacrificial victim: she fought and struggled to escape from the room.

	Offend you in my life; never loved Cassio	

Offend you in my life; never loved Cassio
But with such general warranty of heaven   60
As I might love. I never gave him token.

OTHELLO   By heaven, I saw my handkerchief in's hand!
O perjured woman! thou dost stone my heart,
And mak'st me call what I intend to do
A murder, which I thought a sacrifice.   65
I saw the handkerchief.

DESDEMONA   He found it then.
I never gave it him. Send for him hither.
Let him confess a truth.

OTHELLO   He hath confessed.

DESDEMONA   What, my lord?

OTHELLO   That he hath used thee.

DESDEMONA   How? Unlawfully?

OTHELLO   Ay.   70

DESDEMONA   He will not say so.

OTHELLO   No; his mouth is stopped.
Honest Iago hath ta'en order for't.

DESDEMONA   O, my fear interprets. What, is he dead?

OTHELLO   Had all his hairs been lives, my great revenge
Had stomach for them all.   75

DESDEMONA   Alas, he is betrayed, and I undone!

OTHELLO   Out, strumpet! Weep'st thou for him to my face?

DESDEMONA   O banish me, my lord, but kill me not!

OTHELLO   Down, strumpet!

DESDEMONA   Kill me tomorrow; let me live tonight!   80

OTHELLO   Nay, if you strive –

82   **But** only; just *(let me live)*

 Being done...pause Now that I have
 started, I cannot stop.

84   ***Calls within*** *from within the tiring-house;*
 backstage

92   **like** likely

93   **The noise was high** the commotion
 (surrounding the attack on Cassio) was
 loud

101   **yawn at alteration** split wide open with
 the change in nature (*it was commonly
 believed that the natural world reacted to
 terrible events affecting humans, a
 powerful idea in Shakespeare's* Julius
 Caesar)

Othello in performance

88 What does *So, so* signify? Following lines 86–87, most actors take it to mean that, to
prevent Desdemona from suffering further, Othello administers the final pressure required to
smother her. Others point out that, as it is medically impossible for a person to recover from
suffocation and then die (see 117–125), Othello must actually stab her at this point. This is
perhaps overliteral and fails to allow for the fact that Shakespeare's medical knowledge might
not have been that extensive; it also goes against Othello's pledge that he will not shed
Desdemona's blood (3–5). Most actors therefore opt for suffocation. But does he suffocate
her with a pillow or strangle her with his bare hands (which, some suggest, is implied by line
200)? Shakespeare doesn't specify; yet the manner in which Othello kills his wife can be
central to how we feel about him here.

Othello's language

91–101 As Emilia's knocking is heard, Othello's brief, staccato questions and exclamations
betray his agitation (91–97). But this emotional turmoil is different from the psychological
breakdown of Act 4 (see, for example, 4.1.36–45), as the dignified and sonorous language
shows (98–101).

5.2

DESDEMONA But half an hour!

OTHELLO   Being done, there is no pause.

DESDEMONA But while I say one prayer!

OTHELLO   It is too late.

Smothers her.

EMILIA at the door.

EMILIA [*Calls within*] My lord, my lord! What, ho, my lord,
           my lord!

OTHELLO What noise is this? Not dead? Not yet quite dead? 85
           I that am cruel am yet merciful;
           I would not have thee linger in thy pain.
           So, so.

EMILIA [*Within*] What, ho! My lord, my lord!

OTHELLO   Who's there?

EMILIA [*Within*] O, good my lord, I would speak a word
           with you.   90

OTHELLO Yes, 'tis Emilia. – By and by. – She's dead. –
           'Tis like she comes to speak of Cassio's death.
           The noise was high. Ha! No more moving?
           Still as the grave. – Shall she come in? Were't good? –
           I think she stirs again. No. – What's best to do? 95
           If she come in, she'll sure speak to my wife.
           My wife! My wife! What wife? I have no wife.
           O, insupportable! O heavy hour!
           Methinks it should be now a huge eclipse
           Of sun and moon, and that th'affrighted globe   100
           Should yawn at alteration.

EMILIA   [*Within*] I do beseech you
           That I may speak with you, O good my lord!

OTHELLO I had forget thee. O, come in Emilia.
           Soft, by and by. – Let me the curtains draw. –

Draws bed hangings, then opens door.

Emilia enters to report the death of Roderigo, and discovers the dying Desdemona

109	**error** straying off its normal course	119	**Out and alas** *an expression of grief*
115–116	**murder's...harsh** murder has not had its desired effect and I cannot enjoy the sweetness of revenge	125	**Commend me to** give my love to

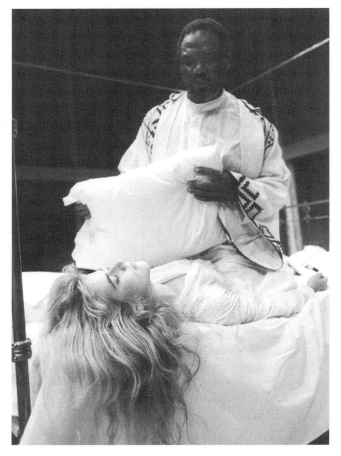

Willard White as Othello and Imogen Stubbs as Desdemona (RSC, 1989)

Desdemona

124 Is it out of love for Othello that Desdemona claims to have killed herself? Her willingness to take the blame has been condemned by some critics.

Where art thou?

Enter EMILIA.

What's the matter with thee now? 105

EMILIA O my good lord, yonder's foul murders done!

OTHELLO What? Now?

EMILIA But now, my lord.

OTHELLO It is the very error of the moon.
She comes more nearer earth than she was wont 110
And makes men mad.

EMILIA Cassio, my lord, hath killed a young Venetian
Called Roderigo.

OTHELLO Roderigo killed?
And Cassio killed?

EMILIA No, Cassio is not killed.

OTHELLO Not Cassio killed? Then murder's out of tune, 115
And sweet revenge grows harsh.

DESDEMONA O, falsely, falsely murdered!

EMILIA O Lord! What cry is that?

OTHELLO That? What?

EMILIA Out and alas, that was my lady's voice!
Help! Help, ho! Help! [*Draws back bed hangings.*]
     O lady, speak again! 120
Sweet Desdemona! O sweet mistress, speak!

DESDEMONA A guiltless death I die.

EMILIA O who hath done this deed?

DESDEMONA Nobody – I myself. Farewell.
Commend me to my kind lord. O, farewell! 125

She dies.

5.2 *Accused of the murder, Othello tells Emilia that he had acted on information provided by Iago*

126 **how should she be** how is it possible for her to have been

129 **like a liar** like the liar that she is

130–131 **the more angel...devil** her innocent death makes her seem even more like an angel and you more devilish

132 **folly** unchaste behaviour *(her supposed adultery)*

133 **belie** slander

136 **top** *a version of 'tup'; see note to 1.1.86*

else if you think that isn't true

139 **this extremity** final extreme act of justice

140 **wedlock** marriage

143 **Of one...chrysolite** out of one pure, perfect topaz *(a precious stone)*

Emilia

140 *My husband?...:* Emilia's repetition of this phrase (140, 144, 147) and her seeming inability to say anything else conveys her unwillingness to accept the information and the beginnings of her struggle to recognise its implications.

OTHELLO	Why, how should she be murd'red?

EMILIA	Alas, who knows?

OTHELLO	You heard her say herself, it was not I.

EMILIA	She said so. I must needs report the truth.

OTHELLO	She's like a liar gone to burning hell! 'Twas I that killed her.

EMILIA   O, the more angel she,   130
And you the blacker devil!

OTHELLO	She turned to folly, and she was a whore.

EMILIA	Thou dost belie her, and thou art a devil.

OTHELLO	She was false as water.

EMILIA   Thou art rash as fire to say
That she was false. O, she was heavenly true!   135

OTHELLO   Cassio did top her. Ask thy husband else.
O I were damned beneath all depth in hell,
But that I did proceed upon just grounds
To this extremity. Thy husband knew it all.

EMILIA	My husband?

OTHELLO   Thy husband.

EMILIA   That she was false to wedlock?   140

OTHELLO   Ay, with Cassio. Had she been true,
If heaven would make me such another world
Of one entire and perfect chrysolite,
I'd not have sold her for it.

EMILIA   My husband?

OTHELLO   Ay, 'twas he that told me on her first.   145
An honest man he is, and hates the slime
That sticks on filthy deeds.

EMILIA   My husband?

5.2 *When Iago enters with Montano and Gratiano, Emilia angrily challenges him to refute Othello's accusation*

148 **iterance** repetition

149 **made mocks with** made a mockery of; played games with

153 **pernicious** destructive; poisonous

155 **fond of** foolishly infatuated by

most filthy bargain *in that she exchanged her position in Venice, and Brabantio's love, for the murderer Othello*

159 **Peace...best** You had better be quiet.

161 **gull...dolt** credulous fool...idiot

163 **I'll make thee known** I'll reveal what you have done

168 **lay...neck** say it was your fault they committed murder

Othello in performance

146–152 In a piece of painful dramatic irony, the word *honest* seems to return to haunt Othello here. Some actors have played line 152 as though Othello realises what he is saying halfway through, pausing between the two 'honests' in appalled recognition of the truth. Others take Othello's groan at line 196 as the moment when he realises. But both of these, though each is dramatically effective, are difficult interpretations to sustain, given that Othello continues to express his faith in Iago up to line 215.

OTHELLO	What needs this iterance? Woman, I say thy husband.
EMILIA	O mistress, villainy hath made mocks with love!
	My husband say she was false?
OTHELLO	He, woman. 150
	I say, thy husband. Dost understand the word?
	My friend, thy husband; honest, honest Iago.
EMILIA	If he say so, may his pernicious soul
	Rot half a grain a day! He lies to th'heart.
	She was too fond of her most filthy bargain. 155
OTHELLO	Hah?
EMILIA	Do thy worst.
	This deed of thine is no more worthy heaven
	Than thou wast worthy her.
OTHELLO	Peace, you were best.
EMILIA	Thou hast not half that pow'r to do me harm 160
	As I have to be hurt. O gull! O dolt!
	As ignorant as dirt! Thou hast done a deed –

OTHELLO touches his sword.

> I care not for thy sword; I'll make thee known,
> Though I lost twenty lives. Help! Help ho! Help!
> The Moor hath killed my mistress ! Murder!
>   Murder!   165

Enter MONTANO, GRATIANO, IAGO and others.

MONTANO	What is the matter? How now, general?
EMILIA	O, are you come, Iago? You have done well,
	That men must lay their murders on your neck.
GRATIANO	What is the matter?
EMILIA	Disprove this villain, if thou be'st a man. 170
	He says thou told'st him that his wife was false.
	I know thou didst not; thou'rt not such a villain.
	Speak, for my heart is full.

175 **apt** plausible; likely

181 **charm** put a spell on *(to make it silent; i.e. be quiet!)*

192 **charge** order

194 **proper** fitting; correct

198 **lift up eye** *i.e. to heaven, in order to pray*

Emilia

190 It is not clear what Emilia means by *I thought so then*. Is she implying that she suspected Iago at 4.2.129–132 of being the *cogging, cozening slave* slandering her mistress *to get some office*? Or perhaps she had doubts even earlier when handing over the handkerchief to Iago (3.3.313–314)? If we follow either of these interpretations, it is difficult to account for her reaction of extreme shock at line 216.

IAGO	I told him what I thought, and told no more
	Than what he found himself was apt and true. 175
EMILIA	But did you ever tell him she was false?
IAGO	I did.
EMILIA	You told a lie, an odious damnèd lie!
	Upon my soul, a lie! A wicked lie!
	She false with Cassio? Did you say with Cassio? 180
IAGO	With Cassio, mistress. Go to, charm your tongue.
EMILIA	I will not charm my tongue; I am bound to speak;
	My mistress here lies murdered in her bed.
ALL	O heavens forfend!
EMILIA	And your reports have set the murder on. 185
OTHELLO	Nay, stare not, masters. It is true indeed.
GRATIANO	'Tis a strange truth.
MONTANO	O monstrous act!
EMILIA	Villainy, villainy, villainy!
	I think upon't – I think I smell't! – O villainy!
	I thought so then. – I'll kill myself for grief. – 190
	O villainy, villainy!
IAGO	What, are you mad? I charge you get you home.
EMILIA	Good gentlemen, let me have leave to speak
	'Tis proper I obey him, but not now.
	Perchance, Iago, I will ne'er go home. 195
OTHELLO	O! O! O!

Falls on the bed.

EMILIA	Nay, lay thee down and roar,
	For thou hast killed the sweetest innocent
	That e'er did lift up eye.

5.2 *When Othello mentions the handkerchief, Emilia reveals that she had found it and given it to Iago*

199	**scarce did know** hardly recognised
203	**Thy match was mortal...** your marriage caused his death
204	**Shore** cut; sheared *(an allusion to the classical belief that one of the Fates would cut a person's thread of life at the allotted time)*
	Did he live had he been alive
205	**do a desperate turn** kill himself
206–207	**Yea, curse...reprobation** Yes, drive away his guardian angel and fall into damnation *(because suicide was considered a mortal sin for which a person would go to hell)*

211	**gratify...works** reward his love-making
212	**recognizance** token
217	**Zounds...peace!** By God's wounds *(a powerful oath)* be quiet!
	'Twill out the truth must be revealed
218	**liberal as the north** as freely as the north wind blows
222	**Fie!** You should be ashamed of yourself!
223	**dull** stupid
224	**by fortune** by chance

Structure: the time scheme

209–210 Othello's belief that Cassio and Desdemona have *the act of shame A thousand times committed* contributes further to our sense of 'long time'.

OTHELLO	O, she was foul!

Rises. To GRATIANO.

OTHELLO I scarce did know you, uncle. There lies your niece,
Whose breath, indeed, these hands have newly
　　stopped.　　　　　　　　　　　　　　　　　　200
I know this act shows horrible and grim.

GRATIANO Poor Desdemon! I am glad thy father's dead.
Thy match was mortal to him, and pure grief
Shore his old thread in twain. Did he live now,
This sight would make him do a desperate turn;　205
Yea, curse his better angel from his side,
And fall to reprobation.

OTHELLO 'Tis pitiful; but yet Iago knows
That she with Cassio hath the act of shame
A thousand times committed. Cassio confessed it;　210
And she did gratify his amorous works
With that recognizance and pledge of love,
Which I first gave her. I saw it in his hand.
It was a handkerchief, and antique token
My father gave my mother.　　　　　　　　　　215

EMILIA O God! O heavenly God!

IAGO Zounds, hold your peace!

EMILIA 'Twill out, 'twill out! I peace?
No, I will speak as liberal as the north.
Let heaven and men and devils, let them all,
All, all, cry shame against me, yet I'll speak.　　220

IAGO Be wise, and get you home.

EMILIA I will not.

IAGO threatens EMILIA with his sword.

GRATIANO Fie! Your sword upon a woman?

EMILIA O thou dull Moor, that handkerchief thou speak'st of
I found by fortune, and did give my husband;
For often with a solemn earnestness –　　　　　225

Realising the truth, Othello attempts to kill Iago, who, in the scuffle, fatally stabs Emilia and makes his escape, pursued by the others

226 **belonged to** was appropriate to

231 **coxcomb** fool

232–233 **Are there...thunder** Aren't there any thunderbolts, other than those used for thunder? *(an allusion to the belief that wicked people would be destroyed by thunderbolts hurled by the gods)*

233 **Precious** *used to intensify the word 'villain'*

237 **notorious** blatant *(not 'well known')*

242 **puny whipster** feeble whippersnapper; insignificant person *(someone who is too prone to whipping out his sword at the least provocation)*

243 **But why...honesty?** But why should a man retain a reputation for honour after the honour itself has gone? *(i.e. when he no longer deserves it)*

244 **bode** foretell

245 **play the swan** *swans were believed to sing just once: before their death*

Othello

241 Othello's *I am not valiant neither* might be a comment on Montano's description of Iago (so that Othello is saying, 'I am a damned slave as well'); or possibly a recognition that, along with losing all his other virtues, he has lost his courage and manliness also, proved by the fact that he has been easily disarmed by Montano – though it seems unlikely that he would describe his predecessor as governor of Cyprus as a *puny whipster* (242).

More than indeed belonged to such a trifle –
He begged of me to steal't.

IAGO   Villainous whore!

EMILIA   She give it Cassio? No, alas, I found it,
And I did give't my husband.

IAGO   Filth, thou liest!

EMILIA   By heaven, I do not, I do not, gentlemen.   230
[*To* OTHELLO] O murd'rous coxcomb! What should
    such a fool
Do with so good a wife?

OTHELLO   Are there no stones in heaven
But what serves for the thunder! Precious villain!
[*The Moor runs at* IAGO, *but is disarmed by* MONTANO. IAGO
    kills his wife.]

GRATIANO   The woman falls. Sure he hath killed his wife.

EMILIA   Ay, ay. O, lay me by my mistress' side.   235

                                              Exit IAGO.

GRATIANO   He's gone, but his wife's killed.

MONTANO   'Tis a notorious villain. Take you this weapon,
Which I have recovered from the Moor.
Come, guard the door without. Let him not pass,
But kill him rather. I'll after that same villain,   240
For 'tis a damnèd slave.

                          Exit with all but OTHELLO and EMILIA.

OTHELLO   I am not valiant neither;
But every puny whipster gets my sword.
But why should honour outlive honesty?
Let it go all.

EMILIA   What did thy song bode, lady?
Hark, canst thou hear me? I will play the swan,   245
And die in music. [*Sings*] 'Willow, willow, willow.'
Moor, she was chaste. She loved thee, cruel Moor,

248 **So come my soul** as I hope my soul will come *(i.e. may my soul never enjoy the bliss of heaven if I'm lying)*

251 **ice-brook's temper** tempered (hardened) by being plunged into an icy stream

253 *Within in the tiring-house; offstage*

254 **perforce** necessarily; inevitably

256 **naked** unarmed

265 **butt** goal

266 **seamark...utmost sail** beacon for my final voyage

267 **lost** pointless

268 **Man but a rush** aim only a reed

270 **ill-starred** ill-fated

271 **at compt** at the final reckoning *(on Judgement Day)*

278 **steep-down** with sides like precipices

Othello in performance

275 Most actors take Othello's cry of *O cursèd, cursèd slave* to apply to himself, rather than Iago.

So come my soul to bliss as I speak true.
So speaking as I think, alas, I die.

She dies.

OTHELLO I have another weapon in this chamber;   250
It was a sword of Spain, the ice-brook's temper.
O, here it is. – Uncle, I must come forth.

GRATIANO [*Within*] If thou attempt it, it will cost thee dear.
Thou hast no weapon, and perforce must suffer.

OTHELLO Look in upon me then and speak with me,   255
Or, naked as I am, I will assault thee.

Enter GRATIANO.

GRATIANO What is the matter?

OTHELLO   Behold, I have a weapon;
A better never did itself sustain
Upon a soldier's thigh. I have seen the day
That with this little arm and this good sword   260
I have made my way through more impediments
Than twenty times your stop. But O vain boast!
Who can control his fate? 'Tis not so now.
Be not afraid, though you do see me weaponed.
Here is my journey's end, here is my butt,   265
And very seamark of my utmost sail.
Do you go back dismayed? 'Tis a lost fear.
Man but a rush against Othello's breast,
And he retires. Where should Othello go
Now? How dost thou look now? O ill-starred
    wench,   270
Pale as thy smock! When we shall meet at compt,
This look of thine will hurl my soul from heaven,
And fiends will snatch at it. Cold, cold, my girl?
Even like thy chastity.
O cursèd, cursèd slave! Whip me, ye devils,   275
From the possession of this heavenly sight!
Blow me about in winds, roast me in sulphur,
Wash me in steep-down gulfs of liquid fire!
O Desdemon! Dead Desdemon; dead. O! O!

5.2 *Iago is brought back, but refuses to explain his actions*

283 **that's a fable** *i.e. 'it's only a myth that the devil has cloven hoofs'*

287 **in my sense** the way I feel; to someone who feels as I do

289 **in the practice** because of the plots

294 **consent in** plan together

Othello

291–292 To the last, Othello retains his belief that he was motivated, not by revenge, but out of a sense of honour and justice (see, for example, 4.1.208, 5.2.1–6, 5.2.17, 5.2.64–65 and 5.2.138).

Iago in performance

300–301 Iago's dismissive final words give actors the opportunity to explore a wide variety of interpretations. Does Iago appear satisfied with the outcome of his actions? If so, what kind of satisfaction is it? Does he exult? Is he apparently distressed (Kenneth Branagh, 1995)? Or does he, like Ian McKellen (RSC, 1989; see photograph on page 246), appear completely impassive?

Act 5 Scene 2

Enter LODOVICO, CASSIO, wounded, MONTANO, and IAGO, as prisoner, with OFFICERS.

LODOVICO	Where is this rash and most unfortunate man? 280
OTHELLO	That's he that was Othello; here I am.
LODOVICO	Where is that viper? Bring the villain forth.
OTHELLO	I look down towards his feet – but that's a fable. If that thou be'st a devil, I cannot kill thee.

Wounds IAGO.

LODOVICO	Wrench his sword from him.

OTHELLO's sword is taken from him.

IAGO	I bleed, sir, but not killed. 285
OTHELLO	I am not sorry neither. I'd have thee live; For in my sense, 'tis happiness to die.
LODOVICO	O thou Othello that was once so good, Fall'n in the practice of a cursèd slave, What shall be said to thee?
OTHELLO	Why, anything: 290 An honourable murderer, if you will; For naught I did in hate, but all in honour.
LODOVICO	This wretch hath part confessed his villainy. Did you and he consent in Cassio's death?
OTHELLO	Ay. 295
CASSIO	Dear general, I never gave you cause.
OTHELLO	I do believe it, and I ask your pardon. Will you, I pray, demand that demi-devil Why he hath thus ensnared my soul and body?
IAGO	Demand me nothing. What you know, you know. 300 From this time forth I never will speak word.
LODOVICO	What, not to pray?

302 **Torments** torture

303 **thou dost best** you're wise to remain silent

307 **imports** is about

310 **heathenish...gross** barbaric and disgusting

311 **discontented paper** letter expressing discontent

314 **But that, belike** except that, in all likelihood

in the interim meanwhile *(i.e. before Roderigo could send the letter)*

315 **satisfied him** gave him a satisfactory explanation

pernicious caitiff poisonous slave

320 **wrought to his desire** worked out according to his plan

322 **upbraids** complains to

323 **Brave** provoke

whereon it came as a result of which it came about

324 **cast** dismissed *(as lieutenant)*

even now only a moment ago

327 **forsake** leave

329 **this slave** Iago

331 **hold him long** keep him a long time dying

Dramatic structure

305 This is not the only Shakespeare play in which the denouement is assisted by the sudden appearance of some convenient letters: in *The Merchant of Venice*, Portia acknowledges the implausibility by telling everybody 'You shall not know by what strange accident I chancèd on this letter' (5.1). At least here Lodovico explains where the letters came from.

GRATIANO	Torments will ope your lips.	
OTHELLO	[*To IAGO*] Well, thou dost best.	

LODOVICO Sir, you shall understand what hath befall'n,
Which, as I think, you know not. Here is a letter   305
Found in the pocket of the slain Roderigo;
And here another. The one of them imports
The death of Cassio to be undertook
By Roderigo.

OTHELLO O villain!

CASSIO   Most heathenish and most gross!   310

LODOVICO Now here's another discontented paper
Found in his pocket too; and this, it seems,
Roderigo meant t'have sent this damnèd villain;
But that, belike, Iago in the interim
Came in and satisfied him.

OTHELLO   [*To IAGO*] O thou pernicious caitiff!   315
How came you, Cassio, by that handkerchief
That was my wife's?

CASSIO   I found it in my chamber;
And he himself confessed it but even now
That there he dropped it for a special purpose
Which wrought to his desire.

OTHELLO   O fool! Fool! Fool!   320

CASSIO There is besides in Roderigo's letter,
How he upbraids Iago that he made him
Brave me upon the watch; whereon it came
That I was cast; and even but now he spake,
After long seeming dead – Iago hurt him –   325
Iago set him on.

LODOVICO You must forsake this room and go with us.
Your power and your command is taken off,
And Cassio rules in Cyprus. For this slave,
If there be any cunning cruelty   330
That can torment him much and hold him long,

332	**rest** remain	346	**Albeit...mood** although unused to tender feelings
335	**Soft you** just a moment		
338	**unlucky** fateful	348	**med'cinable gum** sap used as medicine *(a reference to the myrrh tree, associated with incense)*
339	**extenuate** lessen; underplay		
342	**wrought** worked upon	349	**Aleppo** *an ancient city in Syria*
343	**Perplexed** bewildered	351	**traduced** slandered; insulted
344–345	**the base Indian...** *possibly an allusion to some legendary native American who was unaware of the value of the pearl he owned (but this is much debated by scholars)*	354	**period** conclusion
		358	**Spartan dog** *Spartan dogs were famous for their ferocity.*
345	**subdued** overcome by emotion	359	**fell** deadly

Othello in performance

How does Othello begin his final speech? Willard White (1989) was typically quiet and dignified, whereas Olivier (1964) proudly reminded the Venetians that he had *done the state some service, and they know't*. He laid particular stress on *unlucky* (338). Then, 'the last speech was spoken kneeling on the bed, her body clutched upright to him as a shield for the dagger he turns on himself' (Ronald Bryden). In the 1995 film, Cassio secretly slips Othello a knife at line 329, presumably understanding that, as a soldier, he would prefer suicide to a life of degradation and regret.

Iago in performance

'I threw myself on his dying body...I did this for two reasons: first, shock and surprise at Othello's suicide; and second, to follow the hate/love theme right through to the end' (David Suchet, who played Iago in 1985). Ian McKellen's Iago (1989), by contrast, remained on the surface completely unmoved.

It shall be his. You shall close prisoner rest
Till that the nature of your fault be known
To the Venetian state. Come, bring away.

OTHELLO   Soft you, a word or two before you go.   335
I have done the state some service, and they know't.
No more of that. I pray you, in your letters,
When you shall these unlucky deeds relate,
Speak of me as I am. Nothing extenuate,
Nor set down aught in malice. Then must you
        speak   340
Of one that loved not wisely, but too well;
Of one not easily jealous, but being wrought,
Perplexed in the extreme; of one whose hand,
Like the base Indian, threw a pearl away
Richer than all his tribe; of one whose subdued
        eyes,   345
Albeit unusèd to the melting mood,
Drops tears as fast as the Arabian trees
Their med'cinable gum. Set you down this.
And say besides that in Aleppo once,
Where a malignant and a turbaned Turk   350
Beat a Venetian and traduced the state,
I took by th'throat the circumcisèd dog
And smote him – thus.

He stabs himself.

LODOVICO   O bloody period!

GRATIANO   All that is spoke is marred.

OTHELLO   I kissed thee ere I killed thee. No way but this,   355
Killing myself, to die upon a kiss.

He dies falling on DESDEMONA.

CASSIO   This did I fear, but thought he had no weapon;
For he was great of heart.

LODOVICO   [*To IAGO*] O Spartan dog,
More fell than anguish, hunger, or the sea,
Look on the tragic loading of this bed.   360

Lodovico gives Cassio the responsibility for Iago's punishment and returns to Venice

362 **keep** guard

363 **seize upon** legally confiscate; take possession of

364 **succeed on** descend to; are to be handed down to

lord governor Cassio *(see 4.1.233)*

365 **censure** judgement; trial

367 **straight** immediately

368 **heavy** sorrowful

Ian McKellen as Iago (RSC, 1989)

This is thy work. The object poisons sight;
Let it be hid.

Bed curtains drawn.

               Gratiano, keep the house,
And seize upon the fortunes of the Moor,
For they succeed on you. To you, lord governor,
Remains the censure of this hellish villain,   365
The time, the place, the torture, O enforce it!
Myself will straight aboard, and to the state
This heavy act with heavy heart relate.

Exeunt.

Exam practice

Extracts

1. Reread 5.1.1–64 ('...Murder! Murder!'). How far is Roderigo's and Iago's interaction in this extract illustrative of the relationship they have had in the play as a whole? In your answer you should:
   - examine in detail the language and characterisation of both Iago and Roderigo
   - give your own opinions on Iago's attitude to Roderigo, and what Roderigo himself says about the planned attack on Cassio
   - show some awareness of the figure of the 'gull' in Shakespeare's plays more generally (see note on page 12).

2. Reread 5.2.1–57 ('...I say, amen'). What might the thoughts and feelings of an audience be as they watch this part of the scene? In your answer you should:
   - show in detail how characterisation, atmosphere and dramatic qualities are created by Shakespeare's choice of language
   - express your own thoughts and feelings about the scene at this point in the play, as well as suggesting how other audiences might respond to it
   - show some awareness of dramatic climax and Shakespearean tragedy.

3. Reread 5.2.167–235 ('O, are you...my mistress' side'). In what ways does this extract develop your understanding of Emilia and her role in the play? In your answer you should:
   - make detailed reference to Emilia's language, actions and characterisation
   - express your own reactions to Emilia's behaviour as well as suggesting how other audiences might respond to her, both here and in the rest of the play
   - show some awareness of Elizabethan attitudes to the relationship of a wife to her husband.

Extended writing

4. How far would you agree with Othello's description of himself in his final speech (5.2.335–348: 'Soft you...med'cinable gum')? In your answer you should:
   - examine in detail Othello's language, statements and underlying beliefs
   - give your own opinion on the accuracy or otherwise of his self-assessment
   - show an understanding of the Shakespearean tragic hero.

Performance

5. In groups of six, 'block' the characters' positions and movements – i.e. plan where they should stand and what moves they should make – at the beginning of 5.1 (up to 65, when Iago moves to Gratiano and Lodovico after stabbing Roderigo). It will help to read the notes on pages 206 and 208. Make notes on the blocking and then discuss how Iago's movements help us to observe the ways in which he stage-manages the whole episode and reacts to the unexpected arrival of Gratiano and Lodovico.

6. In small groups, freeze-frame the final moment of the play. Pay particular attention to Iago: should he be exulting over his fallen enemies, for example, or be distressed or impassive...? (Reread David Suchet's comment on page 244.) Discuss which version best fits your interpretation of the character, and what you think Iago is feeling and thinking as the play ends.

Willard White as Othello and Imogen Stubbs as Desdemona (RSC, 1989)

Shakespeare's world

The Renaissance

The age during which Shakespeare lived and worked is traditionally known as the Renaissance, though some people these days prefer to call it the 'early modern' period. It was a moment in European cultural history when extraordinary changes were taking place, especially in the fields of religion, politics, science, language and the arts.

Religion and politics

- In the century following the Reformation in 1534, people in Shakespeare's England began to view the world and their own place in it very differently.
- Queen Elizabeth felt that she had to stand alone against a strongly Catholic Europe and maintain the Protestant religion in England established by her father Henry VIII.
- People began to think about the relationship between themselves as individuals and the authority of the state, while not everybody any longer accepted the idea that queens or kings ruled by 'divine right' (on God's authority).
- There were divisions in the Protestant Church, with extremist groups such as the Puritans disapproving of much that they saw in society and the Church.
- During this time people began to question the traditional beliefs in rank and social order – the ideas that some people should be considered superior simply because they were born into wealthy families; or that those in power should always be obeyed without question.
- England had become a proud and independent nation, and a leading military and trading power, especially after the defeat of the Spanish Armada in 1588.
- As trade became increasingly important, it was not only the nobility who could become wealthy. People could move around the country more easily and a competitive capitalist economy developed.
- James I succeeded Elizabeth in 1603. He was a Scot, interested in witchcraft, and a supporter of the theatre, who fought off the treasonous attempt of the Gunpowder Plot in 1605.

Science and discovery

- Scientists began to question traditional authorities (the accepted ideas handed down from one generation to the next) and depended instead upon their own observation of the world, especially after the development of instruments such as the telescope. The Italian Galileo (1564–1642) came into conflict with the Church for claiming that the Earth was not the centre of the universe.
- Explorers brought back new produce, such as spices, silks and gold, and created great excitement in the popular imagination for stories of distant lands and their peoples.

Language

- The more traditional scholars still regarded Latin as the only adequate language for scholarly discussion and writing (and liked it because it also prevented many 'uncultured' people from understanding philosophy, medicine, etc).
- But a new interest in the English language came with England's growing importance and sense of identity.
- The English language began to be standardised in this period (into Standard English), but it was still very flexible and there was less insistence on following rules than there is nowadays.
- English vocabulary was enriched by numerous borrowings from other languages. Between 1500 and 1650, over 10,000 new words entered the language.
- Shakespeare therefore lived through a time when the English vocabulary was expanding amazingly and the grammar was still flexible, a time when people were intensely excited by language.

Key dates and Shakespeare

1558 Elizabeth I becomes Queen.
1564 William Shakespeare born in Stratford-upon-Avon.
1565 The explorer John Hawkins introduces sweet potatoes and tobacco into England.
1567 Mary Queen of Scots abdicates in favour of her year-old son, James VI.
1576 James Burbage opens the first successful playhouse (The Theatre) in London.
1580 Francis Drake returns from a circumnavigation of the world.
1582 Pope Gregory reforms the Christian calendar; Shakespeare marries Anne Hathaway.
1587 Mary Queen of Scots executed for a treasonous plot against Elizabeth; Drake partly destroys the Spanish fleet at Cádiz and war breaks out with Spain.
1588 Philip II of Spain's Armada is defeated by the English fleet.
1592 Before this date Shakespeare arrives in London; another writer, Robert Greene, writes about 'Shake-scene', the 'upstart crow' who has become a popular playwright.
1592–1593 Plague kills over 10,000 Londoners.
1593 Playwright Christopher Marlowe killed.
1594 The Lord Chamberlain's Men is formed; Shakespeare joins them as an actor and playwright.
1596 Shakespeare's only son, Hamnet, dies, age 11.
1599 Globe Theatre opens on Bankside.
1603 Elizabeth I dies and is succeeded by James VI of Scotland as James I of England; he grants the Lord Chamberlain's Men a royal patent and they become the King's Men.
1605 Gunpowder Plot uncovered.
1607 First permanent English settlement in America at Jamestown, Virginia.

1608 The King's Men begin performing plays in the indoor Blackfriars Theatre.
1610 Galileo looks at the stars through a telescope.
1611 Authorised Version of the Bible published.
1616 Shakespeare dies, 23 April.
1618 Sir Walter Raleigh executed for treason; physician William Harvey announces discovery of blood circulation.
1620 Pilgrim Fathers sail from Plymouth to colonise America.
1623 First Folio of Shakespeare's plays published.
1625 James I dies and is succeeded by Charles I.

Playwrights

Shakespeare was not writing in a dramatic vacuum; during his working life, and for a period beyond it up to the closure of the playhouses, there was a veritable industry of playwriting which produced several playwrights to rival Shakespeare in stature.

- **Christopher Marlowe** (1564–93) was born in the same year as Shakespeare, but his life was tragically cut off when he was mysteriously stabbed, possibly for his atheistic views or his involvement with the secret service. Marlowe wrote a series of great dramas with titanic heroes, most of them created for Edward Alleyn, leading actor with the Admiral's Men at the Rose. These included *Tamburlaine* and *Dr Faustus*, which has a terrifying concluding scene in which the hero is dragged off to hell. Had Shakespeare died as young as his rival, there is little doubt that Marlowe would now be considered the greater dramatist.
- **Ben Jonson** (1572/3–1637), like his friend Shakespeare (whom he loved and admired 'on this side idolatry'), began his theatre career as an actor. A fiery character, he killed a fellow actor in a duel and also spent time in prison for offending the authorities in his plays. Shakespeare himself acted in Jonson's first success, *Every Man in his Humour* (1598), a satire mocking current affectations. Jonson is best known for his two great comedies *Volpone* (1605) and *The Alchemist* (1610), both biting satires on human greed and foolishness.
- **John Webster** (born c. 1580, died c. 1632) is also thought to have started life as an actor, but little is really known about him. He is famous for two dark and violent tragedies of love, horror and political intrigue set in Renaissance Italy, *The White Devil* (1612) and *The Duchess of Malfi* (1614), both of which have determined women as their central characters.
- Among other popular dramatists were two who collaborated widely with other writers. **Thomas Middleton** (1580–1627) had a hand in numerous plays, but is best known for his major part in *The Changeling* (1622) and his probable authorship of *The Revenger's Tragedy* (1607). **John Fletcher** (1579–1625), a phenomenally prolific playwright, enjoyed a very successful collaboration with **Francis Beaumont** (1584–1616) and wrote at least three plays with Shakespeare: *Henry VIII* (1613), *The Two Noble Kinsmen* (c. 1613) and a lost play, *Cardenio* (acted at court in 1613).

Social, historical and literary context

Venice

'Venice, Cyprus and the sea are therefore more than geographical features of the play; they are part of its dramatic symbolism' (G Salgado).

It has been said that the presence of Venice in *Othello* is so strong that it almost becomes another character. There are a number of facts about Venice – as well as a range of associations – that educated members of Shakespeare's audience would have been aware of:

- Venice was a republic with a reputation for religious and political tolerance.
- It was an extremely successful commercial centre with contacts around the Mediterranean.
- Italians generally were supposed to be cunning, with a love of plots and deceptions. Italy was the country of Machiavelli.
- Venetian women had a reputation for being sophisticated and sexually active. It was notorious for prostitutes.
- Venice was famous for the fairness of its laws; it was a place of order and justice.
- In the sixteenth century, Venice had been involved in a long struggle against the Turks.

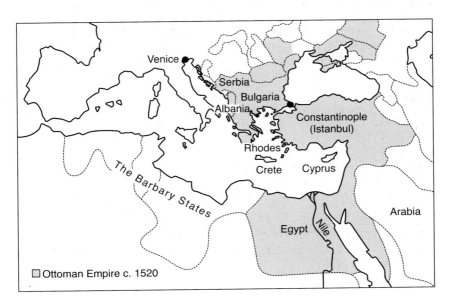

Venice and the Ottoman Empire in 1520

253

Social, historical and literary context

These key references help to show the importance of Venice in the play: 1.1.136; 1.2.98; 1.3; 1.3.49; 2.1.165–176; 3.3.201–204 (see notes on pages 10, 20, 22, 24, 62 and 118).

Cyprus

At the time when this story was set (1570–71), the Turks were just beginning to attack Cyprus, which had belonged to Venice for over a century. By the time of the first performance of *Othello* (between 1602 and 1604), Cyprus had been in Turkish hands for over thirty years.

A critical perspective:
- Some people see the movement of the characters from Venice to the threatened outpost of Cyprus as a reflection of the characters' psychological change from rationality and order to emotional turmoil and chaos (the change itself paralleled in the storm).
- The night brawling that Iago instigates in 2.3 might therefore be seen as foreshadowing the psychological disorder that Othello is about to experience.

Othello and race

In 1601 Africans in London were sufficiently numerous for Queen Elizabeth to comment on the fact. But, although Othello is repeatedly referred to in the play as a 'Moor', there is little agreement about what the word means in terms of his ethnicity or appearance. Unfortunately the two Moors in other plays of Shakespeare don't help us to form a picture of Othello: the Prince of Morocco in *The Merchant of Venice* is described as a 'tawny Moor' (2.1 stage direction) – in other words, comparatively light-skinned; while Aaron in *Titus Andronicus* is a 'coal-black Moor' (3.2). Othello could be either – or something else entirely.

In addition to the occasions on which 'black' and 'Moor' are used as neutral titles – for example Desdemona's 'the Moor my lord' (1.3.187); and even Iago's 'health of black Othello' (2.3.29) – references to Othello's colour and ethnicity come under a range of headings:
- *Insulting comments*: 'the thick-lips' (1.1.63); 'old black ram' (1.1.85); 'Barbary horse' (1.1.109); 'sooty bosom' (1.2.69); 'erring barbarian' (1.3.354).
- *References to ugliness, frightening appearance or difference*: 'to fear, not to delight' (1.2.70); 'what she feared to look on' (1.3.98); 'beauties...the Moor is defective in' (2.1.231–232); 'heave the gorge, disrelish and abhor the Moor' (2.1.234–235); 'shake and fear your looks' (3.3.207); 'matches Of her own clime, complexion, and degree' (3.3.229–230).
- *Othello's own disparaging comments about his blackness*: 'Haply for I am black' (3.3.262); 'begrimed and black As mine own face' (3.3.385–386).

Some of Shakespeare's audience might well have formed their image of Moors from Abd el-Ouahed ben Messaoud ben Mohammed Anoun, the Barbary ambassador who was in London on an official visit to Queen Elizabeth between August 1600 and February 1601.

- *Links between Othello's blackness and the devil*: 'what she feared to look on' (1.3.98); 'And you the blacker devil!' (5.2.131).
- *Statements which, while favourable to Othello, recognise that his blackness is a barrier to be overcome*: 'I saw Othello's visage in his mind' (1.3.248); 'Your son-in-law is far more fair than black' (1.3.286).

The sources of *Othello*

Shakespeare found the story in a collection of tales called the *Hecatommithi*, by an Italian writer called Giraldi Cinthio. This collection, first published in 1565, was very popular and provided stories for other dramatists; Shakespeare himself used it again as the source for *Measure for Measure*. There may have been an English version of the book in Shakespeare's lifetime, but none has survived; he may have read it in the original Italian, or in a French translation of 1583.

Cinthio's collection is divided into ten 'decades', each of ten stories. Each group deals with a single topic and the story on which *Othello* is based comes from the third decade, which is devoted to 'The Unfaithfulness of Husbands and Wives'.

Shakespeare seems to have taken a great deal of his plot from Cinthio, but he changed and developed it in a number of ways. For example, in the original tale:
- the characters are wooden and only the heroine, *Dis*demona, is named
- Brabantio and Roderigo do not appear at all
- the Iago character is simply a handsome villain whose love for Disdemona is thwarted
- he steals the handkerchief himself (while Disdemona is holding his three-year-old daughter)
- the Emilia character knows of her husband's plot, but is afraid to speak out
- the Moor and the villain beat Disdemona to death with a sand-filled stocking, and then pull the roof down on her bed in an attempt to avoid detection.

Among other possible sources, Shakespeare might also have been influenced by a story originally found in the *Histoires Tragiques*, by the French writer Belleforest, published in 1580. For example, the French story has as its background the Turkish wars and contains a murder scene similar to 5.2 of *Othello* which ends with the husband committing suicide across his dead wife's body.

Plays with similar themes

Jealousy

Sexual jealousy is a common theme in plays of this period, though in Shakespeare the passion does not always have tragic consequences: the jealous Ford in *The Merry Wives of Windsor* is merely ridiculed, while Claudio (in *Much Ado About Nothing*) is rewarded with the woman whose reputation he has disgracefully slandered. The green-eyed monster also features to a greater or lesser extent in several of the comedies, as well as in tragic heroes and heroines such as Antony and Cleopatra. But Shakespeare's most detailed exploration of jealousy outside *Othello* occurs in one of his last plays, *The Winter's Tale*. In this disturbing tragicomedy, the jealous delusions of King Leontes lead to the death of his son and a sixteen-year estrangement from his daughter and his wife.

One of the funniest treatments of jealousy is found in Ben Jonson's *Every Man in his Humour*, where Kitely's 'house is so stored with jealousy there is no room for love to stand upright in' (4.6).

Soldiers and male comradeship

Much Ado About Nothing (see above), written two to five years before *Othello*, also features a group of men whose lives have been dedicated to the military life and who do not adapt easily to peacetime. Like Othello, Claudio and Don Pedro are more prepared to believe the lies of another soldier, the scheming Don John, than the truth of Hero, a woman who, like Desdemona, is known to be virtuous. Even Hero's father Leonato initially accepts the slanders uttered against her, asking doubters 'Would the two princes lie? And Claudio lie...?' (4.1) In both plays it is as though the comradeship and trust which are so central to soldiers' success and safety in battle, can become the most dangerous of weaknesses in peacetime, open as they are to exploitation by unscrupulous Machiavels like Iago and Don John.

The characters

These notes provide references for discussion and essay writing. Nearly all the points are summaries of fuller notes in the text.

They can form the basis for quotation banks of:
• characters' key qualities
• moments of change, crisis or revelation
• issues for debate.

Othello

1.1
13 We get Iago's view of Othello before we see the man ourselves.

1.2
58 Othello's calmness and authority.

1.3
48–49 The language used by the Duke and senators when referring to Othello.
76–94 Othello's language: stately and formal expressions from Latin and the Romance languages; military terms.
81–82 Is he being modest, or does he genuinely believe that he lacks eloquence?
83–85 Othello's pride in his profession.
122–123 He is a practising Christian.
127–144 Othello's heroic past intrigues the Venetians.
257–260 Othello plays down the sexual aspect of their relationship.

The characters

2.3

9–10 Eagerly looking forward to the consummation of their marriage.

201–213 In a temper but still in control. Yet infuriated when he fails to get a straight answer to a straight question.

3.3

90–92 Othello's last complete affirmation of his love for Desdemona. Is he in the power of feelings that he cannot control?

179... His view of himself: a man who, once his suspicions have been aroused, would take immediate practical steps to find out the truth and act instantly.

240 Does Othello seem to have sunk very low very quickly?

258–259 How important is his awareness that he is an outsider?

345–355 Some of Othello's grandest language. He creates a picture of all the magnificence and glory that he is destined never again to enjoy; and, significantly, it is all associated with his career as a soldier.

357 He now uses the crudest and most brutal language to describe Desdemona's alleged behaviour. He now depends totally upon Iago to give him 'ocular proof', while cursing him for having put him on the rack.

366 His inability to see what Iago is doing to him.

386–388 Is he seriously contemplating suicide?

3.4

31... Dissembling language to Desdemona with sexual connotations.

76–96 His increasing loss of control is reflected in the language.

4.1

36–45 Othello's mental and physical degeneration are represented in his language and self-awareness that he is falling apart physically.

94–168 One of the lowest points in Othello's decline and degradation?

103–105 Iago's image of Othello's lack of worldly-wisdom. Is it an accurate picture?

177–205 The conflict in Othello between his love for Desdemona and his jealous fury.

208 From this point onwards, Othello thinks of the approaching murder as an act of justice.

236 Othello shames himself publicly. Is this, in fact, his lowest point?

4.2

1... Othello's degradation continues as he cross-examines Emilia. He is now so convinced of Desdemona's guilt, that he rejects evidence which might count in her favour.

40 Othello has to fight back his love for Desdemona.

52–54 The prospect of public mockery is a nightmare.

60–61 Othello's language includes coarse animal imagery heard earlier from Iago (in contrast to the religious imagery of line 62).

5.2

1 'It is the cause...': Desdemona's supposed infidelity: it will be a just sacrifice, rather than a revenge murder.

5 Othello's language now regains some of its former majesty.

21–22 His action will be like God punishing those he loves.

62–65 He is inflamed by Desdemona's repeated denials: the 'sacrifice' is being polluted by thoughts of revenge.

91–101 Look at the ways in which this emotional turmoil is different from the psychological breakdown of Act 4.

146–152 In a piece of painful dramatic irony, the word 'honest' seems to return to haunt Othello.

241 'I am not valiant neither'.

291–292 Othello retains his belief that he was motivated by a sense of honour and justice.

Iago

1.1

54 Iago 'makes remarks which appear at first hearing well turned and significant, and on examination turn out to mean very little.' (M R Ridley)

62 'I am not what I am': he is not what he appears to be.

68 Iago's use of animal imagery. Also 1.1.109–114 and see 1.2.49.

1.2

49 Imagery from ships and the sea; sexual language to describe human relations. What is the effect of this imagery?

1.3

280 'honesty'

377–398 **First soliloquy**

2.1

290–316 **Second soliloquy**

311 Iago's sexual jealousy now extends to Cassio.

2.3

26–44 He knows which of Cassio's weaknesses to exploit. Plays the bluff, good-natured 'mate' and employs a range of persuasive techniques.

104–105 Is he goaded by Cassio's drunken and comic assertion that 'The lieutenant is to be saved before the ancient'?

138 Iago masks his duplicity.

151–152 He makes the most of his opportunities.

216–242 He demonstrates his skill with words and his ability to imply much by apparently saying little.

264–268 He is capable of offering contrary views on the same subject, to suit the listener or the context.

The characters

308–309 Iago's confidence that other people view him as a loyal friend.

312 Opportunist that he is, Iago takes advantage of Cassio's reluctance.

318–321 His understanding of other people's characters and his readiness to exploit their greatest virtues.

326 Iago applies 'honest' to himself within a sentence laden with trust words.

331–332 Is Iago rubbing salt in Cassio's wounds?

334–360 **Third soliloquy**

348 Iago explodes the hypocrisy of his own argument.

351–360 Iago's plan has now become clear to him – at least in its opening phases.

374–375 Another example of his proverbial sayings which look straightforward, but don't stand close examination.

3.3

35 Iago's first step in the deception.

70–71 His jealousy of Cassio possibly increased.

93 His 'temptation' of Othello begins (see the notes on page 112).

125, 129 He gives the impression of having reservations and doubts.

144–151 He cleverly makes his statements sound hesitant and reluctantly expressed by speaking in long, complex sentences.

155–161 He cunningly implies a reference to sexual 'reputation' and the mockery that a cuckold has to endure.

155–167 He quickly raises the stakes.

196 He goes a stage further, moving to a specific suggestion about Desdemona and Cassio.

201 He creates a sense of insecurity in Othello.

218–220 He urges Othello not to take a particular course of action, knowing that he is putting the idea firmly into his head.

226 He implies that Othello is being a credulous fool.

228 He pounces upon Othello's thought.

230 He highlights three aspects of Desdemona likely to make Othello feel alien and inferior.

234 He draws back from a direct accusation.

237 He slily exploits Othello's insecurity concerning his origins and colour.

244–245, 252–255 Further examples of Iago urging one course of action with the intention that Othello will do the opposite.

389–406 Matter-of-fact language and explicit and crude references to torment Othello.

473 More 'reverse intention' from Iago.

477 Iago has now achieved both his aims.

478 'I am your own for ever.' Does this mean 'I am your loyal servant'? or 'You have become possessed with my spirit'? (Or both?)

3.4

185 The handkerchief – Iago has worked quickly and efficiently.

4.1
34–35 Iago's cunning wordplay.
74–75 Another of his cryptic remarks, this time about cuckolds.
87–88 His words force Othello to contemplate the nature of Desdemona's alleged infidelity.
89–91 He knows that he can manipulate Othello.
148 Typically he thinks quickly and exploits Bianca's arrival to the full at line 172.
161 Knowing when to quit while he is ahead, Iago urges Cassio to run after Bianca.
163 He checks Cassio's planned movements for the evening.
206 Why does he say 'Do it not with poison...'?
267–268 Another cryptic utterance.
272–274 He appears to be a loyal and discreet servant, while clearly implying that Othello beats his wife.

4.2
203 Iago adapts his tactics to suit Roderigo's changing behaviour.

5.1
18–22 Iago seems to put envy of Cassio's 'daily beauty' above fear of exposure as a motive for killing him.
46 He stage-manages the whole scene. He has pre-planned Cassio's departure from Bianca's lodging, exploits the arrival of the authority figures and asks Bianca designedly incriminating questions.
52 Lodovico comments on Iago's finer qualities.

5.2
300–301 What do Iago's dismissive final words imply?

Desdemona

1.3
94–96 Brabantio's view of his daughter's modesty.
157–165 Desdemona was, in Brabantio's phrase, 'half the wooer' (174).
179–187 A daughter's conflicting duties towards her father and the man she loves.
246–247 She feels an emotional subjugation to Othello.
253 She is not afraid to assert her rights as a married woman.

2.1
120–121 Is her explanation of her behaviour in this scene convincing?
165–176 Is she being flirtatious with Cassio?

3.4
81–85 Why does Desdemona lie about the handkerchief?
149 She feels that she has failed to live up to expectations as a soldier's wife.

The characters

4.1
243 She ought to have the audience's sympathy, but does her seeming passivity distance us?

4.2
113, 117–118 Her child-like innocence.

5.2
124 Is it out of love for Othello that Desdemona claims to have killed herself?

Emilia

3.3
301–302 Does she think that Iago is going to raise her alleged infidelity again?

3.4
50–96 Why does she remain silent about the handkerchief?
101–104 Bitter sentiments and a hard-headed, down-to-earth attitude towards love and marriage.
156–159 What does her understanding of jealousy suggest about her?

4.2
119 Emilia's down-to-earth directness acts as a stark contrast to Desdemona's innocence.
129–132 Emilia's speculations are spot on. Does she know what Iago has done?
144–146 Iago has accused Emilia of a sexual relationship with Othello.

4.3
67–68 Emilia's bawdy joke typifies the contrast between her and Desdemona.
90–107 Emilia's plea for women. What is the effect of raising this feminist issue here?

5.2
140 'My husband?...' Emilia at first seems unwilling to accept that it was Iago who informed Othello that Desdemona had been unfaithful.
190, 216 When does she know for sure what Iago has done?

Cassio

1.2
51 Is Cassio unaware of the marriage or pretending ignorance?

2.1
98–99 His view of his upbringing.

2.3

16–18 The contrast between Cassio's and Iago's descriptions of Desdemona – what does it suggest of their different characters?
104–105 Is Cassio being funny or serious?
293–294 Cassio describes the moods that have 'possessed' him as 'devils'.

5.1

18–22 Iago's fear of Cassio's 'daily beauty' – what does Cassio say or do in the play that show this?

Language and structure

Shakespeare's verse

Metre

It is possible to describe where the heavy stress falls in any English word. For example, these three words (from 1.1) have their heavy stress on the first syllable: **lov**ing, **bom**bast, **squad**ron; while in these the heavy stress is on the second syllable: ab**hor**, De**spise**, E **vades**.

All Shakespeare's verse has a pattern of light and heavy stresses running through it, known as the metre. You can hear the metre if you read these lines out loud, over-emphasising the heavily stressed syllables:
- That **nev**-er **set** a **squad**-ron **in** the **field** (1.1.19)
- And **I**, of **whom** his **eyes** had **seen** the **proof** (1.1.25)
- Wears **out** his **time**, much **like** his **mas**-ter's **ass** (1.1.44).

No actor would ever perform the lines in that monotonous way, but they would certainly be aware that the metre was always there, helping to give the verse form and structure.

Sometimes, to point out that a syllable has to be sounded to make the metre work, it will be accented, like this:
- Wherein the tog**èd** consuls can propose (1.1.22)
- The wealthy, curl**èd** darlings of our nation (1.2.67).

Some lines contain weakly stressed syllables which are spoken with less emphasis, as is the case with '-ing' in the first foot of this line:
- And, **throw**ing | but **shows** | of ser- | vice **on** | their **lords** (1.1.49).

Varying the metre

Most of the lines in Shakespeare's plays are not as regular as the first three quoted above. In fact, most will have an irregular stress pattern, like this one:
- As **mas**- | terly as **he**. | **Mere prat**- | tle with**out** | **prac**tice (1.1.23).

Language and structure

The repeated heavy stresses and the alliteration help to emphasise Iago's disgust at Cassio's lack of real soldierly experience.

Occasionally a line will contain an extra syllable (11 rather than 10):
- And I | – God **bless** | the **mark!** | – his **Moor-** | ship's **ancient** (1.1.30).

Here the extra syllable at the end can be used by the actor to convey the feeling of anticlimax at being Othello's ensign, rather than his lieutenant.

Some lines are very noticeable, because they are clearly short. The brevity of Iago's reply:
- O **sir**, con**tent** you (1.1.38)

makes the line stand out. It serves as an introduction to Iago's explanation why he continues to follow Othello – 'to serve my turn upon him'.

A collection of heavy stresses together can add emphasis:
- What a | **full for-** | tune does | the **thick-** | **lips owe** (1.1.63).

Here Roderigo's indignation and insult are conveyed both through the repeated heavy stresses and through the alliteration (**f**ull **f**ortune) and assonance (th**i**ck-l**i**ps).

Dividing the line into feet

Just as music has a number of beats in a bar, so Shakespeare's verse has five 'feet' in a complete line, made up of stressed and unstressed syllables. A five-feet line is called 'pentameter' (pent = five; meter = measure):

1st | *2nd* | *3rd* | *4th* | *5th foot*

This **on-** | ly **is** | the **witch-** | craft I | have **used** (1.3.168).

Iambic pentameter

A foot which contains an unstressed syllable followed by a stressed one (the standard 'beat': dee-**dum**) is called an 'iamb'. Verse which has five iambs per line as its standard rhythm is called 'iambic pentameter'. Iambic pentameter which does not rhyme is also sometimes known as 'blank verse'. This is Shakespeare's standard verse form.

Special effects can be gained by the choice of words within a given line. Here, Iago forces Othello to contemplate the physical horror of Desdemona's supposed infidelity through studied use of monosyllables:
- For I will make him tell the tale anew:
  Where, how, how oft, how long ago, and when
  He hath, and is again to cope your wife (4.1.86–88).

The layout of the verse

A single foot can contain syllables from different words, and any one word can be broken up by the foot divisions:

	1st	2nd	3rd	4th	5th	foot

- The **na-** | tive **act** | and **fi-** | gure **of** | my **heart** (1.1.59).

This is why a single line of verse is sometimes set out rather oddly in different lines of print, if it is shared between two or more characters, as happens in 5.2:

EMILIA	**My hus**band?		
OTHELLO	**Thy hus**band.		
EMILIA		That **she**	was **false**	to **wed**lock?

} These three speeches make up line 140.

Rhyme

Shakespeare sometimes uses rhyme for the ends of scenes, where a 'rhyming couplet' can have the effect of rounding things off, as it does in 1.2:
- For if such actions may have passage free,
  Bondslaves and pagans shall our statesmen be. (1.2.97–98)

In *Othello*, there is also an interesting passage wholly in rhyming couplets (1.3.199–216). The Duke starts them off as a means of conveying some proverbial wisdom:
- When remedies are past, the griefs are ended
  By seeing the worst, which late on hopes depended. (1.3.199–200)

Brabantio is not appeased and responds with some couplets of his own, parodying the Duke's jingling rhythm and rhyme to convey his cynicism and bitterness:
- So let the Turk of Cyprus us beguile:
  We lose it not so long as we can smile. (1.3.207–208)

Verse and prose

It is never totally clear why Shakespeare chooses to write some scenes, or passages, in verse, and others in prose.

Although there are many occasions in Shakespeare's plays where the more serious scenes, involving great passions, are in verse, while those about ordinary people and comedy are in prose, there are also significant examples where this is not the case. *Othello* is written substantially in verse. But Iago's speech on passion and reason ('Tis in ourselves that we are thus, or thus...'; 1.3.316–330) is a good example of serious philosophical statement – albeit for corrupt ends – conducted in prose. Perhaps that is why this speech is not in verse: to signify its lack of integrity.

Structure: the double time scheme

Many critics have commented on the 'double time scheme' of *Othello*, in which the events seem to happen in 'short time', in order to heighten the intensity of the drama and give an impression of the headlong nature of the tragedy; while a longer background time is established to add plausibility to the idea that a reasonable

Language and structure

period has elapsed during which an affair might have taken place and Othello's jealousy evolved. The following references show how the play establishes both the urgency of 'short time' and the dramatic plausibility of 'long time'.

'Short time'

There are a number of lines which, when taken together, help to establish the sense of 'short time'. This is how it works.

We know that, when the play begins, Othello and Desdemona have just married. Before they have any time in which to be together, the Duke sends Othello off to deal with the Turkish threat to Cyprus. Act 2 begins with news that the Turkish fleet has been destroyed and soon we witness Othello's reunion with Desdemona (2.1.181). Shortly afterwards, Iago explains the plot against Cassio to Roderigo, telling him to be available that same evening ('Watch you tonight...', 269). A herald announces celebrations 'from this present hour of five till the bell hath told eleven' (2.2.10–11) and then we see Cassio's drunken brawl and dismissal in 2.3, which clearly takes place that same night. Then, following Iago's suggestion, Cassio determines to see Desdemona 'betimes [early] in the morning' (327); and shortly afterwards, Iago says 'By the mass, 'tis morning!' (376). When they meet again (in 3.1), Cassio confirms that 'the day had broke before we parted' (31). Putting all these together, it is clear that we are now only at the beginning of Day 2. The only points at which there could then be a break in time are between 3.3 and 3.4 or between Acts 3 and 4; but in both cases the dialogue strongly suggests continuity of action.

There is no possibility of a break after the beginning of Act 4. Lodovico arrives and is invited to supper 'tonight' (4.1.257), and we see him being escorted back to his lodgings, presumably after the meal, at the beginning of 4.3. Earlier, Cassio confirms to Iago that he intends to accept Bianca's invitation to supper 'tonight' (4.1.159–164) and Iago then sets up Roderigo to lie in wait for Cassio and attack him 'between twelve and one' (4.2.235), which he does in 5.1. Othello receives news of the attacks as he is killing Desdemona (5.2.106).

In addition to creating tension and urgency, this short time is necessary to make the plot credible, because 'If Iago's plot does not work fast, then it will not work at all' (M R Ridley). As Iago is acutely aware, 'the Moor May unfold me to him [Cassio]; there stand I in much peril' (5.1.20–21).

'Long time'

This short time, of course, if allowed to stand alone, would make nonsense of the story: when could there have been time for the supposed adultery to take place? This is why, alongside the references which indicate 'short time', are those which help to imply that events have had some considerable time during which to unfold. For example, Bianca's question at 3.4.170–171 ('What, keep a week away...?') tells us that Cassio (and therefore Othello and Desdemona) must have been on Cyprus for some while – at the very least, a period longer than the week that Bianca complains about.

Other 'long time' references are:
- Emilia's statement that Iago had asked her to steal the handkerchief 'a hundred times' (3.3.291–292) and 'so often' (3.3.308)
- Othello's reference to Desdemona's 'stol'n hours of lust' (3.3.336)
- Iago's claim that Othello had a similar seizure 'yesterday' (4.1.53)
- his promise to make Cassio reveal '...how long ago...' he has 'coped' Desdemona (4.1.87)
- Cassio's reference to Bianca having accosted him 'the other day' (4.1.134)
- the letter relieving Othello of his command – which presumably would not happen until he had been there some time (4.1.232–233)
- Othello's questions to Emilia, implying that she must have had time during which to observe Desdemona, and her replies (4.2.1–10)
- and, most especially, Othello's belief that Cassio and Desdemona have 'the act of shame A thousand times committed' (5.2.209–210).

Imagery

The most powerful and interesting strands of imagery in the play are those built upon oppositions. These oppositions play a central role in creating the play's emotional intensity.

Black and white, heaven and hell, night and day

Such references, of which these are only a selection, occur throughout:
- Iago tells Brabantio 'an old black ram Is tupping your white ewe' (1.1.85–86)
- according to the Duke, Othello is 'far more fair than black' (1.3.286)
- Iago combines the oppositions when he declares 'Hell and night Must bring this monstrous birth to the world's light' (1.3.397–398)
- later, cracking witty barbs against women, he quips 'If she be black, and thereto have a wit, She'll find a white that shall her blackness fit' (2.1.130–131)
- Desdemona is Othello's 'fair warrior' (2.1.181)
- explaining his methods of deception, Iago explains 'When devils will the blackest sins put on, They do suggest at first with heavenly shows' (2.3.349–350)
- and he describes his planned slander of Desdemona as turning 'her virtue into pitch' (2.3.358)
- Desdemona's reputation 'that was as fresh As Dian's visage, is now begrimed and black As mine own face' (3.3.384—386)
- Emilia is accused of having 'the office opposite to Saint Peter' and keeping 'the gate of hell' (4.2.90–91)
- Emilia would not deceive her husband 'by this heavenly light', but might 'do't as well i'th' dark' (4.3.67–68)
- for Othello, Desdemona becomes a catalogue of contradictions: a beautiful 'weed' (4.2.66–67), a 'goodly book, Made to write "whore" upon' (4.2.70–71) and a 'pearl' thrown away by a 'base Indian' (5.2.344)
- when Othello claims that the lying Desdemona has 'gone to burning hell', Emilia replies 'O, the more angel she, And you the blacker devil!' (5.2.129–131).

Illusion and reality

Most strikingly, the deceitful and wicked Iago is perceived as 'honest' – 'I am not what I am' (1.1.62), a man in whom 'Knavery's plain face is never seen till used' (2.1.316); while Othello, who 'thinks men honest that but seem to be so' (1.3.394) sees the chaste Desdemona as a whore. Elsewhere:

- Iago scorns the 'duteous and knee-crooking knave' in favour of those who 'Do themselves homage' (1.1.41–51), refusing to let his 'outward action' demonstrate the 'native act and figure' of his heart 'In complement extern' (1.1.58–60)
- Brabantio sees Othello's appearance as something 'to fear, not to delight' (1.2.70, 1.3.98, etc)
- the Turks set up a diversion in order to keep the Venetians 'in false gaze' (1.3.19)
- Desdemona 'has deceived her father, and may thee' (1.3.289)
- later, she explains 'I am not merry; but I do beguile The thing I am by seeming otherwise' (2.1.120–121)
- Iago tries to persuade Roderigo that Cassio is 'putting on the mere form of civil and humane seeming for the better compass of his salt and most hidden loose affection' (2.1.241–244); and that Desdemona's courteous gestures are 'Lechery, by this hand!' (257–261)
- on the positive side, Cassio judges Desdemona to have 'An inviting eye; and yet methinks right modest' (2.3.23)
- Iago explains that Venetian women 'do let heaven see the pranks They dare not show their husbands' (3.3.202–203); and reminds Othello that Desdemona 'did deceive her father, marrying you; And when she seemed to shake and fear your looks, She loved them most. ...such a seeming To seel her father's eyes up close as oak' (3.3.206–210)
- Othello cannot believe at first that the appearance is merely an illusion 'If she be false, O then heaven mocks itself!' (3.3.277)
- but Iago reminds him that 'Her honour is an essence that's not seen; They have it very oft that have it not' (4.1.16–17).

The oppositions are important because, in addition to representing the reality of Iago's evil masked by the illusion of 'honesty', they help to show the ways in which a character such as Othello is pulled in two directions ('I think my wife be honest, and think she is not', 3.3.382; 'O Iago, the pity of it, Iago...I will chop her into messes!' 4.1.194–199). Iago too is so aware that his rival 'hath a daily beauty in his life That makes me ugly' (5.1.19–20), that he is prepared to kill him for it.

Criticism

There are many views on *Othello*, especially concerning the relative degrees of blame to be attached to Othello and Iago. The following extracts represent some of the main points of critical discussion which have arisen over the years.

Samuel Taylor Coleridge, 1818/19

The Romantic poet Coleridge invented a phrase for Iago's behaviour – and in particular his soliloquy in 1.3 – which has had a great influence on subsequent views of Iago's character. He termed it: 'the motive-hunting of a motiveless malignity'.

A C Bradley, 1904

Bradley was the best known of the critics who viewed Othello as noble, glamorous and poetic, 'the most romantic figure among Shakespeare's heroes', almost free of blame for the terrible events which take place, deceived by a man who is wickedness incarnate.

> Othello's mind, for all its poetry, is very simple. He is not observant. His nature tends outward. He is quite free from introspection, and is not given to reflection. Emotion excites his imagination, but it confuses and dulls his intellect...His trust, where he trusts, is absolute. Hesitation is almost impossible to him. He is extremely self-reliant, and decides and acts instantaneously. If stirred to indignation, as 'in Aleppo once', he answers with one lightning stroke. Love, if he loves, must be to him the heaven where either he must live or bear no life. If such a passion as jealousy seizes him, it will swell into a well-nigh incontrollable flood. He will press for immediate conviction or immediate relief. Convinced, he will act with the authority of a judge and the swiftness of a man in mortal pain. Undeceived, he will do like execution on himself.

F R Leavis, 1952

Leavis completely disagreed with Bradley's view of Othello as noble and blameless; Leavis felt that Othello was totally responsible for the murder and that the role of Iago was 'subordinate' and had been overrated.

> He is truly impressive, a noble product of the life of action – of
>
>> The big wars
>> That make ambition virtue.
>
> 'That make ambition virtue' – this phrase of his is a key one: his virtues are, in general, of that kind; they have, characteristically, something of the quality suggested. Othello, in his magnanimous way, is egotistic. He really is, beyond any question, the nobly massive man of action, the captain of men, he sees himself as being, but he does very much see himself:
>
>> Keep up your bright swords, for the dew will rust them.
>
> In short, a habit of self-approving self-dramatization is an essential element in Othello's make-up, and remains so at the very end.
> It is, at the best, the impressive manifestation of a noble egotism. But, in the new marital situation, this egotism isn't going to be the less dangerous for its

Criticism

nobility. This self-centredness doesn't mean self-knowledge: that is a virtue which Othello, as soldier of fortune, hasn't had much need of. He has been well provided by nature to meet all the trials a life of action has exposed him to. The trials facing him now...are of a different order.

William Empson, 1951

[Random House UK Limited: an extract from *The Structure of Complex Words* by William Empson (Chatto and Windus, 1951)]

Empson decided that the best way in which to contrast Othello and Iago was not to speak about 'character' at all, but to concentrate upon the varied life of one of the key words in the play – 'honest'.

The fifty-two uses of *honest* and *honesty* in Othello are a very queer business; there is no other play in which Shakespeare worries a word like that. *King Lear* uses *fool* nearly as often but does not treat it as a puzzle, only as a source of profound metaphors. In *Othello* divergent uses of the key word are found for all the main characters; even the attenuated clown plays on it; the unchaste Bianca, for instance, snatches a moment to claim that she is more honest than Emilia the thief of the handkerchief; and with all the variety of use the ironies on the word mount up steadily to the end...Everybody calls Iago honest once or twice, but with Othello it becomes an obsession; at the crucial moment just before Emilia exposes Iago he keeps howling the word out. The general effect has been fully recognized by critics, but it looks as if there is something to be found about the word itself...

The word was in the middle of a rather complicated process of change, and what emerged from it was a sort of jovial cult of independence. At some stage of the development (whether by the date of *Othello* or not) the word came to have in it a covert assertion that the man who accepts the natural desires, who does not live by principle, will be fit for such warm uses of *honest* as imply 'generous' and 'faithful to friends', and to believe this to disbelieve the Fall of Man. Thus the word, apart from being complicated, also came to raise large issues, and it is not I think a wild fancy to suppose that Shakespeare could feel the way it was going...

Most people would agree with what Bradley, for example, implied, that the way everybody calls Iago honest amounts to a criticism of the word itself; that is, Shakespeare means 'a bluff forthright manner, and amusing talk, which get a man called honest, may go with extreme dishonesty'...

One need not look for a clear sense when he toys with the word about Cassio; the question is how it came to be so mystifying. But I think a queer kind of honesty is maintained in Iago through all the puzzles he contrives; his emotions are always expressed directly, and it is only because they are clearly genuine ('These stops of thine', Othello tells him, 'are close dilations, working from the heart') that he can mislead Othello as to their cause.

OTHELLO: Is he not honest? (*Faithful, etc.*)
IAGO: Honest, my lord? (*Not stealing, etc. Shocked.*)

OTHELLO:	Honest. Ay, honest. (*'Why repeat? The word is clear enough.'*)
IAGO:	My lord, for aught I know...(*'In some sense.'*)
IAGO:	For Michael Cassio,
	I dare be sworn I think that he is honest.
OTHELLO:	I think so too.
IAGO:	Men should be what they seem;
	Or those that be not, would they might seem none!
OTHELLO:	Certain, men should be what they seem.
IAGO:	Why then, I think Cassio's an honest man. [3.3.103–129]

Othello has just said that Cassio 'went between them very oft', so Iago now learns that Cassio lied to him in front of Brabantio's house when he pretended to know nothing about the marriage.

   Iago feels he has been snubbed, as too coarse to be trusted in such a matter, and he takes immediate advantage of his discomposure. The point of his riddles is to get 'not hypocritical' – 'frank about his own nature' accepted as the relevant sense; Iago will readily call him honest on that basis, and Othello cannot be reassured. 'Chaste' (the sense normally used of women) Cassio is not, but he is 'not a hypocrite' about Bianca. Iago indeed, despises him for letting her make a fool of him in public; for that and for other reasons (Cassio is young and without experience) Iago can put a contemptuous tone into the word; the feeling is genuine, but not the sense it may imply. This gives room for a hint that Cassio has been 'frank' to Iago in private about more things than may honestly be told. I fancy too, that the idea of 'not being men' gives an extra twist. Iago does not think Cassio manly nor that it is specially manly to be chaste; this allows him to agree that Cassio may be honest in the female sense about Desdemona and still keep a tone which seems to deny it – if he is, after so much encouragement, he must be 'effeminate' (there is a strong idea of 'manly' in *honest*, and an irony on that gives its opposite). Anyway, Iago can hide what reservations he makes but show that he makes reservations; this suggests an embarrassed defence – 'Taking a broad view, with the world as it is, and Cassio my friend, I can decently call him honest.' This forces home the Restoration idea – 'an honest dog of a fellow, straightforward about women', and completes the suspicion. It is a bad piece of writing unless you are keyed up for the shifts of the word.

A P Rossiter, 1961

Rossiter pointed out that 'jealous' in Shakespeare's time had at least two meanings; in addition to our modern sense, it often meant merely 'doubtful' or 'concerned' – at most, 'suspicious'. Building on that, he examined Othello's final speech.

   If it be agreed that Othello's lines [5.2.342ff.] contain an ambiguous term, 'jealous', then we can estimate what is being said, and, with that, its bearing on the whole Othello and on the whole play. If 'jealous' means *suspicious*, the lines can be taken at face value. Othello is 'not *given* to suspicion': he is trusting (Iago agrees there), and all his dealings with Iago demonstrate it. But a man who denies an ambiguous term may be denying either of its distinct senses. If he is

Criticism

simultaneously aware that he can truthfully deny the one, but not the other, then he is an equivocator. If he could, perhaps should, be aware of what he is falsely denying even in making a true denial of its equivoke, he is a self-deceiver, or is self-deceived. 'The fiend', we can say, if we like, 'equivocates with him (or within him).' The fault in him is not hypocrisy, but lack of insight, self-knowledge: i.e., of sincerity in its deepest sense of integrity. If 'jealous' means capable of or subject to extreme *sexual jealousy*, then Othello is, to say the least, deceived; for 3.3 has been a long revelation of just that: proneness to sexual jealousy. While Iago's game has been made the easier by Othello's *not* being jealous in the sense he still prefers to insist on [in 5.2].

The integrity of the '*noble Othello*' depends enormously on taking without adulteration:

> Of one not easily jealous, but, being wrought,
> Perplex'd in the extreme....

His defence as not sexually jealous will hinge on when he can be said to have been 'wrought'. For that, there is nothing to do but to go back to [3.3.35] and from there follow the character-deployment in detail. But I will anticipate by suggesting that in 'not easily jealous' Othello is right and wrong at once; and add that with his own continual behaviour behind him – and its consequence beside him – he has no good *reason* to be wrong ('excuse' is another matter).

Lisa Jardine, 1983
[Columbia University Press: an extract from *Still Harping on Daughters* by Lisa Jardine (Harvester Wheatsheaf, 1983)]

Lisa Jardine suggests that the drama of Shakespeare's time is male-dominated and that Desdemona is punished for her independence, ultimately becoming a passive victim.

The 'plain truths' uttered by female characters in Shakespeare (Emilia's chastising of Othello, Paulina speaking out against Leontes for wronging his queen [*The Winter's Tale*]) bear the mark of the scold's privilege. Indeed, the men concerned openly recognise them as such. As Paulina pours out before Leontes the words no one else dare utter (that his fears that his new born daughter is no child of his are grotesque and unfounded), Leontes calls her 'audacious lady', then 'a mankind witch!...A most intelligencing bawd!', and: 'A callat [scold]/Of boundless tongue, who late hath beat her husband,/And now baits me!' Finally, still failing to stop her speech by force, he accuses her of being a heretic (an 'explanation' for female unruliness evident from the Essex witch trial records):

LEONTES: A gross hag!
And, lozel, thou art worthy to be hang'd
That wilt not stay her tongue.
            ...Once more, take her hence.
PAULINA: A most unworthy and unnatural lord
Can do no more.

LEONTES:	I'll ha' thee burnt.
PAULINA:	I care not.
	It is an heretic that makes the fire,
	Not she which burns in't.

When Iago cannot prevent Emilia from uttering the truths he has no wish to hear, he parries by calling her 'villainous whore' and 'filth'. When Volumnia (Coriolanus's mother) turns on the Romans who have banished her son, they retaliate by terming her 'mad'. In *Troilus and Cressida* the Trojans dismiss Cassandra's unwelcome prophecy that Helen will bring doom upon them as 'brain-sick raptures'...

The female sharp tongue both entices and threatens. A number of critics find the 'shrewdness' of Desdemona, for example, incompatible for her supposed 'innocence'. For instance, M. R. Ridley, in the Arden *Othello*, footnotes [2.1.108–164] as follows:

> This is to many readers, and I think rightly, one of the most unsatisfactory passages in Shakespeare. To begin with it is unnatural. Desdemona's natural instinct must surely be to go herself to the harbour [where Othello has just arrived], instead of asking parenthetically whether someone has gone. Then, it is distasteful to watch her engaged in a long piece of cheap backchat with Iago, and so adept at it that one wonders how much time on the voyage was spent in the same way. All we gain from it is some further unneeded light on Iago's vulgarity.

It is, of course, Desdemona's vulgarity which offends the critic. There is something too-knowing, too-independent about her tone and ready reply. But Desdemona's 'backchat' is 'licence to carp', subsequently to be withdrawn from her when comment gives way to action, in which she must inevitably be the passive victim. When a female character in the drama gives verbal thrust for verbal thrust as Desdemona does in this scene, she is acting out the paradoxes of patriarchy:

DESDEMONA:	Come, how wouldst thou praise me?
IAGO:	I am about it, but indeed my invention
	Comes from my pate as birdlime does from frieze,
	It plucks out brain and all: but my Muse labours,
	And thus she is deliver'd:
	If she be fair and wise, fairness and wit;
	The one's for use, the other using it.
DESDEMONA:	Well prais'd! How if she be black and witty?
IAGO:	If she be black, and thereto have a wit,
	She'll find a white, that shall her blackness hit.
DESDEMONA:	Worse and worse.
EMILIA:	How if fair and foolish?
IAGO:	She never yet was foolish, that was fair,
	For even her folly help'd her, to an heir.
DESDEMONA:	These are old paradoxes, to make fools laugh i' the

273

	alehouse; what miserable praise hast thou for her that's foul and foolish?
Iago:	There's none so foul, and foolish thereunto, But does foul pranks, which fair and wise ones do.

These 'paradoxes' are, in fact, the substance of the 'woman debate'. Desdemona's sharp-tongued involvement in an exchange about womanish wiles (the feminine mystique) sets her up as active temptress, scold, 'husband-beater' and cuckolder: an appropriate talismanic threat. Iago's own insidious tongue has only to play on these traditional fears lurking beneath female 'mystery' to rouse Othello to full jealousy, and finally murder.

Norman Sanders, 1984

Sanders was one of many critics who considered that *Othello* was in important ways different from the other major tragedies of Shakespeare.

> It is the ending of the play that separates it most strikingly from the other tragedies...there is no emphatic re-establishment of public order...the tragic loading of Othello's bed does not affect anyone, Venetian or Cypriot...[there is no] final panegyric that other tragic heroes receive. The real emphasis is on the punishment of the villain; there is no effort to understand the nature of the catastrophe, no attempt to ritualise the hero's end.

Martin Wine, 1984

[Palgrave Macmillan: an extract from *Othello: Text and Performance* by Martin Wine (Macmillan, 1984)]

Martin Wine shows how Iago contrives to make other people see the world through his eyes by forcing them to use his language.

> Of all the characters in the play Iago is the only one who understands the arbitrary nature of language as an endlessly manipulable system of signs that are social and cultural in origin. As master-manipulator of signs, Iago throws into confusion the language of discourse, to the point where Othello does not know what to think anymore: whether his wife is 'honest', whether Iago is 'just'. Iago's success in manoeuvring Othello and others to 'read' the world by his own signs is largely attributable to his conscious manipulation of himself as a 'sign': 'I am not what I am', he admits [1.1.62], an admission that he can afford to make because 'honesty' is his strategy.
>
> If language, however, is what enables us to create our sense of reality, Iago's total appropriation (or, more properly, disappropriation) of the language of discourse creates the very 'chaos' that Othello's love of Desdemona has overcome [see 3.3 90–92]. Signs – words – only signify; they cannot be the equivalent of what or whom they are signifying. What makes communication possible is a faith in language that bridges that silent gap between the word and what it refers to. Love 'speaks' in that silence. But Iago demystifies language. He

speaks in that gap by totally objectifying it. The world for him is a body to be read literally, not a mystery to be accepted and interpreted with love and humility. There are no mysteries for Iago, to whom all Moors are lascivious, all women are whores, and all men, except himself, of course, are asses. Under his spell Othello claims not words shake him but 'Noses, ears, and lips!' [4.1.44]. For Iago, black is black and white is white, and his greatest triumph is to make Othello accept his literal blackness as the reality of his being whereas previously Desdemona had awakened him to his full humanity by seeing his 'visage in his mind' [1.3.248]. Desdemona's 'love' does not depend on external signs as Iago's 'hate' does. He confesses that to deceive Othello, 'I must show out a flag and sign of love' [1.1.153]. Desdemona gives the lie to Iago; to believe in his world as 'real' is to believe in a world drained of meaning, one that is 'merely a lust of the blood and a permission of the will' [1.3.332–333]. Before she leaves him at the start of the temptation scene, Desdemona says to Othello, 'Be as your fancies teach you./Whate'er you be, I am obedient' [3.3 88–89]. Unfortunately, she leaves him to the 'fancies' that Iago now starts teaching him, and Othello's acceptance of them is acceptance of a lunatic world where even time is out of joint: hardly a couple of days on Cyprus and he believes 'That she with Cassio hath the act of shame/A thousand times committed' [5.2.209–210].

David Suchet, 1988

[Cambridge University Press: an extract from *Players of Shakespeare 2* (David Suchet as Iago) ed. Jackson and Smallwood (1988)]

Actors have particular insights into the characters they play. David Suchet was Iago in the RSC's 1985 production and wrote about his preparation for the role.

All my reading made me aware that almost everyone that has either written about Iago or played Iago, is always in search of one thing: *motivation*. The search for motivation in any character is a necessary step to understanding the behaviour of that character. But no one has ever come up with a completely satisfying explanation for Iago's behaviour. Instead we get a series of labels:
1. A smiling villain.
2. The latent homosexual.
3. The devil's emissary.
4. The playwright (i.e. creator of events and observer, who conducts the outcome).
5. The melodramatic machiavel.
Putting these 'labels' on a characterisation is a convenient though simplistic way around the problem, allowing the actor to play the role effectively irrespective almost of his Othello. Hence the play becomes a battle about who is going to win the applause of the critics and of the audience. And hence the play does not work because the play itself can never really come to the surface – only two (or possibly one) bravura performances.

Our rehearsal period was approximately six weeks and we started with a detailed analysis of the play. My personal plan for rehearsal was to try out all the

Criticism

various labels which I have mentioned above. It was a most interesting experience because each way/label came unstuck at certain places in the play and I had to bend the text to make the 'label' work. Having concluded that I would not play just one of the labels I decided to find out not *how* to play Iago but *why* Shakespeare wrote him. What does he provide, why did Shakespeare need him?

To do this I read the play without Iago in it. Basically Othello marries Desdemona, her father is upset, but the Duke appeases him. Othello goes off to Cyprus with Desdemona. When they arrive the wars have ended and (without Iago's machinations) there is no reason why everyone couldn't have had a very nice holiday!

What is missing is what causes all the destruction in the play – Jealousy. Iago *represents* Jealousy, *is* Jealousy. What is Iago jealous about?

1. Not becoming a lieutenant (jealous over Cassio).
2. Jealous that Emilia and Othello have had an affair.
3. Jealous of Emilia and Cassio.
4. Jealous over Desdemona and Cassio.
5. Jealous of Desdemona's power over Othello.

But what struck me was that all these reasons that he states as justifications for his actions are totally unfounded.

1. When Othello makes Iago lieutenant ('Now art thou my lieutenant') Iago does not stop his destructive actions.
2. There is no evidence anywhere in the text, let alone in the scenes where Emilia and Othello are alone, that there has been any form of sexual liaison or indeed of any other kind between them.
3. Because of one line at the sea shore?
4. Because Desdemona is 'fram'd as fruitful/as the free elements' and Cassio has a 'daily beauty in his life which makes me ugly'?

There is no doubt that Iago is *genuinely* jealous of these things; therefore (I wondered) could Iago destroy and kill through jealousy even though the reasons for his jealousy are unfounded? Human beings are given to finding justifications for deeds or actions to make those deeds 'allowable' in their own minds even though they are not always valid justifications. And so it is with Iago.

Then comes another 'Why?', this time in reference to his jealousy. Why is he jealous? When Desdemona is wondering why Othello may be jealous [3.4.155], Emilia/Shakespeare gives us one answer to the problem:

> But jealous souls will not be answer'd so;
> They are not ever jealous for the cause,
> But jealous for they're jealous. It is a monster
> Begot upon itself, born on itself. [3.4.156–159]

In other words, *don't look for reasons for the behaviour of jealous people.* Critics, actors, and audiences will constantly ask 'why does Iago do this or that? why is he jealous?' Emilia, his wife, who knows him better than anyone, gives us the answer – Don't ask!...

So far then, let me sum up the type of man I was beginning to see: a man who is jealous about everything – and finding particulars to justify his feelings (these particulars we know are not valid); a man whose life has changed through his general's marriage; a man who swears revenge; a soldier who makes jokes about his wife; a man who is sexually obsessed and sees life and goodness through splintered, green glasses – love is lust, courtesy is lechery, kissing hands leads not to making love but to pure fucking; a man who has caused one act of chaos (waking up of Brabantio) and is about to cause another; a man who really is confused, mixed up over one person in particular. He has openly slandered Desdemona and Cassio, but what of *Othello* – very little? *Perhaps*, and only perhaps, did it enter my mind that his jealousy could be centred around the one area he has hardly mentioned, Othello, and in particular his mind, the mind Desdemona said she fell in love with. But this is conjecture – more later. So, a pretty mixed-up, pained human being.

Anthony Brennan, 1986

[Taylor and Francis Books Limited: an extract from *Shakespeare's Dramatic Structures* ed. Anthony Brennan (Routledge, 1986)]

Brennan focuses on the ways in which Iago organises roles for his victims and creates psychological separation between them.

In tragedy the audience is often given knowledge that is denied to the characters. Because the audience is not subject to clouded judgement by participation in the action, it has the freedom to understand why catastrophe must occur and must watch helplessly while the characters use their freedom and proceed in ignorance to make assurance of death double sure. This burden of special knowledge with which the playwright invests his audience can be exploited in a great variety of ways. The tension experienced by the audience can be tuned to an almost unbearable level when the audience feels that the characters are ensnared in a trick of plot which simple information could dispel. Many of Shakespeare's tragedies, however, do not aim to produce a sense of helpless frustration in the audience at its inability to interfere in the course of events...

In *Othello* Shakespeare made radical alterations in his source-story to produce an experience of almost unbearable tension which has no parallel in world drama. There is a convention in English pantomime which generously provides the audience with a release denied by Shakespeare in *Othello*. Early on in a pantomime the hero usually talks to the audience warning of the dangers he anticipates from the villains. He asks for the audience's help in looking out for traps that are set for him in his absence and gives a password which must be shouted out to warn him of trouble. The audience thereafter screams out the word whenever the hero is about to stumble into unexpected snares. By feigning temporary deafness the hero can tune up the audience's involvement to a delirium of lusty bellowing in a co-operative triumph over evil. *Othello* achieves its effect by reversing this process so that the audience is relentlessly victimized.

The structure of *Othello* develops in a series of improvised, undeclared playlets in which Iago organizes roles for his victims. The degree of control he

Criticism

maintains over the characters allows him to induce a psychological alienation and separation between some of them. This produces a physical separation which is registered by the finely judged proportions in the character interactions. Iago is helped over all the weak points in his plot by his victims themselves. Even the mere random contingency of events for a while allows all the accidents to knit up the design where it could unravel and expose Iago's villainy. We may smile indulgently at the many recorded instances of unsophisticated audiences shouting out warnings to Othello about the handkerchief, or invading the stage to belabour the unbearable villain Iago. We have to acknowledge, however, that the play's success depends on arousing our impulsive wish to stop the action and that the more, as civilized playgoers, we stifle that impulse the more the play achieves its ascendancy over us. It is not simply that we lack the release valve provided in pantomime but rather that we are confronted again and again by our helplessness. We have no access to a hero who needs our help, rather we have access to the villain sharing his plans and explaining to us why the characters must fall into the roles he has shaped for them.

What makes Iago unbearable is his ability to combine two roles very familiar to an Elizabethan audience. He is very much like the intermediary, commentator friends, those blunt, honest figures who try to make the tragic heroes see the true nature of their situations – Enobarbus, Kent, Lear's Fool, Menenius Agrippa, Apemantus, Mercutio. He is a soldier, a rough diamond who is foul-mouthed, cynical, and has a low opinion of women. Because he admits to his limitations he is trusted. The role of blunt soldier and honest friend conceal a descendant of the Vice-figure, a man who is an amoral rag-bag of confused motivations invested with a cynicism so profound that he must pervert or destroy any sign of virtue. Shakespeare wrote of other tragic heroes who reject the judgement of their blunt advisers because their very natures make them incapable of cautious restraint. They must embrace their fates even at the cost of the destruction fearfully prophesied for them. Othello, however, accepts the version of reality thrust upon him by his 'honest' friend in the belief that he is saving himself from miserable embroilment in a corrupt world. Thus in most of the tragedies it is the commentating figure who, in the limitations in his understanding, enables us to come to terms with the full complexity of the fate with which the tragic hero is coping. In *Othello* it is the hero who is separated off from the full complexity of the circumstances in the world in which he exists. The very deliberate organization of the play to produce an unbearable tension around Iago as a strategist of separation can be seen in the radical changes Shakespeare makes in the source-story. Cinthio's novella contains, on the face of it, very little promise of dramatic tension. Shakespeare made many alterations of detail especially in tightening up the time-scheme of the sequence of events, in changing the military rank of the originals of Othello and Cassio, and in developing a significant political framework in which his Moor could be featured. He invents a romantic courtship between Othello and Desdemona and the objections of Brabantio to his daughter's secret alliance. He does not make any radical changes in the characters on which Desdemona and Cassio are based. Shakespeare's most significant changes in developing his scenic structures are in the dramatic methods he finds of unfolding Iago's dominating agency in the story.

Karen Newman, 1988

Karen Newman is interested in looking at *Othello* as a play which seems to argue against ('stands in a contestatory relation to') some of the ruling beliefs ('hegemonic ideologies') concerning race and gender in Shakespeare's time.

> Was Shakespeare a racist who condoned the negative image of blacks in his culture? Is Desdemona somehow guilty in her stubborn defence of Cassio and her admiring remark 'Lodovico is a proper man'?...
>
> Shakespeare was certainly subject to the racist, sexist, and colonialist discourses of his time, but by making the black Othello a hero, and by making Desdemona's love for Othello, and her transgression of her society's norms for women in choosing him, sympathetic, Shakespeare's play stands in a contestatory relation to the hegemonic ideologies of race and gender in early modern England. Othello is, of course, the play's hero only within the terms of a white, elitist male ethos, and he suffers the generic 'punishment' of tragedy, but he is nevertheless represented as heroic and tragic at a historical moment when the only role blacks played on stage was that of a villain of low status. The case of Desdemona is more complex because the fate she suffers is the conventional fate assigned to the desiring woman. Nevertheless, Shakespeare's representation of her as at once virtuous and desiring, and of her choice in love as heroic rather than demonic, dislocates the conventional ideology of gender the play also enacts.

Edward Pechter, 1999

[University of Iowa Press: an extract from *Othello and the Interpretative Tradition* by Edward Pechter (1999)]

In asking how it is that the play has had such a powerful effect over audiences throughout the centuries since its earliest performances, Pechter examines the idea of Shakespeare's alleged 'universality'.

> How has *Othello* sustained its extraordinary power to affect audiences over four centuries? What is it about the play that accounts for this remarkable continuity of response? Its themes and subject matter must be relevant here. Love and jealousy, sexual desire and creaturely difference (racial or otherwise) – these seem to be subjects of deep and ambivalent fascination throughout human history, mattering greatly to all societies that have left us records of their interests. It might be claimed that *Othello* is resonating on a universal register, transcending the partialities of particular audiences and appealing to an essential humanity shared across cultural differences. In fact, of course, it has been so claimed: this idea – not just about *Othello* but about Shakespeare's plays generally – goes back to Ben Jonson at the beginning of the First Folio ('He was not of an age, but for all time!'), and similar claims were often – even routinely – made through the end of the nineteenth century. They have been subjected to a skeptical scrutiny in the twentieth century and a downright hostile one in our own time; but the idea of Shakespeare's transcendent appeal remains generally

familiar, and substantial vestiges of it survive, however qualified, even among those current critics who are most skeptical about the existence of an essential humanity and most committed to a materialist explanation for the transmission of cultural values.

Too many smart people have committed themselves to one version or another of Shakespeare's universality for us to dismiss it out of hand. But it doesn't seem to get us very far; once we declare it, what next? Moreover, contemporary suspicion about universals is justified; they can be vague and amorphous abstractions, obscuring important differences. Whatever race means now, for instance (and it's hardly an identical meaning for all of us), it seems implausible to assume that it meant the same thing for audiences four hundred years ago (who presumably had to endure internal contradictions of their own). Neither could the concept of gender difference as the constituting feature of male and female identity or of sexual desire. There is good evidence to believe that Shakespeare's audience did not identify human nature in terms of a core racial or sexual self. In fact, the very concept of an inner core of being, however identified, is probably something Shakespeare's audience would not have recognized, at least not in our sense as the self-evident motivating factor by which to understand human action.

Performance

From its earliest days, *Othello* has been an extremely popular play. The first recorded performance was at Whitehall in front of King James I in 1604; since then it has never been off the English stage. Over the centuries the play has been a fascinating example of developments in theatrical practice and audience attitudes, especially in terms of the changing representations of women and of non-white characters. For example, in Shakespeare's time, the female roles were, of course, all played by boys; when the theatres were reopened at the Restoration, the first known example of an actress on the English stage was in the part of Desdemona (in 1660).

In the eighteenth century the play did not escape the tampering suffered by many of Shakespeare's tragedies in an effort to make them more suitable for the sensibilities of the age; in particular, the role of Othello was adapted to give the character the highest degree of nobility. Othellos tended to be of one of two kinds: either thoughtful and sensitive, or passionate and wildly jealous. The most famous actor of the second kind was Edmund Kean (1787–1833), of whom William Hazlitt wrote: 'there was all the fitful fever of the blood, the jealous madness of the brain: his heart seemed to bleed with anguish, while his tongue dropped broken, imperfect accents of woe'. Kean showed an emotional range which awoke feelings in his audience of both sympathy and fear. A famous Iago of the nineteenth century was the American Edwin Booth (1833–93), who demonstrated a demonic pleasure in the evil outcome of his plottings.

Famous Desdemonas at that time included Ellen Terry in 1881, who played the part with such tenderness that she even made her Iago (Henry Irving) cry. But some actresses performed the role with more assertiveness, notably Helen Faucit (1817–98), who asked 'How could I be otherwise than "difficult to kill"?'

The 'oppositions' in the play (see pages 267–268) have offered great opportunities for theatrical representation. Thoughtful Othellos have frequently been contrasted with physical Iagos, splendid Venices have been set against stark Cypruses. But the most obvious opposition – Othello's blackness against the predominant white – has been problematic. For most of this play's history the Moor has been played by a white actor 'blacking up'. Where that has happened, the actor has often depended upon marks of 'difference' other than skin colour (exotic clothing and ornamentation, for example, or alien gestures). Because they have been preserved on film, the best-known examples of white actors in the role are the portrayals by Orson Welles in 1952 and Laurence Olivier in the 1960s. Olivier's interpretation – of a narcissistic Afro-Caribbean Othello – now strikes many people as dated and patronising; and the close-ups cruelly expose the problems of 'blacking up'. Although there were isolated instances in the mid-twentieth century of black actors playing Othello (most famously Paul Robeson in 1930 and 1959), the first influential breakthroughs came with the casting of Willard White for the RSC in 1989 and the American movie star Laurence Fishburne in the 1995 film. Patrick Stewart's performance as a white Othello in a black society (in 1997) explored the racial dimensions in a new and unusual way.

Many actors in recent times have been keener to play Iago than Othello, given the character's ambiguity (and, no doubt, the fact that the part is longer). Olivier in 1937 famously portrayed an Iago motivated by homosexual love for Othello, an interpretation followed in part by David Suchet in 1985 and Kenneth Branagh in 1995; Bob Hoskins (BBC TV, 1981) played Iago as a psychopath; while Ian McKellen's extraordinary portrayal (RSC, 1989) brought out, among other things, the Ensign's strange and brutal relationship with his wife (played by Zoë Wanamaker).

Othello on video

Five versions of *Othello* are widely available on video.

1952, directed by Orson Welles (Mercury Productions)
Othello: Orson Welles
Iago: Micheál MacLiammóir
Desdemona: Suzanne Cloutier
Emilia: Fay Compton

1964, directed by Stuart Burge (a film of the National Theatre production, directed by John Dexter)
Othello: Laurence Olivier
Iago: Frank Finlay
Desdemona: Maggie Smith
Emilia: Joyce Redman

1981, directed by Jonathan Miller (BBC Television)
Othello: Anthony Hopkins
Iago: Bob Hoskins
Desdemona: Penelope Wilton
Emilia: Rosemary Leach

1989, directed by Trevor Nunn (a film of the Royal Shakespeare Company stage production)
Othello: Willard White
Iago: Ian McKellen
Desdemona: Imogen Stubbs
Emilia: Zoë Wanamaker

1995, directed by Oliver Parker (Castle Rock Films)
Othello: Laurence Fishburne
Iago: Kenneth Branagh
Desdemona: Irene Jacob
Emilia: Anna Patrick

There is also a Russian film from 1955, directed by Sergei Yutkevitch.

The plot of *Othello*

Act 1

1.1: The play starts at night in a street in Venice. Roderigo, a young gentleman, is complaining to Iago, a soldier. He is displeased that Iago has not told him about the sudden marriage between Othello, Iago's superior officer and General of the Venetian forces, to Desdemona, the young daughter of a powerful senator, Brabantio. Roderigo is upset because he had hoped to win Desdemona for himself. Iago claims that he knew nothing of the marriage and explains why he has every reason to feel resentful towards Othello: the post of Othello's lieutenant has been given to Michael Cassio. Iago is angry because, as an experienced soldier who had been with Othello for some time, he expected to be promoted. He confides that he is only staying with Othello for his own advantage. Urged on by Iago, Roderigo wakes Brabantio and informs him that his daughter has eloped. When the old man goes off to check this claim, Iago leaves Roderigo – he doesn't want Othello to know that he has been betraying his secret. Brabantio, led by Roderigo, sets off to arrest Othello.

1.2: Iago has found Othello and tells him how angry he was to see Roderigo telling Brabantio about the elopement. Othello takes it calmly, confident in his status. Cassio arrives with an urgent message from the Duke, summoning Othello to a meeting. There is an emergency relating to Cyprus and Othello's advice is needed. Before they can set off, however, Brabantio intercepts them. Accusing Othello of having bewitched Desdemona, Brabantio attempts to arrest him. Othello explains that he is wanted by the Duke, and Brabantio decides that they will both go, confident that the Duke will give him a sympathetic hearing.

1.3: In the palace council chamber, the senators are in a state of turmoil as conflicting reports come in about the Turkish fleet. Just as they receive confirmation that the Turks are headed for Cyprus, Othello and Brabantio arrive. Brabantio announces that his daughter has been stolen and repeats his allegations that Othello must have used witchcraft or love potions. Othello admits that he has married Desdemona, but denies that he is guilty of any offence. While Desdemona is sent for, Othello tells the assembled senators about their courtship. The Duke tries to persuade Brabantio to accept the situation. But the old man will not be moved and, when his daughter arrives and acknowledges that she now owes obedience to her husband rather than her father, it is with great bitterness that Brabantio gives her up. The meeting moves on to the urgent business of the Turkish invasion fleet. Othello is asked to take charge of the island's defence and Desdemona asks permission to accompany her new husband. Othello has to set sail immediately, but he arranges that Iago's wife, Emilia, will attend on Desdemona.

Iago is left alone with a disconsolate Roderigo, who is threatening to drown himself for love of Desdemona. Iago advises Roderigo to collect as much cash as he can and join the army going to Cyprus. Desdemona will soon tire of Othello, he says, and then she will look for someone younger. When he is alone, Iago explains to us that he is merely using Roderigo. He restates his hatred of the Moor, expressing his suspicions that Othello has had an affair with his wife, and begins to ponder how he can take revenge and get Cassio's post at the same time. An idea forms: he will deceive Othello into believing that Cassio is too familiar with Desdemona.

Act 2

2.1: The scene switches to Cyprus. A terrific storm has blown up and there are concerns about the ships carrying Othello and the other Venetians. Cassio's ship puts in safely, bringing news that the Turkish fleet has been destroyed by the storm. Cassio and Montano, the governor, discuss Othello's marriage. Desdemona arrives in the ship which also carries Iago and Emilia, and distracts herself by inviting Iago to make witty comments about women. As Cassio talks privately with Desdemona, Iago makes observations about him in a cynical aside. The third ship brings Othello and there is a joyful reunion for the newly married couple. As he observes it, Iago vows to destroy their happiness.

Othello and the others depart, leaving Iago behind to sort out the luggage. He calls the disguised Roderigo to him. Desdemona, he says, will soon tire of Othello and look for someone similar to her in age, behaviour and background. Cassio will be the obvious man, he argues. Having given Roderigo good reason to want Cassio out of the way, Iago explains his plan. He tells Roderigo to provoke Cassio to a fight later that evening. Iago will stir up a riot and Cassio, blamed for the disorder, will be stripped of his lieutenantship. With Cassio out of the way, Roderigo will have a clear run at Desdemona. Roderigo agrees and leaves Iago alone to deliver his second major soliloquy. In it he claims that Cassio loves Desdemona, and that she might plausibly love him in return. He explains that he loves her too, though he admits that his feelings have more to do with lust; but he wants her as an act of revenge for the imagined affair between Othello and Emilia. If he can't have Desdemona, his plan will be to drive Othello into an incurable jealousy by means of a plot involving Roderigo and Cassio (whom he also suspects of having cuckolded him).

2.2: A herald reads a proclamation declaring that the evening is to be given over to celebrating the defeat of the Turkish fleet.

2.3: That evening, Othello puts Cassio in charge of the guard. When Othello and Desdemona retire to enjoy the first night of their marriage, Iago tries to engage Cassio in conversation about Desdemona. Knowing that Cassio gets drunk easily, Iago pressures him into drinking a toast to Othello with a bunch of Cyprus gallants, including the governor, Montano. Within a short time Cassio is half drunk, and he goes out to take charge of the watch. Iago prompts Roderigo to follow Cassio, in line with their plot. Just as Montano is expressing the view that Othello ought to be informed of Cassio's weakness, Roderigo runs back in, pursued by an enraged Cassio. Roderigo has said something insulting to Cassio and he is determined to exact revenge. Montano attempts to restrain Cassio, but is wounded by him, and in the confusion Iago instructs Roderigo to go out and ring the alarm bell. Hearing the clamour, Othello arrives in time to stop the fight. He demands to know who started the fracas. Iago claims not to know; the now sober Cassio is so upset as to be incapable of speech; and Montano, weak from loss of blood, refers Othello back to Iago for a report of what happened. Othello is furious and threatens dire punishment for the culprit. When Iago is asked directly, he feigns reluctance to incriminate Cassio, but gives a report of the sequence of events which damns him. Othello immediately strips Cassio of his lieutenantship and instructs Iago to calm things down around the streets of Cyprus.

Cassio is distraught and, left alone with Iago, bewails the loss of his reputation. Iago advises him to approach Desdemona; she is a kind-hearted person and will gladly plead on Cassio's behalf. Cassio accepts this advice and leaves, determining to see Desdemona early the next morning. For the third time, Iago shares his thoughts with us: while Desdemona pleads for Cassio's reinstatement, Iago will deceive Othello into believing that she is doing so because of her lust for Cassio. Roderigo returns, complaining bitterly that he is almost out of money, has been beaten up, and is nowhere nearer attaining Desdemona. Iago counsels him to be patient. He dispatches Roderigo and concludes his soliloquy: he will get Emilia to persuade Desdemona to support Cassio, while he arranges for Othello to discover Cassio pleading privately with Desdemona.

Act 3

3.1: The next morning, Cassio hires some musicians to play outside Othello's window, but a servant (the 'clown') comes out to send them away. Cassio bribes the clown to fetch Emilia and then Iago arrives. Iago offers to help Cassio by getting

Othello out of the way so that Cassio can speak to Desdemona in private. Emilia arrives and reports that Othello and Desdemona have already been discussing Cassio's case.

3.2: Othello gives Iago some papers to deal with and explains that he intends to inspect the fortifications.

3.3: Desdemona promises Cassio she will do all she can on his behalf. As Othello comes into view, Cassio takes his leave, giving Iago his first opportunity to create suspicion in Othello's mind. Desdemona admits openly that she has been speaking to Cassio and pleads with Othello to recall him. Othello finally agrees. As Desdemona leaves him, he expresses the all-embracing nature of his love for her.

Iago begins to poison his thoughts, asking seemingly innocent questions about Cassio and Othello's courtship of Desdemona in the knowledge that Othello will read something more into them. Othello asks Iago to tell him openly what is on his mind. Knowing that it will intrigue Othello further, Iago refuses to reveal his thoughts. But he reminds Othello of the importance of a man's reputation and advises him to beware of jealousy. Othello's denial that he could ever be jealous is exactly what Iago wants to hear. It gives him the opening he needs to warn Othello about Desdemona's relationship with Cassio. Iago reminds Othello that Desdemona deceived her father and behaved unnaturally when she rejected young men of her own culture and class in favour of – he implies – an alien. Othello, now crushed, asks Iago to tell him if he sees anything else and also to instruct Emilia to observe what is going on. Already Othello is asking himself why he ever got married. Iago advises Othello not to reinstate Cassio, explaining how significant it will then be if Desdemona keeps pleading on his behalf.

Iago departs, leaving Othello to speculate miserably on the possible reasons for Desdemona's unfaithfulness: his blackness, lack of social skills and age. Already he is talking of loathing her, but, when she appears to call him to dinner, he refuses to believe that such a creature could be false. When he complains of a headache, she tries to bind his head with a handkerchief, but he brushes it away and neither of them notices it when it drops to the ground. Emilia picks up the handkerchief and gives it to Iago, but with some misgivings. Left alone, Iago confides that he plans to drop the handkerchief in Cassio's lodgings in the hope that it will cause some mischief.

Othello returns, already eaten away by Iago's poison. He turns on Iago for destroying his peace of mind and demands visible proof. Iago tells him what happened when he recently shared a bed with Cassio. Othello solemnly vows revenge; but Iago still has his ace to play. He tells Othello that he has seen Cassio wipe his beard with Desdemona's strawberry-patterned handkerchief. Othello dismisses all last vestiges of love for his wife and cries out for bloody vengeance. Iago pledges his loyal service to his 'wronged' master and agrees to kill Cassio. Othello makes Iago his lieutenant.

3.4: Desdemona asks the clown to find Cassio: she wants to tell him of her hopes that he will soon be reinstated as lieutenant. She anxiously asks Emilia about the lost handkerchief. When Othello enters, he behaves strangely and, claiming that he has a cold, asks for a handkerchief. When Desdemona cannot produce the one he specifies, he tells her that it had special powers, and that to lose it would mean the loss of his love. Angered by her attempts to change the subject by pleading for Cassio, he storms off, leaving Emilia to interpret his behaviour as jealousy. When Cassio arrives with Iago, Desdemona reports that she has not dared to plead on his behalf because of Othello's strange and angry mood, and Iago goes supposedly to check what might be the matter. Emilia is not convinced that Othello's disturbed state of mind is caused by some problem to do with his governorship; she muses on the nature of jealousy and the fact that some people do not need a reason for it. As soon as the women leave, Cassio is accosted by Bianca. He gives her the handkerchief that he has found in his lodgings, asking her to copy the embroidery for him.

Act 4

4.1: Iago now becomes bolder with Othello, claiming that he has seen Desdemona in bed with Cassio, and he keeps reminding Othello of the handkerchief. Othello has some kind of seizure and falls to the ground. Iago gloats, but, when Cassio enters, he pretends to be concerned. Othello stirs and Iago dispatches Cassio, arranging to see him later. Pretending to comfort Othello, Iago reminds him that there are many men unaware that they are cuckolds – at least Othello knows the truth. He reveals that Cassio had entered while Othello was unconscious and says that he has arranged to return to talk with Iago. He instructs Othello to conceal himself and overhear their conversation in which Iago will ask Cassio to recount details of his affair with Desdemona. As Othello hides, Iago explains to us that he will, in fact, question Cassio about Bianca, knowing that Cassio's amused and cynical reaction will enrage the eavesdropping Othello.

Cassio enters and laughs when Iago raises Bianca's claim that Cassio has promised to marry her. Bianca enters. Othello observes her angrily returning the handkerchief – she suspects it is from some other lover of Cassio's – and running off. Before Cassio leaves in pursuit, Iago checks that Cassio intends to dine with Bianca that evening. Othello emerges from hiding and Iago reinforces his belief that Desdemona must have given the handkerchief to Cassio, who in turn gave it to a prostitute. Othello now knows he must kill Desdemona. Iago promises to kill Cassio before midnight.

Trumpets announce the arrival of Lodovico from Venice. He enters with Desdemona and gives Othello a letter from the Venetian senate. Desdemona tells Lodovico of the rift that has opened up between Cassio and her husband. When Desdemona expresses her pleasure at the letter's contents – the senate have recalled Othello and are making Cassio governor in his place – Othello strikes her and sends her away. Lodovico questions Iago about the change in Othello. With mock reluctance, Iago takes the opportunity to besmirch Othello's name.

4.2: Othello questions Emilia. She denies having seen anything suspicious between

Desdemona and Cassio – which serves only to make Othello believe that Emilia is party to their deception. He sends her out of the room and accuses Desdemona of being a whore. When he leaves, Desdemona is in a daze and tells Emilia to make the bed up that night with her wedding sheets. Iago enters and offers feigned sympathy for Desdemona. Emilia claims that some villain has poisoned Othello's mind in order to 'get some office'.

Iago is accosted by Roderigo who threatens to make himself known to Desdemona. Iago promises that, if Roderigo is willing to show his courage and resolve for one more night, he will enjoy Desdemona the night following. He suggests that Roderigo should lie in wait for Cassio when he leaves Bianca's, and kill him.

4.3: After a banquet later that evening, Othello offers to accompany Lodovico back to his lodgings. He tells Desdemona to get to bed and to dismiss Emilia. As Emilia helps her mistress to get undressed, she wishes that Desdemona had never met Othello, but Desdemona stands up for him. Nonetheless, Desdemona is in a sombre mood, talking of death. She recalls that a maid of her mother's, having been deserted by her lover, used to sing a song of 'Willow'. The two women discuss unfaithful wives.

Act 5

5.1: It is later that evening in a street outside Bianca's lodgings. Iago gives Roderigo instructions about how to attack Cassio and then explains his plans to us. The death of either man will suit him, and preferably both. Roderigo botches the attack which follows, but, in the chaos, Iago wounds Cassio in the leg. The noise draws Othello to the scene, and he leaves believing that Iago has fulfilled his promise to kill Cassio. Lodovico then arrives with Gratiano (Brabantio's brother). While they tend Cassio, Iago, masked by the darkness, stabs Roderigo. When Bianca emerges from her lodgings, Iago accuses her of conspiring to kill Cassio, and he dispatches Emilia to report what has happened to Othello. Iago realises that the night to come will either make him secure or lead to his downfall.

5.2: The final scene takes place in Desdemona's bedchamber. Othello enters carrying a light and he considers the awful finality of the act he is about to commit. Desdemona's beauty almost convinces him to abandon his plan, but he persists, believing that he is engaged in an act of justice. When Desdemona wakes, Othello tells her to pray as she is about to die. She passionately refutes his accusation that she had been unfaithful with Cassio, but Othello claims that Cassio had admitted his guilt and reveals that Iago has killed him. In her desperation she begs for time to pray, but Othello will hear no more and smothers her.

There is a shout from outside: it is Emilia, come to report the attack on Cassio. Gazing at his dead wife, Othello experiences the enormity of his loss. He opens the door for Emilia, and, as she tells him about Cassio and Roderigo, Desdemona stirs. Emilia rushes to her mistress, but Desdemona lives long enough only to assert her innocence and claim that she herself was responsible for her death. But Othello admits that he killed her and tells Emilia that Iago can confirm Desdemona's infidelity with Cassio. Emilia curses Othello, unable to believe that Iago would have said such a thing. When he threatens her, her cries draw Montano and Gratiano to the scene. They are accompanied by Iago, who defiantly asserts that he told Othello only what Othello found to be true. Emilia angrily reveals that Iago's allegations have led to the murder of Desdemona; Othello admits his responsibility, citing his wife's repeated infidelity with Cassio as the reason. When he mentions the handkerchief, Emilia is devastated and she reveals how it came into Iago's hands. Othello attacks Iago, but is disarmed, and in the melee Iago stabs Emilia and runs from the room, pursued by Montano. As she dies by her mistress's side, reiterating Desdemona's innocence, Emilia recalls the song of 'Willow'.

Othello takes a sword, concealed in the chamber, and calls out to Gratiano who is guarding the door. When Gratiano enters, Othello realises that he has lost all power to act against him. Lodovico arrives, with Montano, the wounded Cassio and Iago, now a prisoner. Othello attempts to kill Iago, but succeeds only in wounding him before he is disarmed. Othello admits his part in the plot against Cassio; but Iago refuses to explain a thing, claiming that he will never speak again. Two letters have been found on Roderigo which help to fill in the details. Cassio explains how he found the handkerchief and Lodovico announces that Othello must return to Venice as a prisoner, leaving Cassio as governor. As they turn to go, Othello halts them. He reminds them of the loyal service he has given to the Venetian state and asks for his story to be told in a fair and balanced way. It will be a tale, he says, of a man who loved 'not wisely, but too well'. He finishes his speech and stabs himself.

As the representative of authority, Lodovico has the concluding words. He dictates that Othello's house and fortunes will go to Gratiano (as Desdemona's uncle) and that Cassio must ensure that Iago is tried and tortured. He himself will set sail to inform the Venetian state of the tragic events which have taken place.

Study skills

Referring to titles

When you are writing an essay, you will often need to refer to the title of the play. There are two main ways of doing this:
- If you are handwriting your essay, the title of the play should be underlined: Othello
- If you are word-processing your essay, the play title should be in italics: *Othello*.

The same rules apply to titles of all plays and other long works including very long poems, novels, films and non-fiction, such as: *Animal Farm* and *The Diary of Anne Frank*. The titles of shorter poems and short stories are placed inside single inverted commas; for example: 'Timothy Winters' and 'A Sound of Thunder'.

Note that the first word in a title and all the main words will have capital (or 'upper case') letters, while the less important words (such as conjunctions, prepositions and articles) will usually begin with lower case letters; for example: *The Taming of the Shrew* or *Antony and Cleopatra*.

Using quotations

Quotations show that you know the play in detail and are able to produce evidence from the script to back up your ideas and opinions. It is usually a good idea to keep quotations as short as you can (and this especially applies to exams, where it is a waste of time copying chunks out of the script).

Using longer quotations

There are a number of things you should do if you want to use a quotation of more than a few words:

1. *Make your point.* ———— At the end Othello asks that people
   should speak: ————— 2. *A colon introduces the quotation.*

3. *Leave a line (optional).* ————
4. *Indent the quotation.* ———— Of one that loved not wisely, but too well;
6. *Keep the same line-* Of one not easily jealous, but being wrought,
   divisions as in Perplexed in the extreme; ———— 5. *No quotation marks.*
   the script.
7. *Continue with a* ———— The word 'jealous' here...
   follow-up point, perhaps commenting on the quotation itself.

Using brief quotations

Brief quotations are usually easier to use, take less time to write out and are much more effective in showing how familiar you are with the play. Weave them into the sentence like this:
• In describing himself as 'not easily jealous', Othello seems to be...

If you are asked to state where the quotation comes from, use this simple form of reference to indicate the *Act, scene* and *line*:
• As a man 'unusèd to the melting mood' (5.2.346)...

In some editions this is written partly in Roman numerals – upper case for the Act and lower case for the scene; for example: (V.ii.346), or (V.2.346).

Further reading

Criticism since 1980

John Drakakis, ed., *Shakespearean Tragedy* (Longman, 1992) contains a variety of different critical perspectives on *Othello*.

Lisa Jardine, *Still Harping on Daughters: Women and Drama in the Age of Shakespeare* (Harvester Press, 1983) focuses on the sexual politics of the play.

John Wain, ed., *Othello* (Casebook, Macmillan, 2nd edition, 1994) includes, in addition to earlier criticism, Karen Newman's examination of gender and race in *Othello*, '"And wash the Ethiop white": Feminity and the Monstrous in *Othello*'; and Anthony Brennan's 'Iago, the Strategist of Separation', an illuminating study of Iago's methods.

Edward Pechter, *Othello and Interpretive Tradition* (University of Iowa Press, 1999) is an account of the play's capacity to generate interest, as recorded in its long and rich history.

Harold Bloom, in *Shakespeare and the Invention of the Human* (Fourth Estate, 1998), argues against the F R Leavis view and reinstates Othello as a figure of nobility.

Earlier criticism

A C Bradley, *Shakespearean Tragedy* (1904; 3rd edition, ed. J R Brown, Macmillan, 1992) gives a view of a noble and romantic Moor.

F R Leavis, *The Common Pursuit* (Chatto and Windus, 1962) contains the chapter 'Diabolical Intellect and the Noble Hero' in which Leavis attacks Bradley's conception of the Moor and plays down the role of Iago.

G Wilson-Knight, *The Wheel of Fire* (Methuen, 1959) includes 'The *Othello* Music'.

William Empson, *The Structure of Complex Words* (Chatto and Windus, 1951) contains the essay 'Honest in *Othello*', in which Empson explores the ways in which the word is played with throughout.

Performance

There are essays by Ben Kingsley and David Suchet about the 1985 RSC *Othello* in: Russell Jackson and Robert Smallwood, eds, *Players of Shakespeare 2* (Cambridge University Press, 1988).

Keith Parsons and Pamela Mason, eds, *Shakespeare in Performance* (Salamander Books, 1995) contains an informative and nicely illustrated overview of the history of the play in performance (pp 162–169).

Russell Jackson, *The Cambridge Companion to Shakespeare on Film* (Cambridge University Press, 2000) includes an excellent introductory essay about Shakespeare in the cinema (pp 15–34), a very useful survey of three *Othello* films (pp 144–155) and a section on the Orson Welles *Othello* (pp 189–193).

Martin Wine, *Othello: Text and Performance* (Macmillan, 1984) is especially interesting on the language and, in particular, Iago's speeches.

Language

Frank Kermode, in *Shakespeare's Language* (Penguin, 2000), has fascinating things to say about the complexity of the language in *Othello*, including Iago's 'filth'.

See also William Empson, above.

Shakespeare's life

The most readable and up-to-date account of Shakespeare's life and work is Park Honan's *Shakespeare: A Life* (Oxford University Press, 1998).

Shakespeare's theatre

Andrew Gurr, *The Shakespearean Stage: 1574–1642* (Cambridge University Press, 3rd edition, 1992) is both encyclopedic and extremely readable.

Exam practice and discussion

1. How far would you agree with one critic's view that 'Othello may be a resolute and capable general but the events of the play suggest that he is out of his depth in matters of the heart'?
2. How helpful to an understanding of Othello's tragedy is the idea that his obsession with his honour serves to both destroy and redeem him?
3. Would you agree that, when we consider Othello's background and his status as an outsider, it is clear that 'to some extent the seeds of the final tragic outcome are already present in the tragic hero and his situation' (Gamini Salgado, 1975)?
4. What have you discovered about Desdemona which makes her more than just the passive victim of Othello's tragic error? What might the critic have had in mind who wrote that her character is 'compounded of many contrasting but not contradictory qualities'?
5. How far would you agree that 'the significance of the play is deepened by what it shows [Desdemona's] individual inner experience to be – especially what it shows of her love for Othello and her ways of responding to him throughout the action' (J Adamson, 1980)?

Exam practice and discussion

6. How far would you agree with the view that the love between Othello and Desdemona is built upon very shaky foundations? In your answer you should:
   - discuss both Othello's and Desdemona's accounts of their courtship, considering the conditions under which it was conducted and what it was that appears to have attracted each lover to the other
   - give your own opinion, as well as suggesting other possible interpretations
   - show an understanding of the attitudes of Shakespeare's time to gender, and to the relationships between daughters and fathers, and wives and husbands, referring to other works of Shakespeare where it would be useful.

7. What do Iago's actions and speeches reveal about his attitudes to women? In your answer you should:
   - make detailed references to the language Iago employs, for example in his exchange with Desdemona and his description of Cassio's behaviour (2.1.108–176), and in his scene with Emilia (3.3.299–318)
   - express your own responses to Iago's comments about women and the way he treats them
   - show some awareness of the attitudes towards women in Shakespeare's time.

8. 'Iago reveals more about himself through the language he uses than through his apparently open admissions.' How far do you agree with this view? In your answer you should:
   - discuss Iago's language, focusing on such features as his repeated use of animal imagery, expressions for the sexual act and statements such as 'I am not what I am'
   - express your own judgement of the critical claim in the question, discussing how far you agree with it and why
   - show some knowledge of the language in Shakespeare's time, including the areas of experience from which imagery could be drawn, referring to other works of Shakespeare where it would be useful.

9. 'Iago's soliloquies are the key to our understanding of both his motives and his methods.' How far do you agree with this view? In your answer you should:
   - discuss the methods that Iago is employing and the motives he offers us in his soliloquies
   - give your own response to the critical view expressed, weighing how far you can agree with it and why
   - show an understanding of the ways in which a Shakespearean character can be presented and especially of the nature of soliloquy.

10. Janet Dale played Emilia in the 1985 RSC production. This is David Suchet's description of her interpretation: 'She played Emilia as a woman desperately needing and wanting Iago's love, and therefore one who would do anything to please him or his fantasy (sexual or otherwise); she is thus a woman who knows Iago's weaknesses and is prepared to put up with them, believing that basically he is a good man. Her confusion then when she learns about his (eventual) truly malignant doings...is very genuine.'
    (a) What evidence is there to support her interpretation of the role?
    (b) Which other very different interpretations could be convincing and plausible?

11. How far would you agree that 'Othello shows us how a woman's character and reputation can be manipulated and distorted by men'?

12. What do you understand by the 'double time scheme' in Othello, and what purposes does it serve?

13. Othello has sometimes been described as 'an exploration of jealousy'. Which features of the play support this description?

14. 'It is essential to the development of the play's tragic situation that Othello, Iago and Cassio are soldiers.' How far do you agree with this view? In your answer you should:
     * discuss characters and their motives
     * give your own response to the critical view expressed, weighing how far you can agree with it and why
     * show an understanding of Elizabethan attitudes to gender, honour and status as well as an awareness of Shakespearean tragedy.

15. How far would you agree that 'Othello is a tragedy of incomprehension, not at the level of intrigue but at the very deepest level of human dealings...No one in Othello comes to understand himself or anyone else' (John Bayley, 1960)?

16. What do the language and behaviour of the characters reveal about attitudes to race in Shakespeare's time? For example
     * compare the language of Iago, Roderigo and Brabantio with that of the Duke, First Senator, Cassio, Lodovico and Desdemona, when they are referring to Othello
     * consider Othello's status in Venice.
     If you can, look at another of Shakespeare's black-skinned characters: the Prince of Morocco in The Merchant of Venice (2.1 and 2.7). There is also Aaron in Titus Andronicus.

17. It has been said that the imagery in Othello is built up around a series of 'oppositions' such as black and white or hell and heaven. Write an analysis of the imagery and show what light these oppositions throw upon the wider concerns of the play.

Some quotations for discussion

These quotations are a selection of critics' views and assumptions about the play. You are invited to question them, using evidence from the text and from performances that you have seen.

Othello

1. 'Othello's marriage is a political act – a black soldier marrying a white aristocrat cannot be viewed in any other way.'

    What do Othello and Desdemona say themselves about their marriage? How does Cassio view it? What is the Duke's opinion?

2. 'We are forced to come to terms with the idea that Othello is not wholly noble; he is also capable of savagery and crudeness.'

Does he display these qualities anywhere? If he does, how significant a part of his make-up are they?

3. 'Despite appearances, Othello does not actually have a propensity towards jealousy.'

   What does he say himself about jealousy, and can we believe him? Is it his weaknesses we should focus on, or Iago's cunning?

Desdemona

4. 'Shakespeare has not made Desdemona woodenly perfect, but touchingly fallible and human.'

   What are Desdemona's weaknesses and how are they made apparent? Do they help to make her a more rounded character?

Iago

5. 'Iago seeks to replace Desdemona in the Moor's affections because of his latent homosexual love for Othello.'

   Is there really any evidence of homosexual love in the text? How far does such an interpretation fit his behaviour in the play and the things he says in his soliloquies?

6. 'Although he never says explicitly that he hates women or foreigners, his exceedingly low opinion of them, which comes across in many of his speeches, suggests that Iago wants to degrade those he despises.'

   What does he say which indicates this hatred or contempt? How does it come across in his behaviour?

Structure

7. 'Between Acts III and IV is the one place, so far as I can see, where an interval can be credibly inserted.' (M R Ridley)

   Consider other possibilities. In the 1985 RSC production, the interval came after Iago's soliloquy at the end of 2.3; at the RSC in 1989, it was after Desdemona drops the handkerchief at 3.3.288; it lay on the floor throughout the interval and the second half opened with Emilia discovering it.

Discussing critical opinions

These questions refer to the extracts from critical essays on pages 269–280.

1. Are you more inclined to agree with A C Bradley, who considered Othello to be almost blameless, or F R Leavis, who considered that the role of Iago in Othello's downfall had been overrated?

2. How do you view Desdemona and her role in the play, having read the observations of Lisa Jardine and Karen Newman?
3. Do you agree with Edward Pechter's comments concerning Shakespeare's alleged 'universality'? Is he really, as Ben Jonson claimed, 'not of an age, but for all time'?

Personal responses

1. How do you feel at the end of the play? Whose 'tragedy' have you witnessed?
2. How would you apportion blame for what happens? Is Iago totally responsible or should the others share the responsibility? Is Othello too credulous, or too easily jealous, for example? Is Desdemona too passive? Should Emilia, having given the handkerchief to Iago, have kept quiet about it for so long?
3. Do you have any sympathy for Iago?
4. Has the play given you any new perspectives on humanity? Have you learned anything about yourself?
5. Which film, television or stage version of the play have you found most satisfying?
6. Were you aware of the double time scheme (see pages 265–267) when you first watched or read the play? Now that you have learned how it works, what is your opinion of it? Does it succeed, or does the apparent inconsistency irritate you? Or is it one of the things which works on stage, but not on the page?

Analysing the verse

This section is designed to reinforce what you learned about Shakespeare's verse on pages 263–265 – how the underlying iambic pentameter works, and what effects can be achieved by varying it.

1. Speaking about another play that involves sexual jealousy, *The Winter's Tale*, Cicely Berry, RSC voice coach, said: 'If an actor experiments by moving on every punctuation point, he or she will feel that the blood is running so hot or so strong, because of the violence or the sexuality in the play.' Try the activity that Cicely Berry suggests. Walk around, reading out loud Othello's speeches in 3.3.381–388 and 4.1.36–45, changing direction every time you come to a comma, question mark, exclamation mark, dash, semicolon or full stop.

Find each of the lines referred to and look at their context before completing activities 2 to 7:

2. Read the following lines out loud and then write them down, marking the heavy stresses:
   (a) 'Yet she must die, else she'll betray more men.
       Put out the light, and then put out the light.' (5.2.6–7)
   (b) 'Of one that loved not wisely, but too well' (5.2.341)
   (c) 'Myself will straight aboard, and to the state
       This heavy act with heavy heart relate.' (5.2.367–368)

3. What is the effect of:
   (a) the repeated heavy stresses in:
       'The **wind**-shaked **surge**, with **high** and **mon**strous **main**' (2.1.13)
   (b) the repeated questions in:
       'What place? What time? What form? What likelihood?' (4.2.137)
   (c) the use of monosyllables in:
       'He that is robbed, not wanting what is stol'n,
       Let him not know't, and he's not robbed at all.' (3.3.340–341)?
4. Write down the following lines and then divide them into feet and mark the heavy stresses:
   (a) 'Hath thus beguiled your daughter of herself' (1.3.66)
   (b) 'And therefore little shall I grace my cause' (1.3.88)
   (c) 'These sentences, to sugar, or to gall' (1.3.213)
5. Explain how the rhythm enhances the meaning in the following lines:
   (a) 'Most potent, grave, and reverend signiors,
       My very noble and approved good masters' (1.3.76–77)
   (b) 'It is the cause, it is the cause, my soul' (5.2.1)
   (c) 'And smooth as monumental alabaster' (5.2.5)
6. (a) Comment on the effect of dividing two iambic pentameter lines between five speeches at the opening of Act 4 (lines 1–2). What clues might this give the actors as to how the lines could be delivered?
   (b) Do the same with 4.1.230–231 (five speeches shared among three speakers) and 5.2.70–71.
7. What different effects do these two pairs of couplets have when they are spoken in the play?
   DUKE: The robbed that smiles, steals something from the thief;
              He robs himself that spends a bootless grief.
   BRABANTIO: So let the Turk of Cyprus us beguile:
              We lose it not so long as we can smile. (1.3.205–208)

Analysing the imagery

1. What is conveyed in *Othello* through the imagery of opposites (black and white, heaven and hell, good and evil, etc)? Is there a straightforward equation between goodness, whiteness and day, on the one hand, and evil, blackness and night, on the other?
2. In what ways does the imagery of oppositions tie in with other opposites, such as honesty/dishonesty, trust/suspicion, passion/reason, barbarism/civilisation, love/hate, joy/despair, peace/war, loyalty/betrayal, poison/medicine, beauty/ugliness...?
3. Write a brief account of the imagery in *Othello*, including in your piece analyses of the following extracts:
   • 'When devils will...As I do now.' (2.3.349–351)
   • 'Dangerous conceits...sulphur.' (3.3.324–327)
   • 'My name...mine own face.' (3.3.384–386)
   • 'Like to the Pontic...Swallow them up.' (3.3.451–458)
   • 'But there where...grim as hell!' (4.2.56–63).